Fruits of Worship
Practical Religion in Bengal

Fruits of Worship
Practical Religion in Bengal

Ralph W. Nicholas

Chronicle Books
An imprint of DC Publishers

New Delhi
2003

Chronicle Books is an imprint of DC Publishers

Distributed by
Orient Longman Limited
Bangalore Bhubaneshwar Chandigarh Chennai
Ernakulam Guwahati Hyderabad Jaipur Kolkata
Mumbai New Delhi Patna

ISBN 81-8028-006-3

Jacket photograph and design by Rishi Barua

Typeset in Goudy
by Eleven Arts, New Delhi
Printed by Pauls Press, New Delhi
Published by DC Publishers
D-27 NDSE Part II, New Delhi 110 049

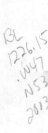

Contents

Introduction

Although they have been trying to do so for almost 150 years, anthropologists and students of religion have not been able to establish a useful definition of 'religion' that covers all of the activities they want to discuss in a culturally neutral way. The reason for this failure is that there is no universal category of 'religion,' even though we think we 'know it when we see it.' I evade this vexing issue by going to the way the Bengalis classify the things I am interested in. The activities discussed in this volume are the ones considered by Bengali Hindus to be 'worship' (pūjā) and they are usually done for the sake of the 'fruit' (*phal*) they bear. The word 'ritual' here refers to what Bengalis (along with many other Hindus) call *karma*. *Karma* is a well-known term that, in its most general, unrestricted sense, means 'action.' Thus, the activity in which a person engages for a livelihood is *karma*, just as much as the activity in which a person is dealing with the gods. There is a distinction between quotidian work (*kāj karma*) and ritual work (*kriyā karma*). There are two forms of *kriyā karma*. *Naimittika karma* are those acts that are done once in a lifetime, what anthropologists call 'the life-cycle rites,' which Hindus also call *samskāras*, the actions that complete and perfect a person from conception to death. Bengalis generally recognize ten of these *naimittika* rites, though they commonly practice only some of these, and each is done only one time in the life of a person. *Nitya karma*, by contrast, refers to acts that are regularly repeated, usually on a calendrical schedule, daily, weekly, fortnightly, monthly, or annually. Unlike the *naimittika karmas*, the *nitya karmas* are extremely numerous and variable among families, castes, villages, and regions even within Bengal, not to say throughout India.

The term 'practical' is meant to call attention to the fact that what is accessible to study is activity or action. Such material is often called 'popular Hinduism,' with an emphasis on the fact that this is the religion of 'the people.' In the sense that these are practices that belong to very ordinary rural people, 'popular' is an apt expression. However, some of the significance of these practices is quite esoteric and need not be part of common understanding. Hinduism does not ask its adherents to recite a creed or make a declaration of faith. People believe many things and provide different intellectual rationales for these activities, and no one seems to be surprised by discrepancies in the interpretation of ritual acts. However, precision in the execution of prescribed acts is considered important; it is the key to fruitful action.

Ritual

The Bengali Hindus say of themselves *bāro māse tero pārbaṇ*, 'in twelve months there are thirteen rituals.' The occasions on which the *nitya karmas* are performed are called *pārbaṇ*, or *pūjā pārbaṇ*, which means 'lunar day of an observance,' or 'lunar day of worship.' That proverb understates the situation very dramatically. In the first article in this collection, I show the various annual cycles of worship that are observed by people in one small area of Medinipur District of West Bengal. The diagrams in that article do not illustrate the many daily, fortnightly, and monthly rituals that are carried out by many pious people, especially the adherents of Gauṛiya Vaiṣṇavism, in that area. Rituals can be added to the set of *nitya karmas*, as new deities become part of the local pantheon, and rituals may be augmented by the worship of additional deities. Theoretically, rituals may be dropped from the cycle as well. Trying to figure out how to tackle an open-ended series of this kind, and to provide something resembling an adequate ethnographic account has been daunting.

Anthropologists are loath to omit details from ethnographic accounts in the well-justified conviction that the details are certain to outlive the theoretical predisposition of the ethnographer and to leave some residue of enduring value for future generations of scholars. Yet the complexity of even the putatively 'simple' society of a village in India is so overwhelming that reporting all of the details is manifestly impossible. What is within reach, and of a value comparable to the details of kinship nomenclature, for example, is a picture of the universe as it is constructed in Bengali culture. Cosmology provides a framework in which all of the details make sense and in which the facts both recorded and unrecorded can be placed. Durkheim said that 'there is no religion that is not at the same time a cosmology.'

Myths

Cosmology, a construction of the way the world is in its totality, is usually implicit in rituals, but it is often made explicit in myths. It seems at first sight difficult to understand myths as forms of practical activity. However, as I try to show, in Bengal it is in performance that the myth has its significance and it is performance that produces fruit. The performance of a myth may be for all purposes equivalent to the forms of worship in which offerings are made to deities.

Myths are narratives that embody meanings that are not obvious at the level of the story, meanings that pertain to the fundamental antinomies of human existence: life and death, health and illness, well-being and suffering. In addition to these existential universals, there are many contradictions that are peculiar to particular cultures, for example, whom one may marry and whom one may not, what one may eat and what is prohibited, purity and defilement, insanity and possession, and so on.

Identifying the myths of the Bengali Hindus is not difficult. They share with Hindus in other regions of India the body of Sanskrit narratives that detail the deeds of the gods. The *Mahābhārata* and *Rāmāyaṇa* are important, and the *Bhāgavata Purāṇa*, narrating the activities of Lord Kṛṣṇa born among the Cattle-keepers on the north Indian plain, is continuously referred to in song, worship, and everyday life among the common people in Hindu Bengal. In addition to the Sanskrit stories, which are all-Indian for the most part, there is a category of myths that are composed in Bengali, are peculiar to Bengal, and which place a distinctive stamp on the Hinduism of Bengal. These are known generically as *Maṅgala Kāvya*, or, roughly 'poems of auspiciousness.' Many of them deal with deities who belong especially to Bengal, including Manasā, the goddess of snakes, Śītalā, the goddess of smallpox and other infectious disease, and Dharma, the creator who appears out of the void at the beginning of the universe. Other gods and goddesses whose careers are narrated in the *Maṅgala Kāvyas*, including Caṇḍī, a manifestation of Durgā or Śakti, and Śiva, are also well established in Sanskrit narratives. However, the stories that are told about their works in the Bengali versions include much that is not related in Sanskrit.

The *Maṅgala Kāvyas* appear in the form of manuscripts composed or copied between about the fifteenth century and the twentieth. Some versions began to be printed in the nineteenth century, and most manuscript copying seems to have come to an end at about that time. However, there are many thousands of *Maṅgala Kāvya* manuscripts in Hindu villages all over West Bengal. Some of these have been collected in libraries, and a few have been published in good scholarly editions. Many others have been inexpensively published in popular editions for use in worship. It is clear that many copies of these texts, both manuscript and printed, were prepared for use in staging the narratives in dramatic form. The form of theater common in rural Bengal, especially before the cinema, is called *yātrā*. Such theatrical performance seems to have been the pre-eminent form of mythic practice in Bengal before the advent of modern media, and it remained current through the period of my research.

Intellectual setting

The influence that Durkheim has had on my thinking about religion will be apparent. I think that *The Elementary Forms of Religious Life* is the single most important book about religion in the social sciences. Although his acquaintance with the Australian Aboriginal societies was based exclusively on what European ethnographers wrote about them, he nevertheless saw clearly the sources, the creation, and the recreation of solidarity in them. He remained a positivist throughout his life, but by examining small-scale, undifferentiated societies, he made great strides in understanding the basis of all social cohesion.

The societies of rural Bengal are much more complex than Australian bands, but they are still small-scale and personal. Yet they became divided in faith and practice beginning with the arrival of Islām at the end of the twelfth century CE. In fact, even before the advent of Islām, there were significant differences between Buddhist and Hindu (or Brahmanical) Bengalis. (By comparison, Christianity, as the religion of European colonialism, had very modest influences on rural Bengalis.) A unified community of belief and practice was not a feature of these small-scale societies for a thousand years before I came to know them. While I don't want to overemphasize the differences between Buddhism and Hinduism in, say, tenth century Bengal, or even between Hinduism and Islām in the nineteenth century, it is a fact that the villages of the countryside, as simple and unsophisticated as they might seem in many respects, were religiously pluralistic.

The social scientific interpretation of pluralistic religious situations began with the work of Max Weber, whose influence on my thinking is equal to that of Durkheim. Among Weber's innumerable contributions to the understanding of the social and cultural functions of religion was his concept of the 'orientation of social action' by the meaning attributed to it by the actor. Religious meaning endows action with significance that transcends the rational ends of everyday life. Weber made use of the differences in religious meaning to interpret the different roles of Protestants, Catholics and Jews in early twentieth century Europe. Rural Bengal, without cities or industries, nevertheless provides a specimen of enormous complexity. Most evident is the difference between Muslims and Hindus. However, among Hindus, the differences between, for example, pious, vegetarian Vaiṣṇavas and lax, meat-eating Śāktas are quite large. And among the vast majority of villagers, who are not of very high caste or education, differences of caste and religious orientation are equally large. While Weber's understanding of Indian society and the Hindu (and Jaina) sects was limited by his lack of direct experience, his grasp of pluralistic religious situations provided me with guidance in understanding rural Bengal.

There is a critical difference between Bengali Hindu religious pluralism and the situation where Christianity is dominant. In the sixteenth century, the Bengali Vaiṣṇava Saint and ecstatic religious leader Caitanya Deva revitalized Bengal Vaiṣṇavism, establishing a movement and a devotional practice that prevails among the great majority of rural Hindu Bengalis today. On full moon nights the villages ring with the sound of the *khol*, the drum that is the special accompaniment to *Hari saṁkīrtan*, and with the untrained, unrestrained, and utterly enthusiastic voices of villagers singing verses memorializing the career of Lord Kṛṣṇa on Earth. This is a form of religious practice that is relatively low in rituals such as offering and sacrifice, and high in expressive praise singing. However, the same people who constitute the *kīrtan* parties are also active in rituals such as those propitiating Manasā, goddess of snakes, and Śītalā, who is both the goddess of smallpox and, frequently, the Village Mother. This form of ecumenism is sometimes puzzling to outsiders. Protestants don't worship with Catholics, nor Christians with Jews, but people self-identified as Vaiṣṇavas nevertheless worship distinctly non-Vaiṣṇava deities, and in the recent past, Muslims often showed up at Hindu ceremonies.

Weber's insistence that social action cannot be interpreted without reference to the meaning attributed to it by the actor is at the heart of what became known as 'symbolic anthropology' in the 1960s and '70s. The proposition that a culture is understandable as a system of symbols and is a unique manifestation of the human capacity to give meaning to things—to symbolize—was advanced with great forcefulness to a generally unreceptive anthropological audience by Leslie A. White, beginning in the 1940s and continuing until his death. Marshall Sahlins carried that conviction forward into the era of symbolic anthropology, and joined it to a form of historical investigation that has exercised great influence on the development of ethnographically grounded anthropology that has so far resisted the post-modern, post-colonial developments in our discipline. Bernard Cohn has been the pre-eminent historical anthropologist of India and has taught many of us how and why to look behind claims of 'tradition' and 'immemorial antiquity.' The view of culture that is known as 'symbolic anthropology' is most closely associated with the work of Clifford Geertz, David M. Schneider, and Victory W. Turner. My indebtedness to each of them for a method of interpretation that is liberally represented here will be obvious from the references. Claude Lévi-Strauss is not known as a symbolic anthropologist but rather as a 'structural anthropologist.' His contribution to the understanding of myths is, in my view, unequalled, and has been the principal influence on my thinking about this subject.

The contents

The essays in this volume were all written between 1965 and 1981. In 1981 I became the chair of the Department of Anthropology at the University of Chicago, and in 1982 I accepted a far more demanding job in academic administration. I could not have envisioned what that would lead to, but I did not finish with administrative responsibilities until I became a Professor Emeritus in 2000. Fortunately, during the last decade I have been closely involved in the work of the American Institute of Indian Studies, which enabled me to keep contact with cultural and intellectual life in India, and to make a number of visits to Calcutta (now known as Kolkata) where I am writing this introduction.

The research was done mostly in the eastern part of Medinipur District, in what was then the Tamluk Subdivision and is now the District of East Medinipur. In 1960 and 1961 I worked there as a Ford Foundation Foreign Area Training Fellow. In 1968–69 I had a Senior Fulbright-Hays Research Fellowship. From 1964 until 1971 I was a member of the faculty of Michigan State University, where the Asian Studies Center was a continuing source of support for me, particularly for the continuation of fieldwork through the Autumn of 1970. Given their age, it may be easy to think of these papers now as historical documents, but, in fact, all ethnographic reports are historical documents. There have been a lot of consequential changes in the lives and circumstances of people in rural West Bengal since I did this work, but there were a lot of changes before I went there, and there are a lot more taking place now.

During the earlier part of my fieldwork and writing, I think I used the term 'traditional,' along with a lot of other words, such as 'community' and 'religion,' without the sense that they might be slicing up the world in a way that the people I wrote about would not recognize. I think I got better about this in later writing, and avoided as many of the unexamined categories as I could while still writing in English. Specifically, I developed a perspective on the continuing history of the people of this area and the sense that their own appeal to 'tradition,' as a means of explaining their own actions, went no deeper than it does in the contemporary English idiom, where it has come to mean little more than 'what we did last time.' Many traditional practices in rural West Bengal have deep roots, but some of them are quite new and are dressed up as archaic to distinguish them from the things regarded as belonging to the contemporary period.

Some of the practices described here are demonstrably innovations. A historical reading of Middle Period Bengali texts documents the appearance of the goddess Śītalā on the Bengali landscape and her progressive acceptance into the pantheon in the eighteenth century. Similarly, the now extremely influential Śiva of Tārakeśvar in Hugli District is generally accepted to have manifested himself first to a certain local cowherd within recent history. Moreover, the extraordinary popularity of Tārakeśvar as a pilgrimage place for Bengal and much of eastern India can be dated to a film about his powers that was popular about 35 years ago. Film and televised versions of mythic narratives now belong to the repertoire of performance, and they have superseded in influence the earlier modes of propagation, from theatrical *yātrā* and oral declamation to printing. The place now occupied by the god Śiva, and his specific manifestation at Tārakeśvar, is the product of yet another historical process in which the local Bengali god Dharma has been gradually pushed aside or absorbed into the all-India Śiva. In other words, the religious practice of rural Bengal has been implicated in complex historical development as far back as one can see.

Acknowledgements

My thinking about religion, myth, and interpretation has evolved, and a part of that evolution is expressed in these essays, which were written between 1968 and 1981. During much of that period I was working with my colleague and friend Ronald Inden on the book *Kinship in Bengali Culture*. A great deal of what I learned in the course of that work is reflected in the later papers in this collection. The thematic organization of the present volume obscures the sequence in which the papers were written, so I have added information about the date of writing to the table of contents.

When I first went to Calcutta in 1960, I was generously and benignly guided by the late Professor Nirmal Kumar Bose, who was then Director of the Anthropological Survey of India. During my first few months in India he taught me much that I did not know, and much that I did not realize I needed to know until later—often much later. Dr Surajit Chandra Sinha was then the Deputy Director and also a wise teacher. I will probably never be able to identify all that I owe to their instruction. When they decided that I was ready for fieldwork, Professor Bose introduced me to Tarasish Mukhopadhyay, a graduate in anthropology from Bangabashi College in Calcutta, a Junior Technical Assistant in the Anthropological Survey, and a native of Tamluk town. Professor Bose proposed that I teach Tarasish something further about anthropology and that he teach me something further about Bengal. We went to the field together and became very closely associated in much later work, extending right up until his untimely death. The exchange between us was very uneven at the beginning, since I had so much to learn about Bengal. However, I suppose it evened out over subsequent years. We worked in the field together in 1968, '69, and '70, and collaborated in a joint study of folklore in the same region that continued through most of the 1970s. That project was directed by Tarun Mitra of the American Institute of Indian Studies Calcutta Center, a fount of knowledge and of opinion about nearly all things Bengali. However, it is to Tarasish that I owe the most for what I know about Bengali society and culture.

I was unmarried when I first went to India. However, throughout the period in which most of this fieldwork was done, my wife Marta was an active participant. The circumstances of life in a Bengali village, the heat, humidity, lack of amenities, and monotonous diet made her life miserable. But when the drums began to sound, she was the first person out the door, with her notebook and tape recorder, dressed demurely, her head covered by the edge of her sari, as a woman who had married into the village. I cannot tell which observations are mine, which are hers, and which belong to Tarasish. The substance of what appears here is as much theirs as mine.

In 1971 I joined the faculty of the University of Chicago. Among the people in Chicago whom I came to know and whose opinion I came to value was Aditi Nath Sarkar, who was then a graduate student in the Department of South Asian Languages and Civilizations. One of our conversations about the goddess Śītalā led us into a research project and to a series of discoveries that are described here in the paper called 'The Fever Demon and the Census Commissioner,' which we wrote together. It was the kind of discovery that required the collaboration of a field anthropologist and a person who could deal with the often obscure Bengali literature of the middle period, before European colonialism influenced Bengali thought and writing. We have now (in 2002) picked up another such problem, one that extends further back in time and that entails analysis of a much more complicated ritual, the Gājan. While I am expressing my gratitude to Aditi Nath, I must also thank him for encouraging me to assemble this book and for encouraging his friend Aloke Roy Choudhury of DC Publishers to publish it. Working with both of them has been among my most agreeable experiences. Thanks are also due to my good friends and fellow Bengal anthropologists Ákos Östör and Lina Fruzzetti, who originally proposed the idea of assembling these papers in a single place.

I must apologize for a couple of failings or misrepresentations. Most Bengali Hindus would agree that the two most important observances in the Bengali year are Durgā pūjā and Gājan (though few educated or high-caste Bengalis know much about Gājan). There is practically nothing about these two major events in a volume that purports to deal with Bengali Hindu practice. The reason for these absences is the scale and complexity of these rituals, which, for my part, will have to be remedied in later work. The work on Gājan, in collaboration with Aditi Nath Sarkar, is already underway. My one contribution so far to the interpretation of Durgā pūjā is contained in the previously unpublished paper 'Caṇḍī' in this volume. My second, and larger, apology is due to all the scholars of Bengal who have published so much valuable new work on these same subjects over the last twenty years. There are several outstanding contributions to the understanding of Bengali Hinduism that have appeared in the years since these papers were published. I started to enumerate and describe these works, but it became apparent that I was creating a vast bibliographical essay that could not be accommodated in this volume.

As will be clear, these essays were published in different places and for very different audiences. Transliteration of Indic words was done differently according to context. Thus, the same deity is sometimes called 'Shiva,' in the common Romanization, 'Siva' transliterated as a Sanskrit name, and 'Sib,' the Bengali version. In the absence of an explicit final vowel, Sanskrit words conclude with the 'implicit vowel' /a/, which is here represented when words are treated as Sanskrit. However, the same word (*tatsama*) in Bengali concludes with the implicit vowel only when the final consonant is a conjunct. I hope I may be forgiven these inconsistencies.

Beginning in 1965 and continuing up to the present, with a few one-year interruptions, there has been an annual meeting of The Bengal Studies Group, an absolutely informal meeting, usually organized by a member who served as the host on his or her college or university campus. The organizer's main tasks have been few beyond the construction of a schedule of papers and, after the conference, editing the papers, which were for many years published as Occasional Papers of the Asian Studies Center at Michigan State University. These publications were not copyright and often served as preliminary versions of work that later appeared elsewhere. Three of the papers in this volume first appeared in these publications. I want to thank the Asian Studies Center at Michigan State University for having done so much to promote the understanding of Bengal. Full information about the original publication and acknowledgements follow:

'The Bengali Calendar and the Hindu Religious Year in Bengal' was first presented at the 1980 Conference on Bengal Studies, held at Oakland University. It appeared in the proceedings of that conference, *The Study of Bengal: New Contributions to the Humanities and Social Sciences*, edited by Peter J. Bertocci, and published by the Asian Studies Center at Michigan State University as its Occasional Paper, South Asia Series No. 31 (1982, pp. 17–29).

'Vaiṣṇavism and Islām in Rural Bengal' was presented at the 1966 Conference on Bengal Studies, held at the University of Missouri in Columbia. It appeared in the proceeding of that conference, *Bengal: Regional Identity*, edited by David Kopf, and published by the Asian Studies Center at Michigan State University as its Occasional Paper, South Asia Series No. 9 (1969, pp. 33–47). This paper was reprinted in *Understanding the Bengal Muslims: Interpretive Essays*, edited by Rafiuddin Ahmed (New Delhi: Oxford University Press, 2001, pp. 52–70).

'Understanding a Hindu Temple in Bengal' was a contribution to the Festschrift *Culture and Morality: Essays in Honour of Christoph von Fürer-Haimendorf*, edited by Adrian C. Mayer (New Delhi: Oxford University Press, 1981, pp. 174–190). It is reprinted here by permission of Oxford University Press in New Delhi.

'The Village Mother in Bengal' was first published in *Mother Worship: Theme and Variations*, edited by James Preston (Chapel Hill: Copyright, University of North Carolina Press, 1982, pp. 192–209). It is used by permission of the University of North Carolina Press.

'The Fever Demon and the Census Commissioner: Śītalā Mythology in Eighteenth and Nineteenth Century Bengal' was written in collaboration with Aditi Nath Sarkar and presented at the 1975 Conference on Bengal Studies, held at the University of Iowa. It appeared in the proceedings of that conference, *Bengal: Studies in Literature, Society, and History*, edited by Marvin Davis, and published by the Asian Studies Center at Michigan State University as its Occasional Paper, South Asia Series No. 27 (1976, pp. 3–68).

'The Goddess Śītalā and Epidemic Smallpox in Bengal' was published in *The Journal of Asian Studies* (vol. 41, pp. 21–44) and is reprinted here with the permission of the Association for Asian Studies.

'Śītalā and the Art of Printing: The Transmission and Propagation of the Myth of the Smallpox Goddess in Rural West Bengal' was first presented in 1971 at a Duke University Conference. It was published in *Mass Culture, Language and Arts in India*, edited by M. L. Apte (Bombay: Popular Prakashan, 1978, pp. 152–180). It is used here by permission of M. L. Apte.

1. *The Bengali Calendar and the Hindu Religious Year in Bengal*

The Bengali calendar is a version of the composite luni-solar calendar used throughout South Asia to determine everything except Muslim observances, which are fixed on the lunar calendar of Islām. Superimposition of a solar year of twelve months upon the cycle of lunar months necessitates some adjustments and manipulations but periodically realigns lunar with the slightly longer solar months so as to keep the year from constantly falling a few days behind the passage of the Earth around the Sun. Thus, the new year always occurs on the same solar day even though it is several lunar days later each year for about three years, after which a lunar leap month (*mala-māsa*, 'dirty month') is introduced to bring the two cycles together again. These features are common to Hindu calendars generally, and do not distinguish Bengal from other parts of India. The problem that I want to deal with is: What makes the Bengali calendar Bengali?

There are some exquisite scholarly answers to that question but they are of concern primarily to the pandits and astrologers who compile the annual almanacs. The perspective of the ordinary person in the countryside who consults an astrologer or reads an almanac is not altogether different from that of the scholar, but it is influenced by the repeated experience of annual cycles in both their reliable tropical regularities and their frequently cataclysmic excesses and insufficiencies. The Bengali calendar that is commonly used among

Hindus—and, devoid of religious rituals, by Muslims as well—is a complicated compound of the ancient scholarly tradition, six or seven centuries of distinctively Bengali experience, by now deeply interpreted in Bengali culture, and more recent experience, such as the advent of smallpox and cholera epidemics.

Taken as a whole, any of the major Bengali Hindu almanacs defies any kind of unitary comprehension. Every significant event since the beginning of the present *yuga*, and quite a few from earlier ones, seems to be recorded there along with the most minute details about what to do and what to avoid on each day. It is, thus, somewhat disconcerting to discover that villagers also know some things that are not mentioned in the almanac. What I shall try to do here briefly is to break up a Bengali Hindu year into a few of its more important cycles in order to show some of the major principles and cultural concerns on which it is constituted. As a specimen, I chose the year 1377 because it is one that I happen to be familiar with that lacks a leap month. I have represented the year in a circular diagram that begins with the vernal equinox in April 1970 and ends with the vernal equinox in April 1971. The fact that the year begins and ends on the same point in the diagram is meant to represent a cyclical conception of the year, which is more characteristic of the rural Bengali perspective than would be any rectilinear representation.

The concentric mandalas of the diagram, reading from the outside inward, show the Bengali lunar months, the Bengali solar months, and, for reference, the Gregorian months. Four of the lines radiating from the center of Diagram 1 (page 19) represent the equinoxes and the solstices, not as they are but as they are considered to be in a calendar that has taken no account of the precession of the equinoxes. The year in Diagram 1 is roughly divided into the three seasons of Bengali agriculture, with the spring merging imperceptibly into the hot weather, the rainy season lasting for approximately four months, and the winter or harvest season merging into the cold weather. Although the *āman* or winter-harvested rice crop has been far and away the most important part of the agricultural year in Bengal, the conceptions of three rice seasons and of innumerable varieties suitable for cultivation in each of them have been present in Bengali culture long before HYVs were heard of. Approximate times from planting to harvest, which vary considerably from one locality to another, are shown around the outside of the diagram.

Diagram 2 (page 20) illustrates a different conception of seasons, one which is also a part of Bengali culture, but is very widely shared with other parts of India. This cycle of six seasons is closely linked to the major observances of the Vaiṣṇava and Śākta years (the latter of which is shown in Diagram 5), observances that are known in somewhat varying forms throughout India and are fixed on the lunar calendar. The cycle of Vaiṣṇava rites shown in Diagram 2 are textually derived from the *Bhāgavata Purāṇa* and heavily influenced by the ritual procedures known from the Jagannāth Temple in Puri. It is interesting to note that the ritual calendar of the Gauṛīya Vaiṣṇavas, who trace their genealogy of gurus to Caitanya, is slightly but systematically different from that which is in general use among Bengali Hindus.

Diagram 3 (page 21) returns to the agricultural year, illustrating the cycle of rites popularly observed by cultivators. This cycle begins with the elaborate Gājan held at the year's end, reordering a cosmos seen to be at the entropic nadir of the year, and fertilizing the earth and water for the new year. The fruits of that fertilization appear nine months later in the Banāi ritual when the principal rice harvest is celebrated. It may seem a bit strange to find Ambubācī, the observance of the menses of the earth, appearing after the ritual fertilization has taken place. Ambubācī belongs to the alternation between the dry and wet parts of the year and, unlike the other main agricultural rites, is fixed on the lunar calendar. During that three-day period digging in the earth is forbidden and farmers may not use their plows; thus, the principal rainy-season plowing for the *āman* crop begins after Ambubācī, fertilizing the earth in an idiom different from that used in the Gājan. Nala Saṃkrānti, which is midway between planting and harvest, corresponding to the *sādh* given a pregnant woman, is oriented to increasing the crop then standing in the fields.

Lakṣmī, the goddess whose name is synonymous with prosperity, is a colorless figure in Sanskrit religious texts. However, she is distinctly personified and personally present in most Bengali Hindu homes. Diagram 4 (page 22) represents three distinguishable cycles of the worship of this fickle goddess. The Kojāgarī Lakṣmī and little Alakṣmī-Lakṣmī pūjās done before Kālī pūjā belong to the cycle of Devī worship followed by high-caste, Śākta-oriented families illustrated in Diagram 5 (page 23). The three Khanda-pālā Lakṣmī pūjās are carried out in conjunction with the three principal rice harvests of the year and visualize the goddess as dwelling in the freshly threshed grain. Again, this is predominantly a high-caste ritual and, although it is distinctively

Bengali, it is set on the lunar calendar. Lakṣmī appears most clearly as a goddess of the house in the small domestic Lakṣmī pūjās done during the period of the main rice harvest on every Thursday, since this is Lakṣmī-vāra, Lakṣmī's day. Although this worship may be performed by a Brahman *purohita*, the women of the house are quite capable of carrying it out themselves and frequently do so. Beautiful *alipanā* diagrams representing her footsteps entering the house and, often, walking straight into the granary, are drawn by women before the ritual. The Banāi pūjā, which culminates the agricultural rites shown in Diagram 3, brings together the domestic and feminine Lakṣmī rituals, with the out-of-door masculine rites, by binding Lakṣmī to the plow and other agricultural implements with a rope of new straw (*bāuni*), keeping her outside the house but enclosed in the courtyard until the end, when she is placed inside the granary for the year.

Diagram 1, 3 and most of 4, then, reflect the year as seen from an agricultural perspective and as interpreted through the deities of Bengali Hinduism. I have put all these together in Diagram 8 (page 26). Diagram 5 returns to the cycle of six seasons and the emphasis on the lunar year known throughout India. The goddess worshipped in Bengal pre-eminently in the totalizing form of Durgā has been a concern of high-caste people. These most elaborate and splendid occasions of the ritual year, centred on Durgā pūjā in the autumn, historically symbolized the protection and control exercised by kings and king-like landholders over their subjects (*prajā*). Needless to say, modern forms of these rituals have taken a very different, democratic approach to social order, but I cannot discuss the interpretation of these complicated rituals here. I only want to note at present that all of the important Śākta worships in Bengal take place during the night of the gods, the time of Viṣṇu's sleep. Because the goddess must first be awakened before she can be worshiped, the rituals involve a great deal of work that could be dispensed with if Bengalis worshiped her at the time they consider seasonally appropriate. The most usual reason given for this 'unseasonal awakening' of the goddess is that she was worshiped in the autumn by Rāma before his invasion of Laṅkā—and this episode does appear in the *Rāmāyana* as told by Krttivāsa, though not that of Vālmiki. But a further examination of the calendar shows Durgā pūjā to be but the grand centerpiece for a series of observances in which danger and death are vividly symbolized and warded off or reversed by the invocation of a powerful goddess—or powerful human protector. Durgā pūjā, and the other Devī pūjās reorder the cosmos during the dangerous night-time of the gods and they do so in ritual modes that are opposite those of the Gājan, the principal ritual of the spring and of the cultivators.

Vrata rites are extremely numerous, common, and poorly studied because they are mostly observed by women inside the home. Few women anywhere in Bengal would observe all the Ṣaṣṭhī Vratas shown in Diagram 6 (page 24), although since she is the goddess who protects children, a woman who lost several children might do all of them. All possible calendrical principles are followed in fixing the occasion of one or another of the *vratas*. It happens that Ṣaṣṭhī Vratas are determined on the lunar calendar with one for each season except for the three that are related to other rituals. Thus, in the autumn, there is a special Ṣaṣṭhī Vrata in conjunction with Durgā pūjā, and, just opposite it in the spring, there is another that is part of the Gājan. There is a special Śītala Ṣaṣṭhī Vrata during the cold season that is observed on the day following Śrī Pañcamī and Sarasvatī pūjā. In the final summing up of the religious year in one rural locality in Midnapur District you will see numerous other *vratas* observed by some women there.

Diagram 7 (page 25) shows two sets of rites, those directed to Śītalā, goddess of smallpox, which are accompanied by the worship of the cholera goddess Olābibi, and those directed to Manasā, goddess of snakes. It appears that smallpox established itself in endemic form in south-western lower Bengal during the eighteenth century and the worship of this goddess was inserted in the calendar at that time. Cholera first appeared in epidemic form in the early nineteenth century and the worship of Olābibi was established some time after that. Snakes and the problem of snakebite have been familiar for a much longer time and, although the goddess Manasā is peculiar to north-eastern India, her rites have been held on one or more of the occasions indicated since the fifteenth or sixteenth century. Smallpox viruses are transmitted through the air and a high level of atmospheric moisture suppresses their transmission very rapidly. Thus, smallpox prevailed in the hot dry weather preceding the rainy season; peak rates for cases and for deaths were in April or May. The worship of Śītalā, which is done by villages collectively, begins with the onset of the hot, dry weather and continues until the beginning of the rainy season. When cholera appeared, cases likewise peaked during the hot, dry months, primarily because the cholera organisms thrive best in the shrinking ponds of this season rather than the fresh water of the rains. Thus, conjoining the worship of Olābibi to that of Śītalā made a kind of utilitarian sense within the framework of premises about goddesses controlling disease. The rainy season, flooding the snakes out of the agricultural fields and onto the high ground inhabited by human beings, replaced one set of calamities with another. Villagers shamelessly turned their attention from Śītalā to Manasā, who has been the other pre-eminent goddess of individual villages. Despite the appearance of crass, self-interested motivation behind the timing of these pūjās, two important lunar dates from the all-India calendar are occasions for Manasā worship, and the eighth day of the dark lunar fortnight in Phālguna now appears in the almanac as Śītalāṣṭamī. Smallpox has been eradicated, cholera is better controlled and there is better therapy, and as the human population has risen, the population of poisonous snakes has diminished. So I can imagine an investigator a century hence, like me struggling to discern the order in a Bengali almanac, puzzling over the dates of these peculiar rites.

The concluding diagram (page 27), labeled 'The Hindu Year in Kelomal,' though it does not reveal the full facts of the calendar in even so inconsequential a rural locality, clearly illustrates why I now laugh when one of my Bengali friends repeats the old *prabād*, '*bāro māse tero pārbaṇ*,' 'in twelve months thirteen rituals.' There are about sixty on that calendar, and I have not said anything about *ekādaśīs*, *pūrṇimās*, or *tulasī* trees, the things most dearly beloved to Bengali Vaiṣṇavas.

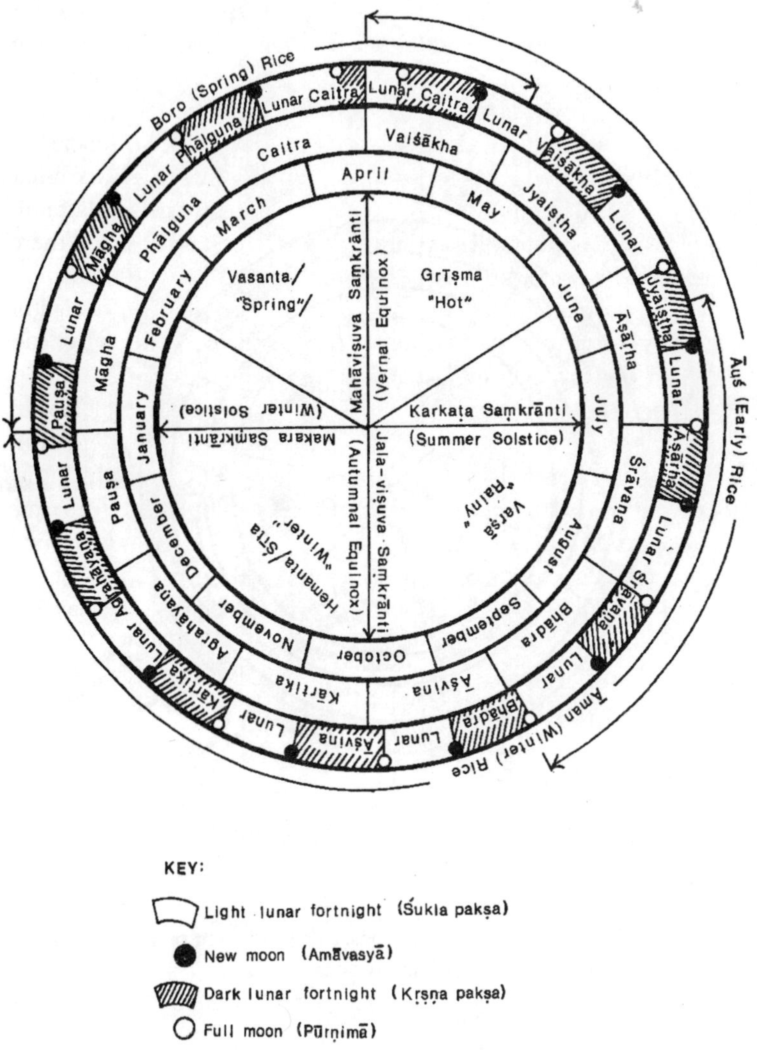

1. The Bengali solar cycle of three seasons and of rice agriculture.

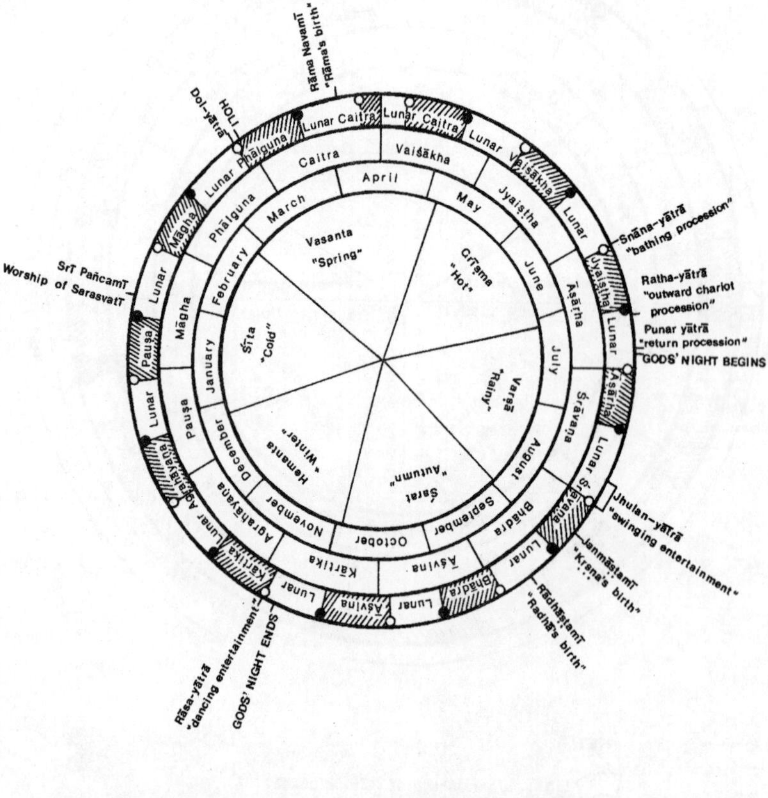

2. The all India lunar cycle of six seasons, a day and night of Viṣṇu, with the cycle of principal annual Vaiṣṇava observances.

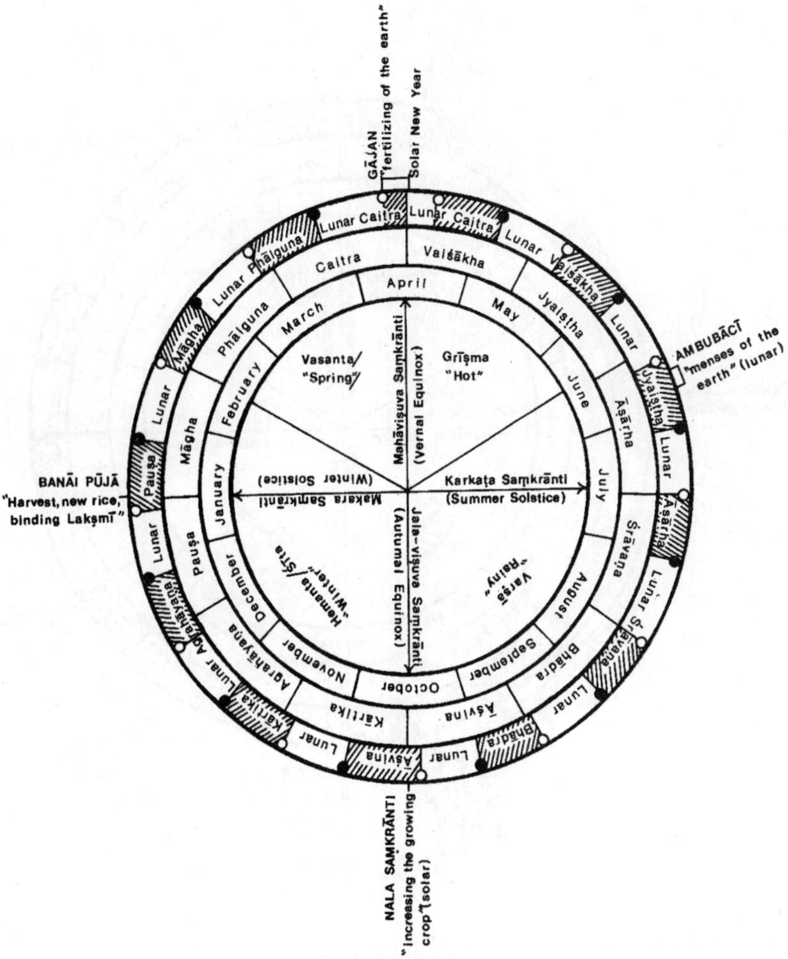

3. The popular (*laukika*) ritual year of agriculture.

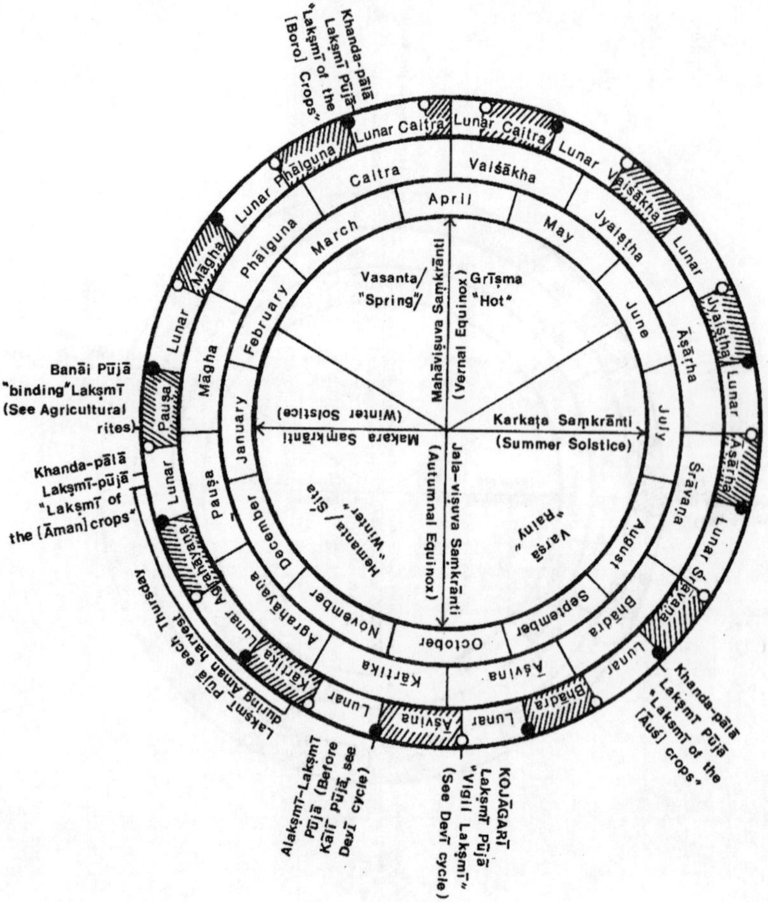

4. The lunar and solar cycles of Lakṣmī worship.

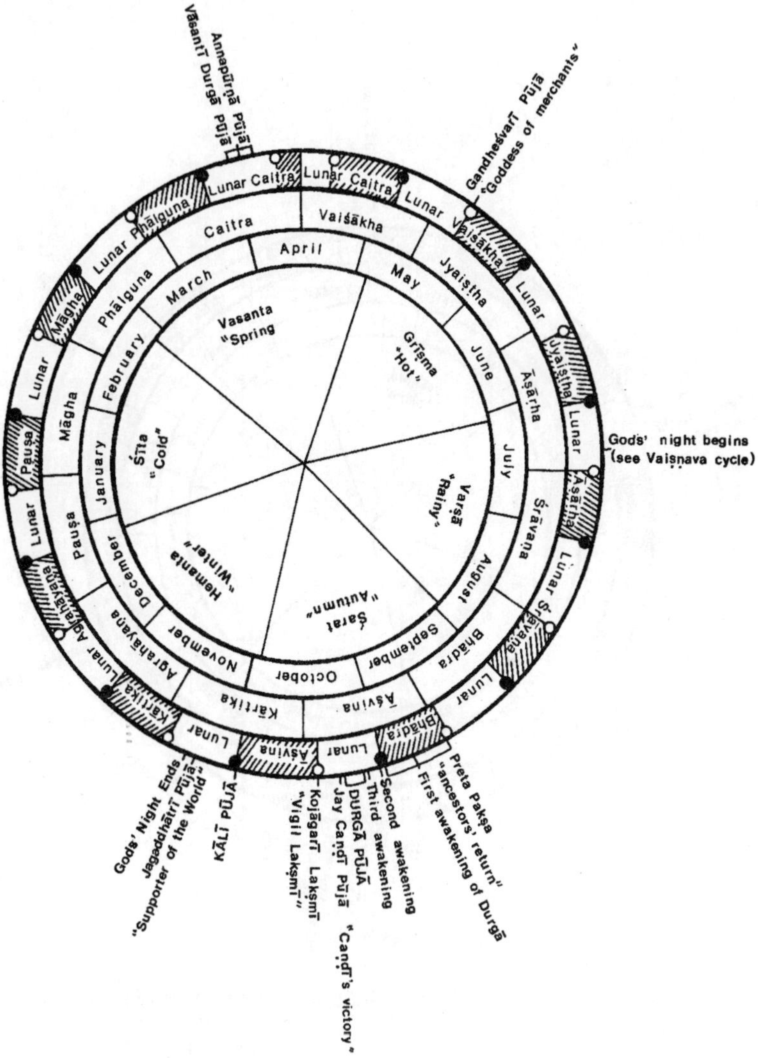

5. The lunar cycle of Devī worship.

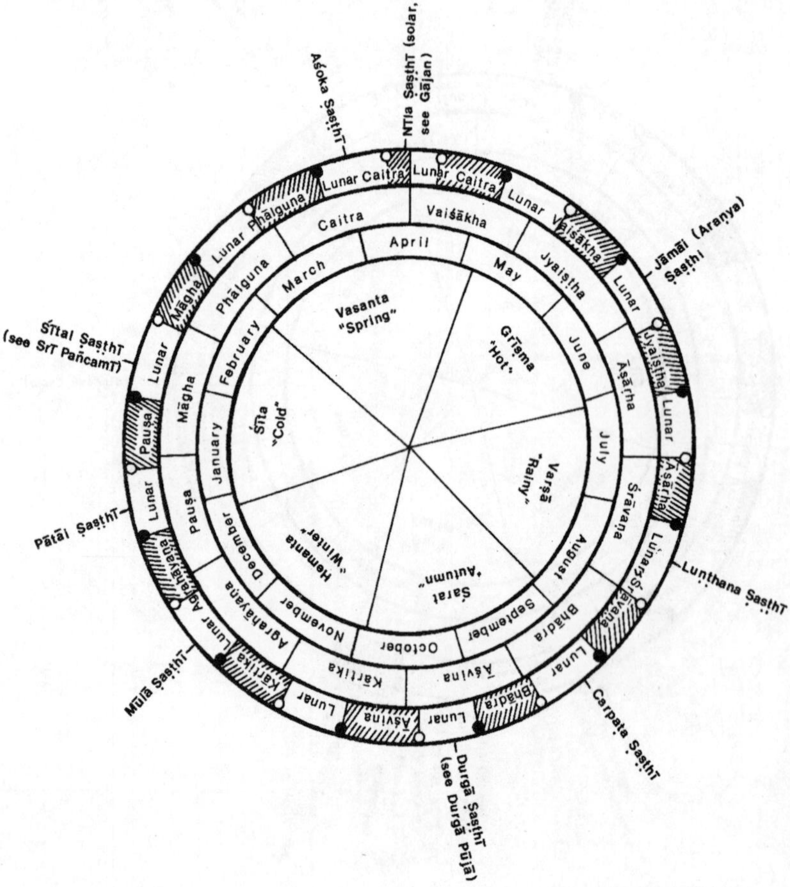

6. The lunar cycle of Ṣaṣṭhī Vratas (illustrating the pattern of *vrata* observances).

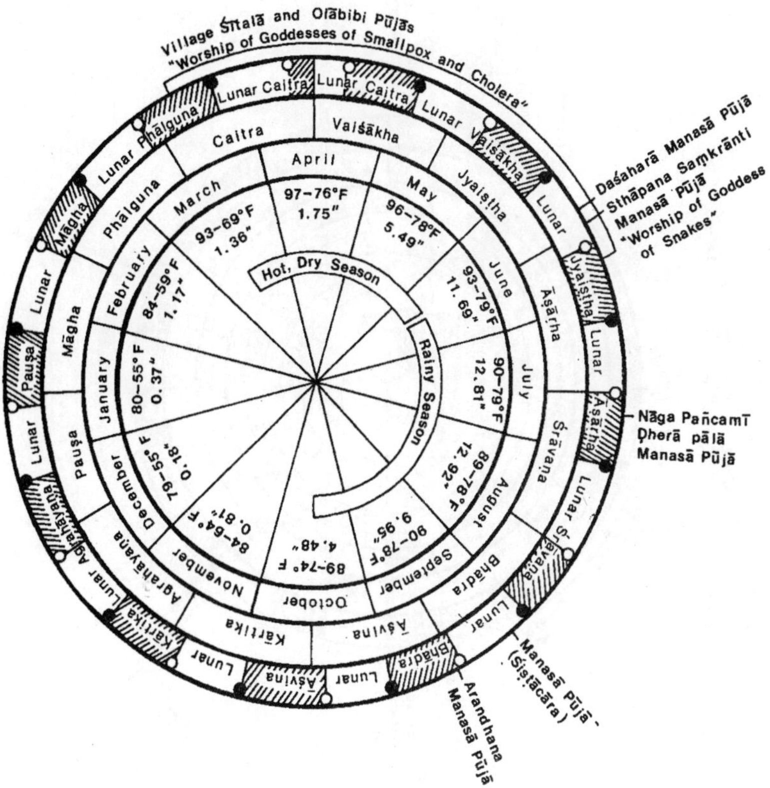

7. The seasonal cycle of the village goddesses of calamities
(Daily average maximum and minimum temperatures and monthly average rainfall recorded at Calcutta, 1881–1940 [Source: 1951 Census of India. West Bengal. Vol. 1, pp. 47–48].)

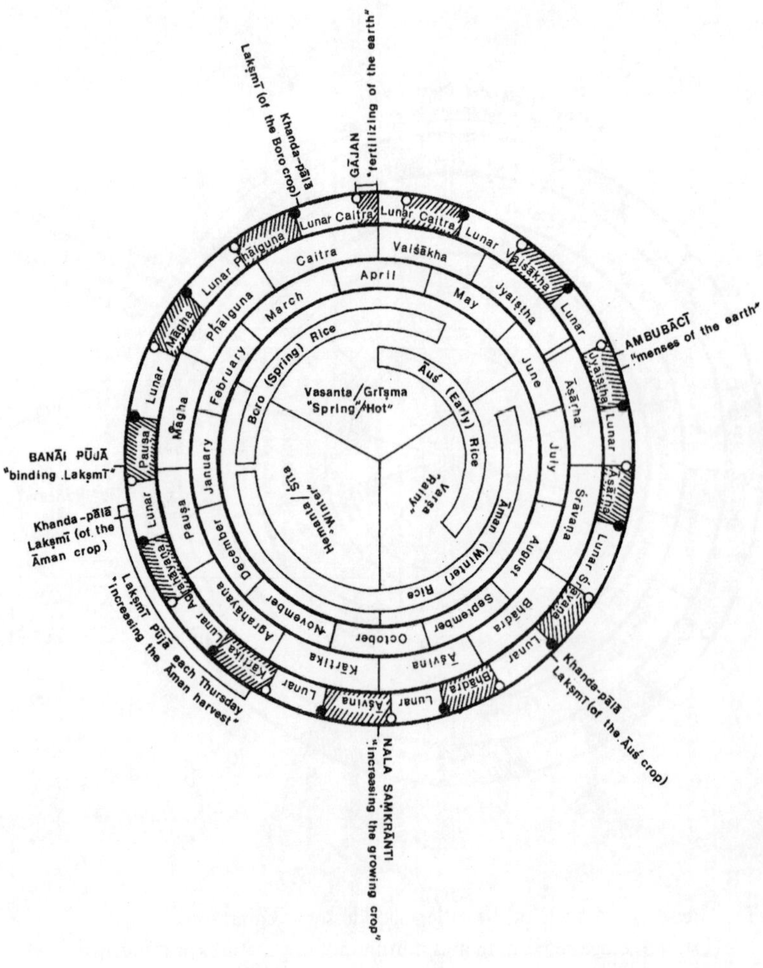

8. Seasons and rituals of the Bengali Hindu agricultural year (Calendars 1, 3 and 4 combined).

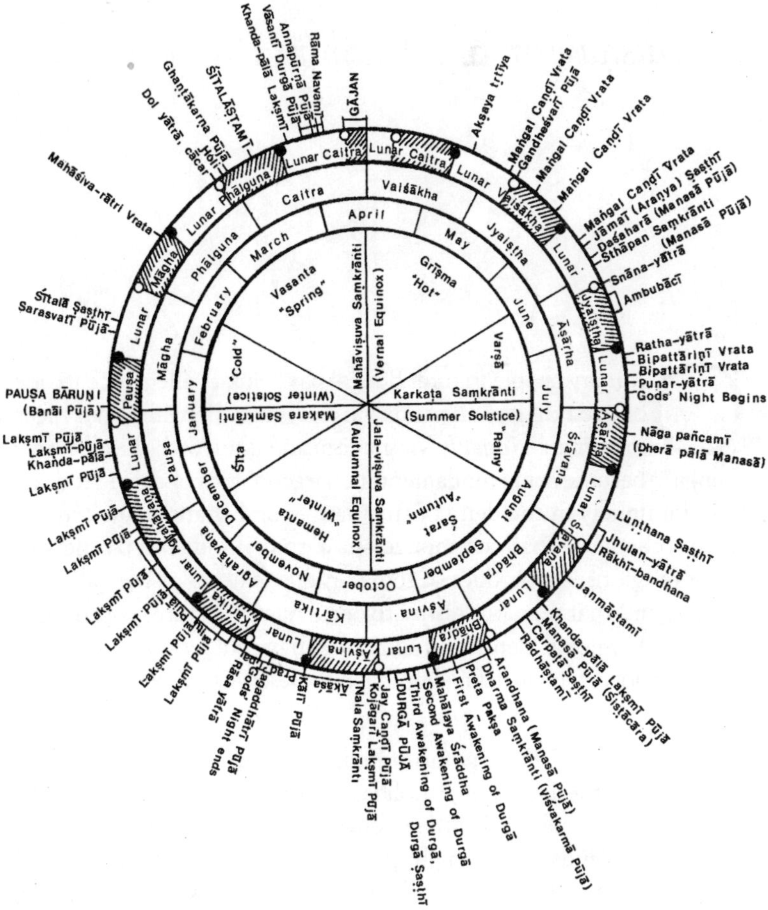

9. The Hindu year in Kelomal (Monthly, weekly, and daily observances are omitted).

2. *Vaiṣṇavism and Islām in Rural Bengal*

Ordinary people in rural Bengal pay primary allegiance to one of two religions: Bengali Vaiṣṇavism or Bengali Islām.[1] It is important to qualify Vaiṣṇavism and Islām with the adjective 'Bengali' because some fundamental characteristics of these sects are found uniquely in the delta of the Ganges and Brahmaputra rivers. In this chapter I shall attempt to show that the distinctiveness of these religions is a product of some unique features of Bengali rural society, and that religious distinctiveness has, in its turn, contributed to Bengal's regional identity. In addition, I have put forward some ideas that I cannot defend in detail, but that may deserve further exploration.

In the autumn of 1960, a group of Bengali friends from Calcutta took me to spend the Durgā pūjā holidays with their relatives in Delhi. Most of the Bengalis in Delhi are employed in Central Government offices. My friends were in high spirits, looking forward to the special vacation granted them for the celebration of what, I was led to believe, is the central festival in the annual ceremonial cycle of Bengal. An ornate image of Durgā in the act of killing the Buffalo Demon (Mahiṣāsur) was placed in a *pandal* outside the Delhi Kālī Bāṛi temple. Worshipers from all strata of political and bureaucratic life attended, dressed in new clothes and wearing their finest ornaments. While the North Indian inhabitants of Delhi flocked to the Rām Līlā grounds to witness again the exploits of that famous incarnation of Viṣṇu, the Bengalis ate the *prasād* of Mother Durgā, Killer of the Buffalo Demon.

Shortly after my visit to Delhi, I took up residence in a small village in Midnapur district. To say that I had some preconceptions about the religious ideas of the villagers is an understatement. Not only had I read a great deal about Bengali religion, but Calcutta acquaintances had told me many things. I was alert to the importance of the Śaktis and Lord Śiva; I had a notion that elements of Tantric Buddhism might be readily visible if I kept my eyes open. The villagers, with what turned out to be a genuine catholicity of interest in deities, fulfilled almost all my expectations. They maintain temples for Śiva and Śītalā, the powerful goddess controlling contagious diseases, particularly smallpox. They make offerings to Manasā, the snake goddess. And almost every family has promised, at one time or another, to sacrifice a goat to the Pañcānanda (five-faced Śiva) of a nearby village if a family member is restored to health. Barren women perform fertility rituals during the annual Pauṣ Bāruṇī Melā at the Barga Bhīmā (Tārā) temple in Tamluk town; this temple stands on the site of a former Buddhist *vihāra* (O'Malley 1911: 221). Even the Muslims have a kind of Śakti in Olābibi, who is thought by some villagers to be the consort of Allah, just as Durgā is the consort of Śiva, and who, like Śītalā, is believed to be responsible for contagious diseases, particularly cholera.

However, as I began to appreciate more of the significance of daily activities and more of the religious symbolism present in ordinary affairs, it became increasingly apparent that the predominant orientation of the Hindu villagers is not toward Śiva and the Śaktis, but toward Lord Kṛṣṇa and his beloved Rādhā. Every household in the village has a *tulasī mañca*, an altar on which a small basil plant, a symbol of Viṣṇu, is grown. In prosperous houses, the altar is sometimes made of cement, and perhaps adorned with a bas-relief of Rādhā and Kṛṣṇa in the embracing *yugalmūrti*. In the homes of the poor, the *tulasī mañca* might be no more than a mud pillar. But in every Hindu household, just after the sun sets, a woman waters the *tulasī* plant in the *mañca*, places a lighted lamp before it, sounds the conch three times to drive away malign spirits, then bows reverentially before the *mañca*. Some devout Vaiṣṇavas cultivate small gardens of *tulasī*; the leaves are used in pūjās, and beads are made from the stems. Very few Hindu villagers of the high and middle castes (known collectively as the *kanthidhārī* castes) go without a tight-fitting necklace of *tulasī* beads.

On the night of the full moon (*pūrṇimā*), as soon as the moon begins to rise, the sound of the Vaiṣṇava drum (*śrī khol*) and cries of 'Haribol' are heard throughout the village. There are two bands of Vaiṣṇava singers (Harisaṁkīrtan *dal*) in the village. On *pūrṇimā* night they visit the houses where supplies of sugar wafers, called *bātāsā*, have been prepared for a Harilut ceremony. They begin to sing slowly, the leader of the *dal* telling a story of Kṛṣṇa's exploits in Bṛndāban. As the mood develops, the *khol*-players begin to finger out well-known rhythms; the small brass cymbals (*karatāl*) begin to ring. All the members of the *dal* begin to repeat the choruses in adoration of Lord Kṛṣṇa. The volume of their singing swells; perspiration drips from the *khol*-players as they dance with their drums slung around their necks, playing more intricate rhythms as the intensity develops. The leader dances with his arms raised straight above his head in the posture of the ecstatic Nityānanda. His voice soars above the others, fervently repeating the name of Hari. The *kīrtan* dies away quickly after the emotional climax is reached. Holding a basket filled with *bātāsā* over his head, the leader throws a handful at a time into the crowd that surrounds him. Children dash about, gathering as many of the sweet wafers as they can; older people taking the offering more seriously, touching it to their foreheads before eating it.

When I saw this demonstration of genuine religious emotion for the first time, I began to appreciate the fact that while these villagers *respect* Śiva and the Śaktis, they are devoted to Kṛṣṇa and Rādhā. If Kālī arouses in a high-caste Calcutta man what Clifford Geertz would call the 'powerful, pervasive, and long-lasting moods and motivations' of religion (Geertz 1965: 4), it is Rādhā and Kṛṣṇa who do it for Hindu villagers. While I know much less about Islām in rural Bengal, I am impressed by a similar devotional quality which appears in it and which suggests that the kind of analysis proposed here is applicable also to it.

The mutual interchange of religious symbols and practices between Hinduism and Islām in Bengal is well known. In the recent past, Hindus and Muslims participated jointly in Muharram processions and in the veneration of Muslim saints (*pir*). Bengali Islām has an elaborate ritual life that certainly did not originate in Arabia or Persia. A systematic survey of religious beliefs and practices in rural Bengal could produce volumes on the syncretism of Hinduism and Islām. There are two reasons why I shall not take up this fascinating phenomenon.

First, religion, like any other component of a culture, is an orderly system of symbols (Geertz 1965: 4). Because symbols in a religious system have unique and complex relations to one another, these elementary constituents cannot be randomly rearranged. Nor can they be taken arbitrarily from one religious system and appended to another. Symbol-borrowing will not take place simply because practitioners of two religions happen to live near one another, or because conversion from one to the other was 'incomplete.' Rites and symbols are to be understood not by the discovery of their origins, but by the discovery of (a) their meanings to the faithful (meanings which may have nothing whatever to do with their origins), and (b) their functions in the systems of which they are parts.

Second, although the phenomenon of religious synthesis—by which I mean the building up of an orderly set of religious symbols somehow 'satisfactory' to a particular human group—would make an exciting study, there is more to be gained at the moment by analysis. This means taking apart the categories 'Hinduism' and 'Islām,' 'Vaiṣṇavism' and 'Śaktism,' 'Sufi' and 'orthodox,' to see what kinds of systems these are. It lies beyond my present undertaking to try to say what kinds of symbolic systems they are. However, I think I can set forth some general ideas about the connections between the Bengali religions and Bengali society.

Society in the Bengal delta

Like every other region in the world, Bengal is unique because it is located on a specific portion of the Earth's surface, and no two portions are exactly alike. However, of the various kinds of natural features over which individual regions are distributed—deserts, mountains, plains, valleys—the river delta is a comparatively rare form. And there is no other delta on Earth the size of the Bengal delta. The Ganges, carrying the water from the southern slopes of the Himalayas, and the Brahmaputra, originating in the drainage of the Tibetan slopes of the same mountains, both find their way to the sea through Bengal. The heaviest rainfall in the world occurs in the north-eastern portion of the South Asian subcontinent, so that even the local Bengali rivers discharge enormous volumes of water. Each of these mighty rivers carries with it a load of silt. Over some millennia, each year's deposit of silt has contributed to the building of the delta, raising the level of the land and extending it a little further southward until today there is a 50,000 square mile deltaic plain. This delta, together with the fringe of non-alluvial raised land that forms a kind of horseshoe around it, is physical Bengal.

Until quite recently, the Bengal delta was a kind of frontier area. There are several common meanings of the word 'frontier.' There is the modern European notion of a line on the surface of the Earth that precisely demarcates one nation from another. The exactitude of these political frontiers is clearly indicated by the contemporary habit of erecting walls or fences along them. Another current conception of 'frontier,' that of the 'ethnic frontier,' is more vague. People who speak the same language, practice the same way of life, and respond to the same cultural symbols are frequently found not only on both sides of a political frontier but also mixed among members of one or more different groups (Leach 1960). Most Americans, however, are likely to associate 'frontier' with the great American West in the nineteenth century. Many of us even have a vague idea about Frederick Jackson Turner's 'Frontier Hypothesis,' which holds that unique features of American democracy are an outgrowth of the inherently democratic society of the frontier. I have intentionally avoided reading Turner again for fear that he would add to my thinking about the Bengal frontier more *a priori* notions about frontier society than he has already given me. There is more to be gained from the analysis of the case at hand than from analogy with another case.

Very briefly (see Nicholas 1962 for details), the conditions for continuous, frontier-type settlement were created in rural Bengal by changes in the courses of major rivers. The Ganges originally flowed down into the Bay of Bengal through a channel on the westernmost side of the delta. The Brahmaputra once flowed down the eastern side of the delta. Where these great rivers reached the deltaic plain, the swiftness with which they were flowing before they entered Bengal was greatly decreased. A slow-moving river cannot carry as large a silt load as a swift river can, so much silt is deposited near the place where the rate of flow is reduced. Thus, the Bengal rivers gradually clogged their own courses, which caused them to shift to new, lower-lying stream-beds. As a consequence, the most important channel of the Ganges has shifted gradually and systematically toward the east, while the Brahmaputra has cut off its easternmost loop. These two rivers now flow the last hundred miles down to the sea through a united course.

The best agricultural land in Bengal is found in the areas where the rivers are most active. Thus, the location of the most productive soil had been changing over the centuries from the northern and western portions of the delta toward the eastern and southern portions. There is much evidence to indicate that the agriculturists moved with the rivers, out of the north and west into the east and south. The fact that new land lay in the lower delta, waiting to be reclaimed, created a kind of longstanding frontier situation in Bengal.

Undoubtedly, a number of factors have conspired to produce what I call the 'ethnic homogeneity of the active delta.' The most frontier-like portions of the delta are simplest in their caste composition. In the areas of the deepest annual floods and the richest soils, single castes tend to predominate over large expanses of territory. Members of the caste-like group of Muslim agriculturists, often known as Śekhs, predominate in all the rural districts of East Bengal. The Hindu pioneers of the delta are primarily Māhiṣya, Pod, and Namaśūdra. Māhiṣyas predominate in the south-western portion of the delta: Midnapur, Howrah, Hooghly, and 24-Parganas; Pods are found primarily in areas near the sea in 24-Parganas and Khulna, as well as in Jessore district; Namaśūdras are most numerous in the south-eastern portion of the delta: Barisal, Faridpur, Khulna, and Jessore. The Śekhs, Māhiṣyas, Pods, and Namaśūdras constitute the great bulk of the population of undivided Bengal. Their techniques as housebuilders, boatmen, fishermen, and 'deep water' cultivators are precisely adapted to the requirements of life in the delta.

These groups have non-Aryan origins; perhaps they are indigenous to Bengal; or perhaps they were driven, by the movement of the Aryans down the Ganges plain, into this land beyond the pale of Aryan civilization. No records suggest that they were ever elaborately divided into specialized caste groups, or that they were profoundly affected by Hindu conceptions of 'proper' social organization. As Hunter (1897: 99) has put it: 'No one can study minutely the local monuments and traditions of the Lower Valley, without coming to the conviction that the Hindu creed, as laid down in Manu and the Brahmanas, is a comparatively modern importation from the north, and that Buddhism was the first form of elaborated religious belief which the Bengali people received.' Superimposed over the relatively simple and unstratified society of delta pioneers is a heterogeneous 'foreign' aristocracy, holding ideas about both religion and society that are quite different from those of ordinary villagers.

Sect and social stratification

It appears to me, on hasty examination of the evidence, that the religion of the rural masses of Bengal has always been different from that of their rulers. In the most recent past—since about the end of the eighteenth century—the effective rulers of rural Bengal have been the zamindārs, mostly members of one of the various sections of the three highest-ranking castes in Bengal: Brāhmaṇ, Baidya, and Kāyastha. The eighteenth and nineteenth centuries, during which the deposition of the Muslims and the Permanent Settlement strengthened the positions of the Hindu zamindārs, constituted 'A period of great Śākta revival over Bengal' (Kennedy 1925: 77). My impression, based upon unsystematic observation of members of these castes in the countryside, in Calcutta, and outside Bengal, is that their primary religious orientation is toward the manifestations of Śakti and, to a lesser extent, toward Śiva. There is not any sense of exclusiveness in what I call their 'orientation'; many a good Calcutta Brāhmaṇ wife is known to be a Baiṣṇabī in daily practice. Such Vaiṣṇava temples as receive regular priestly service receive it from Brāhmaṇs. But I suspect that if an all-Bengal survey of temple-priests were conducted, most would turn out to be Brāhmaṇs serving in Śiva and Śakti temples. Among urban, middle-class Bengalis, Durgā pūjā would certainly be chosen the pre-eminent festival of the annual cycle. And it is probable that a great majority of nominations for the most important temple in Calcutta would go to the Kālī temple at Kālīghāṭ. The nearest Vaiṣṇava temple of importance comparable to that of Kālīghāṭ is at Puri, in Orissa.

People in Radhanagar, the small Midnapur village where I learned about the importance of Vaiṣṇavism in rural life, paradoxically choose Śib gājan as the most significant festival in their annual cycle (see Nicholas 1967: 63–71). This would seem to contradict the argument that deities of the Vaiṣṇava pantheon occupy the place of pride in their religious orientation. But the villagers are more catholic in their religion than high-caste people and city-dwellers; they are not prone to ignore powerful deities. They gladly accept the protection of the two Śiva *liṅga* housed in the Radhanagar temple, though they were installed there not on the villagers' initiative, but by former zamindārs—high-caste men who must have worried about the imperfect religion of the people of Radhanagar.

The inhabitants of Radhanagar join residents of nearby villages in attendance at a Durgā pūjā which is held in the nearest *hāṭ* (bi-weekly market). This pūjā was begun recently by the *hāṭ's* owners, a Brāhmaṇ family of Tamluk, who bear half the cost of the ceremony. The remaining expenses are paid by prosperous betel merchants of the market, who can ill-afford to offend their landlords.

For Bengalis in Delhi, as the story narrated earlier suggests, Durgā pūjā is an important social event: members of the community meet one another and ritually affirm their identity in the alien context of north India. In Punjab and U.P. also, Durgā is a symbol of Bengali identity. Of course, another symbol might serve equally well. But the fact that most of the Delhi Bengalis are high-caste people with some connection to Calcutta was undoubtedly of great importance in the selection of their central symbol.

Residents of Chandipur, a village in Murshidabad district, were complaining, when I arrived to do research there, that village unity no longer existed. Located in one of the oldest portions of the Bengal delta, Chandipur is no longer inhabited primarily—as it once must have been—by one of the castes of the delta pioneers. A complex and differentiated society, made up of nineteen different caste groups, has grown up in the village. At the top of the hierarchy are Bhūmihār Brāhmaṇs who took over as landlords when the last of the indigo planters who had owned the village died (for details see Nicholas 1968). Although not originally a Bengali caste, the Chandipur Bhūmihārs are now thoroughly Bengali. And although their claim to Brāhmaṇhood is not old, they regard themselves and are treated by other villagers as Brāhmaṇs.

The Bhūmihārs were never zamindāri tax collectors; even before Independence they owned their agricultural lands outright. Many Muslim cultivators and members of middle- and low-ranking Hindu castes are either sharecroppers on Bhūmihār land, or work as servants under the supervision of the proprietors, who are forbidden by caste rules to work in the fields themselves.

The time of greatest prosperity in the village is early autumn, when the proceeds from important cash crops, including sugar-cane, jute, and vegetables, are all in hand. Before Independence, it was the custom of the Bhūmihārs to stage an elaborate Kālī pūjā, during which annual payments were made to servants and gifts of cloth were distributed to dependents, both Hindu and Muslim. Increased population density, especially in the post-Partition period, and land ceiling legislation have resulted in a greatly reduced expenditure on the Kālī pūjā. As an aside, it seems to me significant that the Bhūmihārs, non-Bengali newcomers to the local scene at the beginning of the present century, took control of village society previously dominated by a British indigo planter in part by establishing their ritual superiority, then ceased making the 'traditional' presentations that symbolized their superordination. All of this occurred within the lifetimes of some residents of the village. One cannot be too careful about applying the terms 'traditional' and 'modern' to features of Indian village society.

The important point here is that Kālī is the preferred deity of the Bhūmihār Brāhmaṇs of Chandipur, as well as the Bārendra Śreṇī Brāhmaṇs who are landlords in the neighboring village, and Brāhmaṇs and Kāyastha groups all over southern Murshidabad and eastern Burdwan Districts. She and her sisters are the principal deities of the high castes throughout the older portions of the Bengal delta.

As in Radhanagar, religious activity in Chandipur is by no means confined to elaborate seasonal ceremonies, or to the Śaktis. On the contrary, a group of young Chandipur men from middle-ranking castes gather almost nightly for Kṛṣṇa *kīrtan*. As a measure of the non-exclusiveness of cults, it is a Bhūmihār Brāhmaṇ who leads the group. But it is the middle-ranking castes—Barbers, Potters, Cowherds, Weavers, Garland-makers—that provide the most active participants, and whose members most often wear the Vaiṣṇava *tulasī mālā*.

Relatively elaborate Kālī pūjās are still held annually in the *pāṛās* of Chandipur inhabited by the low-ranking Hāṛī scavengers and Mucī leather workers. Castes in the lowest ranks of society appear to be oriented to the Śaktis perhaps even more exclusively than the Brāhmaṇs. In the case of certain low castes, such as Bāgdīs, whose relatively recent origin from hill tribes can be demonstrated, it may be argued that devotion to Śiva and the Śaktis represents the well-known phenomenon of merging the identities of tribal deities with those of deities in a larger system. But Hārīs, Mucīs, and Ḍoms have been playing their unenviable roles in caste society for many generations.

In Radhanagar, there is no *pāṛā* of untouchables comparable to that of the Chandipur Mucīs. In the village just west of Radhanagar, however, there is a neighborhood of Kāorā Hārīs, who work as toddy-tappers, laborers, and midwives. Like all other Hindus in the village, they grow a little *tulasī* plant on a humble earthen altar, but they are not Vaiṣṇava oriented in the same sense as the majority of other villagers. Members of their caste resident in a number of different villages meet annually for a Kālī pūjā, which is alleged to be a wildly drunken affair. One member of the group described this occasion as Manasā pūjā, suggesting that the exact identity of their caste goddess is not fully resolved.

Although I have spoken primarily about some villages which I know in detail, the general pattern of caste stratification and loose sectarian identification is quite widespread. In East Bengal, before 1947, a general picture of society would show small groups of Brāhmaṇ, Kāyastha, and Baidya zamindārs dominant over large groups of Muslim and Hindu Namaśūdra cultivators and fishermen. Most of the middle-ranking artisan and service castes—Potters, Blacksmiths, and Barbers, among others—were Hindus. At the bottom of the system was a stratum of menial castes, nominally Hindu, but largely isolated in their religious life from the remainder of society. Throughout the east, but particularly in the less fertile tracts north of the Padma, were villages of Sāntāl tribesmen, recent immigrants not yet absorbed into the caste hierarchy. Since Partition, most of the zamindārs have left East Bengal, and more of the Namaśūdras and others move to India after each outbreak of communal rioting. The artisan and service castes, however, are still important in the rural economy of East Pakistan (now Bangladesh).

In West Bengal, the position of the high-caste zamindārs has been somewhat affected by zamindārī abolition and land ceiling legislation. In the north-western portion of the delta and in the Rāṛh country, some Brāhmaṇs and Kāyasthas remain in the countryside, continuing to exercise dominance over middle- and low-ranking dependents. This pattern prevails in the Chandipur area, where Muslims constitute a majority of the local population and stand in the same relation to the dominant caste as they did before Partition and before modern land reform legislation. In Radhanagar, and in the active deltaic areas generally, the influence of high castes upon village society was always more intermittent and less intense than in areas with relatively large, resident, high-ranking dominant castes.

Taking a very general view of Bengali rural society, particularly prior to 1947, it seems useful to envision it as composed of three tiers. At the top stand the *bhadralok*—mostly Brāhmaṇs, Kāyasthas, and Baidyas—primarily devoted to the Śaktis and to Śiva. The middle stratum, by far the largest and least differentiated of the three, is composed primarily of a few large groups of cultivators together with artisan and service castes, predominantly either Muslim or Vaiṣṇava in religious orientation. The lowest-ranking groups of menial and laboring castes are primarily Śakti worshipers, though the basis of their religious commitment is surely different from that of the highest castes.

This very broad picture of Bengal rural society, which omits much of the detail that social anthropologists so dearly love, suggests three lines of further enquiry about Vaiṣṇavism and Islām. The first of these is suitable for investigation by a social anthropologist: the fact that Vaiṣṇavas and Muslims occupy the same general structural position in Bengali rural society suggests that their religions perform the same kind of functions in that society. The second line of enquiry—which Dimock (1969) has pursued—deals with the symbolic systems that lie at the center of belief and practice in these religions. If Vaiṣṇavism and Islām serve the same general functions for groups in similar structural positions, there are probably significant similarities between their religious ideas. A third line of investigation, essentially historical, would examine whether there are significant similarities between the methods by which Vaiṣṇavism and Islām were successfully propagated in the Bengali countryside.

The social organization of Islām and Vaiṣṇavism in rural Bengal

One of the most significant similarities between Vaiṣṇavism and Islām, from the point of view of a social anthropologist, is the parallel sets of religious roles that they contain. Perhaps the first of these sets of roles that strikes the outsider is the *bairāgī*-fakir pair. Hardly a day goes by in a village without a visit from a Muslim or Vaiṣṇava mendicant begging for a little food. Though both *bairāgīs* and fakirs are supposed to have given up anything that would attach them to this world, and though they may travel great distances to attend important *melās*, where they sit in long rows to receive alms from the devout, all of the mendicants whom I knew maintained village homes and received their regular support from villagers in a fixed territory. Hindu villagers customarily give a little rice, or perhaps rice mixed with lentils, whether they are addressed by a *bairāgī* or a fakir. Unfortunately, I never witnessed alms-giving in a Muslim neighborhood, and cannot tell whether Muslims respond in the same way, though I believe that they do. The merging of the *bairāgī* and fakir roles is virtually complete in the *bāul*, a religious mendicant whose attire, song, and speech all consciously mix symbols from Vaiṣṇavism and Islām.

The role of the *bairāgī* or the fakir, implying detachment from the world, is held in relation to the general public, which must, of course, remain attached if the mendicant is to get a living. The role of guru or *murshid* is defined in relation to the *celā* or *murid*. Guru is a general term with a number of specialized synonyms: the disciple of a particular Vaiṣṇava guru, for example, may address him as *bābājī* and refer to him as *gosāiñ*. A good *bairāgī* friend in Murshidabad told me:

ṭhākurer ṭhākur āmār baiṣṇab gosāiñ
e kali bhabe torāite ār keha nāi

Lord of lords is my Vaiṣṇava master;
In this world of *kaliyuga*, there is no one else to deliver me.

The *murshid*, the Sufi master, is said to hold much the same relationship to the initiate *murid*. The task of the *murshid* or guru (and guru is, in my experience, the most common term for both Hindu and Muslim religious teachers) is to initiate the *celā* or *murid* into the mystical knowledge of profound religious experience or religious ecstasy. Although some initiates become *bairāgīs* or fakirs, most are mature men with families who remain householding cultivators and constitute the principal sources of material support for their preceptors. The teachers may also instruct the disciple in curing illnesses, magical arts, or other important forms of ritual, but I have the impression that this is highly variable and incidental to the main task.

While most villagers to whom I talked about religious affairs were not particularly respectful toward the teachers who lived nearby and were well known to them, most had the idea that there were teachers who either lived a little distance away or were now dead who did have a more profound capacity. Thus, the local guru or *murshid* might become a *gosāiñ* or *pīr*, as his reputation passed by the usual processes of rumor through the countryside. There is probably no village in Bengal that does not have the tomb of a *pīr* (*dargah*), the tomb of a *gosāiñ* (*samādhi*), or both. The death anniversary of a renowned *gosāiñ* or *pīr* is the occasion of a *kīrtan* or *urs*. Initially the occasion probably attracts only villagers who were attached to the teacher during his lifetime. But then, it seems likely that social process takes control over the rise in the reputation of some and the decline of others. A guru who died in the middle of the agricultural season will not attract many devotees, since there is no rest on the following day for those who would sing *kīrtan* all night, and since supplies for a large feast are not so plentiful. And thus, since the group is smaller, there is less chance that one of the participants will have a unique religious experience, which would add stature to the cult. On the other hand, the renown of a teacher who dies shortly after the winter harvest may well increase over a period of years, and the size of his following may be greater in death than it was in life. (It is possible for the date of celebration of an important death anniversary to be changed to suit the agricultural calendar.)

To summarize what I have said about the parallel sets of roles that are created by Vaiṣṇavism and Islām in rural Bengal, there are three important components of the society in its religious posture: the teacher, the disciple, and the village public. The man who is disciple in the eyes of his teacher, is a *bairāgī* or fakir in the eyes of the public. The man who is teacher to his disciple, is a guru or *murshid* to the public. However, there is nothing distinctively Bengali in this set of relations. Throughout southern Asia there are religious mendicants who rely upon charity for their existence and upon personal instruction for their enlightenment. The guru-*celā* relation might be seen as a special form of the patron-client relation upon which the caste system is built, and, thus as one of the most characteristic forms of social relation, not only in Bengal, but in all of South Asia. Yet, there are forms of social organization within the village public, whether Hindu or Muslim, that are uniquely Bengali. Both of the forms of organization which I shall discuss are related to the peculiar structure of caste in the Bengal delta.

Vaiṣṇava and Sufi 'castes'

When I first went from house to house making acquaintance with the villagers of Radhanagar, I invariably asked people to what caste they belonged. Most people—over 75 percent of the population—were Māhiṣyas, one of the castes of the delta pioneers. A surprisingly large group, however—11 percent—reported themselves as 'Baiṣṭam.' I had not previously been aware that ordinary, settled families of agriculturists and laborers could have Vaiṣṇavism as their only caste affiliation. Therefore, the first men to reply to my caste enquiry with 'Baiṣṭam' were questioned closely by my Bengali co-worker; they invariably asserted that they were '*āsal jātīya Baiṣṇab*,' 'original' or 'pure caste Vaiṣṇava.'

I then went to some knowledgeable men in the village with the question: 'Who are the Vaiṣṇavas?' Everyone, they assured me, was a Vaiṣṇava. What about the man who was the leader of the *saṃkīrtan dal* in the east neighborhood? Oh, he is a 'widow Vaiṣṇava' (*bidhabā baiṣṇab*, locally pronounced *bedo baiṣṭam*). His mother was a Māhiṣya woman, but she became pregnant when she was a widow. When this happens, the villagers compel the widow to call in a *gosāiñ* for a reading of the *Bhāgavata* (*Bhāgabatpaṭh*) in her house. Through *Bhāgabatpaṭh* she becomes a Vaiṣṇavī, and this is the caste of her child. With whom do such children marry? Only other such Vaiṣṇavas.

Gradually, I learned more about the complexities that exist within the group that reported their caste as Vaiṣṇava. Those whose illegitimate ancestry is far enough in the past to be forgotten will not marry those whose origin is recent enough to be known. Not all who say they are *jātīya* Baiṣṇab are descendants of widows; my next-door neighbor was a convert and, although he reported himself and his wife as Baiṣṇabs, he said his children were Māhiṣyas and his son was married to a Māhiṣya girl from a thoroughly respectable family. The watchman in the adjacent village of Govindapur said he was *jātīya* Baiṣṇab, but other villagers said he had been a member of a low-ranking Hindu weaver caste before he moved to the village.

The majority of *jātīya* Baiṣṇabs are known as *bidhabā Baiṣṭams*. Sophisticated villagers even proposed that the distinction between the rustic word *Baiṣṭam* and the more literary form, Baiṣṇab, describes the difference between the descendants of widows and the true devotees who have forsaken a respectable caste. Although most of the *jātīya* Baiṣṇabs, like most other villagers, depend upon agriculture for their livelihood, most of them have no agricultural land, since the paternal ancestor from whom they might have inherited was not a legitimate ancestor. Thus, most of them work as agricultural laborers, although they regard plowing as demeaning and will not do it.

Criteria that are very important in caste ranking—respectability or origin and wealth—are against the *jātīya* Baiṣṇabs being accorded a very high position in the village caste hierarchy. Yet the men whom I interviewed about the relative standings of village castes almost invariably ranked Baiṣṇabs very high—as high as the dominant, respectable Māhiṣyas.

Vaiṣṇavism legitimizes the illegitimate in the microcosm of the village, just as it did for so many members of morally dubious Buddhist sect in the early days of the Caitanya movement (Sen 1954: 351).

There is a long-standing joke in Bengal about the proclivity of rural Muslims to rearrange their descent according to their fortunes. A village leader may claim descent from a Mughal or Afghan, and style himself 'Khan'. If his crops are good and his landholding increases, he may discover that he is directly descended from the Prophet and become 'Sayyad'. The great majority of ordinary Muslim villagers in Bengal, however, call themselves *Śekh* and respond with this term when asked for their caste. To the linguistic sophisticates, *śekh* refers to descendants of Arabs, and, since it is clear that the Muslim cultivators of rural Bengal have little to do with Arabia, their apparent claim to Arabic descent is treated with derision. Too much attention has been paid to etymology, and to the meaning of the Arabic term from which Bengali *śekh* is derived. The important question to ask is: What is the association which people in rural Bengal have with the term *śekh*? Their earliest and most important experience with *śekhs* was their contact with Sufi preachers, who were almost invariably called *śekh*. Pious converts perhaps modelled themselves after those admirable holy men, just as the later Vaiṣṇavas made themselves over in the image of Nityānanda. In order to understand why every Muslim villager I met in Bengal said he was a *śekh*, it is much more important to understand that there is probably no village in Bengal that was not touched by Sufi preachers (Karim 1959: 124), than to know all about the meaning of *shaykh* in Arabic.

The Muslim weavers in Radhanagar village are known to other villagers as Jolā Tā̃ti, a name that has connotations of foolishness. They reported their caste as Nur Musalmān. Nur is an Arabic word meaning 'light,' although it is sometimes used derisively by Bengali Hindus to mean the beard of a Muslim. My informants, however, explained that they were called Nur Musalmān because they got their living through *nurī kām*, which they understood to be the Urdu equivalent of *tā̃tī kāj*, 'weaver work.' In rural Bengal, the 'light of Islām' (nur-ul-Islām) has become a loom. It is appropriate that words of great symbolic importance should be attached to things of great symbolic importance.

Every man in Radhanagar Tā̃tī *pāṛā* preceded his name with the title *śekh* when I took his household census. They are quite clear that they are not *jātīya śekh* like the cultivating Muslims who live in an adjacent village, as the following incident, related by the *pāṛā mālik* illustrates:

Seven or eight years ago, people from Mirābār village came to our *pāṛā* for a religious talk by our guru {*sic*}. An *āsraph* girl from Mirābār asked my daughter-in-law for a drink of water, and when my daughter-in-law began to pour it for her, she said she could not take water from the hand of a *nurīkām*. My daughter-in-law complained to me, and I told the guru. He told the *āsraph* people that they must not maintain distinctions of high and low during religious occasions. The food which is prepared during these occasions is the sacred *sinni*, and it must be eaten by all, lest they become *kafir*. Then he asked the girl who had refused to drink: 'Are these Christians whose water you will not accept?'

Although the caste of the Radhanagar Tā̃tīs is low, and they could never marry with the *āsraph* cultivators of Mirābār, the two groups have in common a guru, a creed, and an identification, however dimly it may be realized nowadays, with the Sufi preachers who brought Islām to the Bengali countryside.

Vaiṣṇavism and Islām intersect the structure of the caste system in several important ways. Perhaps the most important connection between the two is, unfortunately, the one about which, at present, I know least.

Maṇḍalī and *millāt* in frontier society

Earlier I suggested that the Bengal delta might usefully be treated as a kind of slowly opening frontier which was gradually settled by ethnically homogeneous groups of pioneers. Social order is a serious problem in frontier society everywhere. The people of the lower delta are known to be tough and independent. They are famous for their skill with the *lāṭhī*, which is often the only means of establishing a claim to a plot after a flood has changed the boundaries of agricultural land. For centuries, in the lower delta, authority was poorly organized; centers of officialdom were few and widely scattered. It seems likely that Islām and Vaiṣṇavism functioned to provide authority in anarchic frontier society, and that they did so through loosely constituted religious organizations. The Vaiṣṇava form of these organizations is called a *maṇḍalī* (circle, congregation); it is organized around a particular guru, who may be called a *gosāiñ* by his followers, and is frequently constituted of persons from more than one village. The Muslim organization is called by some variant of the Arabic *millāt* (sect, party, religious group) or simply *samāj* (society); it is organized around a particular *mollā*, who may be called a *pīr* by his followers. There seems to be a considerable range in the sizes and territorial extents of individual organizations. Fellow members have closer contacts with one another, both ceremonially and informally, than with non-members.

I do not have any personal experience with *millāt* organizations among Bengali Muslims, but a recent paper by Robert Glasse (1966: 202–4), which describes '*mallot*' groups in western Comilla district, and Peter Bertocci's current research, which involves *samāj* groups in eastern Comilla district, reveal striking similarities to the *maṇḍalī* organizations of Vaiṣṇavas in eastern Midnapur district. Besides meeting for worship and to hear the teachings of the leader, *maṇḍalī* and *millāt* organizations exercise over their members social control of a kind that must have been very important in Bengal's frontier days, when distinct village authority systems had not yet developed.

Radhanagar men are mostly members of a *maṇḍalī* which includes men from about six other villages. They met, while I was living in the village, on the death anniversary of their *gosāiñ*, who had lived in the village north of Radhanagar. The deceased *gosāiñ*'s son presided over the congregation. His father's *samādhi* had been washed with fresh mud and sprinkled with *tulasī* leaves for the occasion; his photograph was hung from a nearby tree. The meeting began the night before I came. Members of *kīrtan dals* from constituent villages had sung the praises of Lord Kṛṣṇa throughout the night, one *dal* taking over when its predecessor was exhausted. Thus, while the singing was constant, most of the men had an opportunity to talk with one another and, especially, to bring up problems that might suitably be settled under the auspices of the *maṇḍalī*.

It was during such a discussion in 1960 that the case of a Radhanagar man was brought up. A widower, this man was having regular sexual relations with a woman of the untouchable washerman caste. He was acknowledged to be a devout man and had several times acted as *pūjārī*, or cook, for *maṇḍalī* feasts. Rules of inter-caste behavior are specifically different for maṇḍalī feasts than for village feasts. In the *maṇḍalī*, all men eat at the same time, sitting on the ground. Members of low and untouchable castes, such as fishermen and Ḍoms, sit a little apart from Māhiṣyas and *jātīya* Baiṣṇabs, but they are fed at the same time as other castes. In the village, a fisherman, if he were invited to a feast, would not get his meal until the Māhiṣyas and Baiṣṇabs had finished theirs. A

Ḍom would be fed only as a beggar, taking whatever food was left and eating outside the walls of the house. Consideration of their principle of religious equality evidently influenced *maṇḍalī* members during earlier discussions on this man's affair. But then a group of fishermen asked the man to cook for a feast that they were having, and he agreed. Not only did he cook, but he also ate with the fishermen. This tipped the scales against him. When he was told that the *maṇḍalī* would discuss what should be done in his case, the man withdrew from the *maṇḍalī* and formally affiliated himself with one nearer the river, where fishermen are more numerous and are given more equalitarian treatment.

It is possible that the *maṇḍalī* was formerly responsible for a wider sphere of social control than it is at present. The *millāt* in East Bengal appears to exercise much greater authority than the *maṇḍalī* that I saw in action. Much more field research will be required before the basic forms and variations which may exist among these organizations is understood. Meanwhile, it is worth noting, once again, that Islām and Vaiṣṇavism in rural Bengal serve very similar social functions through very similar forms of social organization.

Conclusion

It is possible to identify Bengal by a list of the unique properties of its language and literature, its culture and social structure, its history, and even such elemental characteristics as its physical geography and the biological peculiarities of its inhabitants. The encyclopedic approach to the definition of a 'culture area' was typical of American anthropology thirty years ago. Nowadays, most of us do not assemble trait lists of this kind, both because we do not get much intellectual satisfaction from it and because it does not answer any of the questions that we have. Trait lists and the study of religious syncretism have a good deal in common: both assume that cultures or societies can be seen as series of discrete elements which are 'explained' by discovering the origin of each bit in a different prior 'culture.'

There is an alternative assumption, for which the founders of modern social anthropology argued: cultures and societies are systems, the components of which functions together for the maintenance of the whole. Some contemporary social anthropologists, most notably Claude Lévi-Strauss, even hold that each system has a key that reveals the ideal form of all sets of relations within it. While I have worked under the assumption that society in rural Bengal can best be understood as a system, I have not attempted to find a single key to all its parts.

Perhaps the organizing principles of Bengali society and culture will become apparent as we continue our particular investigations. At present, it seems impossible to attribute the formation of Bengali regional identity to a single cause or a unique set of causes. To give primacy to language is to ignore the larger culture of which language is a vehicle, and to avoid the question of why the languages of Bengal and Bihar, for example, became distinct rather than remaining the same. The accounts of historians must begin and end somewhere in time. Histories can tell a segment of the story of the development of regional uniqueness; but each segment is ultimately connected, through the relentlessness of chronology, to earlier uniqueness. The peculiarities of Bengali tastes in literature are just the well-known differences between Bengalis and other people set in a literary context. An exhaustive ethnographic catalog of customs and traits by which Bengalis identify one another would be nothing more than a list of diverse symbolic singularities without a clue to the unitary structure of ideas which may underlie them.

Where can we begin to break into the mass of elements which contribute to regional identity? There is, in every discipline, some method which allows the analyst to synthesize, to see a structural order in the chaos of facts. The method which I have tried to use here is crude: after analyzing some features of rural society and religion, I have tried to see how they are related. There are some important connections between the organization of society in general and the particular organization of religious roles and groups. Vaiṣṇavism and Islām prove to be similar in organization and social location, which leads me to surmise that perhaps they perform many of the same social functions. Their organizational similarity is at least as striking as their apparent symbolic differences.

This discovery is only one modest step toward the wider synthesis which we might seek in our efforts to explain the regional identity of Bengal.

3. *Understanding a Hindu Temple in Bengal*

In the chapter in his *Morals and Merit* on 'Conformity as a Moral Ideal' in Hindu communities, Christoph von Fürer-Haimendorf remarks that

> The concern about the orthodoxy of their fellow-men's beliefs shown at times by the adherents of such religions as Christianity or Islam, is foreign to Hindus. No one thinks of those professing different beliefs as 'heretics', and in doctrinal matters the individual is free to follow any line he may choose (Fürer-Haimendorf 1967: 155).

This observation aptly characterizes what seems to be a pervasive feature of the perspectives on one another's 'religious beliefs' held by Hindus in rural Bengal. However, one or two peculiarities of these perspectives merit further examination. For one thing, although there is no 'orthodoxy'—no central authority, human or textual, against which beliefs can be tested for correctness—people nevertheless often seem to speak in a doctrinaire way about religious matters. In addition, they rarely discuss 'belief' (*viśvāsa*) but they often talk about something else, which I shall call 'understanding.' *Mat*, the term which I render as 'understanding,' may equally well be glossed as 'inclination,' 'disposition,' or even 'opinion,' or 'idea,' depending upon the context. I shall argue that, just as 'Hinduism holds that all morality is subject to social diversification' (ibid.: 158), so too, it holds that all understanding or *mats* are subject to social diversification. An ordinary kind of household shrine and its recent development provide evidence for this case.

The *tulasī* pedestal

Hindu homes in Bengal are usually the homes of several deities as well. A prosperous, high-caste family may maintain a separate building within the house as a temple for its clan deity (*kula-devāta*), normally a form of Vishnu, in which images of Siva, Lakshmi, and perhaps other gods and goddesses also receive the daily ministrations of a Brahman domestic priest (*purohita*). In a less elaborate arrangement, a room in the highest part of the house is set aside as a 'gods' room' (*ṭhākur ghar*), where members of the family as well as the domestic priest may worship the deities. An ordinary household of agriculturalists might have only a deep niche in the thick mud wall of the house where pottery images of Lakshmi, Ganesha, and perhaps, a small brass Siva in the form of a *liṇga* receive offerings of water, vermilion and flowers, and an evening honorific display of light from the mistress of the house. A less well-to-do home may contain only one or two polychrome pictures of deities hung on the wall—but these too are gods and receive some kind of regular service. Only the very poorest households have none of these representations of the gods in them, yet even these have one shrine in common with those of the wealthiest and highest castes: this is the *tulasī mañca*, or 'pedestal of the sacred basil plant.'

Several Puranas relate versions of the myth of the special powers of the *tulasī*, i.e. 'sacred basil' (*Ocimum sanctum*) and its place in Vaishnava worship. The version in the *Brahmavaivartta Purana*, a summary of which follows, is a particular favorite among Bengalis.

In her previous life, Tulasi was a *gopī* in the heaven of Lord Krishna. Radha discovered Tulasi engaged in sexual intercourse with Krishna and cursed her to be reborn as a human. She began her mortal life with a series of ascetic ordeals to obtain the god Narayana (Vishnu) for a husband. Brahma appeared to her and told her that she would have her wish only after her marriage to the modest and virtuous anti-god (*asura*) Sankha-chura, whose faithful and loving wife she duly became. Through his asceticism Sankha-chura had obtained great power: he had conquered the heaven of Vishnu, and was protected by Vishnu's invincible amulet; it was decreed by Brahma that he could not be killed except if his wife be unfaithful to him. Siva was sent by the gods to reconquer heaven from Sankha-chura. The great battle lasted for a year and millions of the anti-god's forces were killed, but Sankha-chura could not be hurt. At last, Vishnu, by his divine transformative power (*māyā*), appeared before him in the guise of a Brahman beggar and prevailed upon Sankha-chura's reverent devotion to Brahmans in order to obtain the invincible amulet. Then Vishnu assumed the form of the anti-god himself and went to the chaste and faithful Tulasi as her husband. He gave away his disguise by engaging in an unusual form of sexual intercourse, but by that time it was too late. Tulasi's chastity was violated and Siva was able to kill Sankha-chura with Vishnu's spear. The deceived Tulasi told Vishnu that she must curse him. Fearful of the curse of a faithful wife (*satī*), he reminded her that she had ardently sought him through her asceticism and prayers, and he asked her to give up her human form and join him as his eternal lover in heaven. If she did this, he promised her that she would appear on earth as the Gandaki River and as the *tulasī* plant, which would be used in the worship of the gods and would convey enormous benefits to all the pure and devoted worshippers who eagerly sought after her. She accepted this proposal, but only after she had cursed Vishnu that, since he possessed a heart of stone, he would be worshipped as a stone. He decreed that his stone would be the *śālagrām* (a dark-coloured fossil ammonite), which is found only on the banks of the Gandaki River (Sen 1919: 129–51).

This tale is retold and alluded to countless times in Bengali Vaishnava devotional lyrics and the plant is used in many different contexts suitable to its powers, which are considered to be very great. Its leaves are sprinkled on the *śālagrām* stone in worship, used to purify the water in which it is bathed, and are indispensible in any worship of Vishnu. In addition, they are thought to be very 'cooling' and are employed in numerous medicinal compounds; some people say that they are antiseptic. Initiation (*dīkṣā*) by a Vaishnava preceptor is often spoken of as the equivalent for Sudras of the sacrificial thread ceremony of the twice-born. An initiated Vaishnava wears a tight necklace (*mālā*) of beads made from *tulasī* wood as a visible sign of devotion to Krishna and as a permanent reminder of the ritual obligations given by the preceptor.

During my fieldwork in the eastern part of Midnapur District[1] I found virtually no Hindu household lacking a *tulasī* pedestal, no matter how poor or unobservant of other Hindu practices it might be. Usually the pedestal is in front of a house, but in some high-caste homes it is located in the courtyard of the house where the women may attend it without exposing themselves to public view. Among the very poor, the pedestal is often constructed of earth, standing not more than a foot high and a foot in diameter. More elaborate ones are typically square pillars, up to about four feet tall and two feet on a side, constructed of brick covered with polished cement, sometimes ornamented with floral stamps, a bas relief figure of Radha and Krishna, or an inscription such as Shri Shri Hari (i.e., Vishnu). There are all sorts of adaptations to circumstances: a poor man with a tiny house plot may simply extend by a few inches one corner of the earthen plinth on which the house sits and grow a *tulasī* plant there; a metal bucket with the bottom rusted out may protect an earthen pedestal from the rain, and so on. No two are exactly alike, but all have in common the purpose of holding and honoring a *tulasī* plant. As an elderly man of Fisher caste put the matter, in an aphorism characteristic of Bengal Vaishnavism, 'A house without a *tulasī* plant is like a cremation ground.'

Vaishnavism in Bengali society

There is little in Bengali Hindu culture today that has not been touched by the influence of Vaishnava 'devotionalism' (*bhakti*). The cultural history of this religious tendency is extraordinarily complex and what I have to say about it here is concerned with only a few aspects of that history as they are seen by contemporary devotees (*bhakta*) rather than as they might be seen through an examination of documentary sources and an analytic view of the texts (cf. De 1961: 26–33).

Bengal came under Muslim rule at the beginning of the thirteenth century. Before that time central authority lay with a Hindu or Buddhist king who encompassed the many rulers of the small kingdoms that were the major social units of the countryside. There were, in each kingdom, central acts of worship (pūjā) in which the king, acting as sacrificer (*yajamāna*), made offerings to a deity—often, perhaps, one of the special forms of the goddess Durga—and then distributed the edible leavings of his offering in the form of the favor (*prasād*) of the deity among his subjects (*prajā*, literally 'offspring'). Ideally, each caste group in the kingdom played a different role in the worship, corresponding to its special occupation and ranked standing in relation to other castes. Such rites symbolically integrated the kingdom by restating at intervals the proper relationships between the king, the Brahmans, who were the worshipers (*pūjaka*) of the deity, and the subjects; and by reiterating the proper order and occupations of the castes. The little kings of the countryside themselves periodically filled the role of subjects in the still larger and more encompassing acts of worship of the King of Bengal (Gaura).

Muslim central authority in Bengal, which prevailed from 1300 until 1757, undermined the hierarchical order of the lesser and greater kingdoms. Although the Muslim ruler took the place of the Hindu king at the center in the exercise of coercive force, he could never enjoy the 'legitimacy' conferred by the hierarchical sharing out of the favor of his supreme deity to the lesser kings and through them, to the subjects. Islam places all believers on an equal footing before their god; not even a king can serve as intermediary between a person and divine favor or mercy. Within the small Hindu kingdoms, the old order remained to some extent intact, and the splendid worship of Durga (and a few other 'royal' deities) still continues today in rural Bengal among the descendants of the Hindu kings and the descendants of their high officials.

The worship of Durga, and of the other powerful goddesses associated with her, is done with extreme formality. Emphasis is placed on procedural correctness and, although a solemn commitment (*saṃkalpa*) to offer the worship is deemed essential, during the long and elaborate rites a worshipful mental attitude is often displaced by anxiety about carrying out the right act at the proper time and in the correct way. There was, by the sixteenth century, some opinion among Hindus in Bengal that the evils which had befallen their society under Muslim rule were due to a lack of sincerity among those who worshiped the 'royal' goddesses with such pomp and splendor. This point of view crystallized around the figure of Chaitanya Deva (1486–1535), a Brahman who was raised and educated in the town of Navadvipa, then the center of Hindu scholarship and ritualism in Bengal.[2]

Chaitanya was an ecstatic; even some of his close followers said that he was mad—but maddened by god. He sometimes seemed to be Krishna incarnate and sometimes his lonely lover Radha seeking her lord in an impassioned frenzy. When such a mood overcame him, he might fall into a faint or dash off into some body of water at peril to his life. Before he left Navadvipa to live in the Vaishnava pilgrimage place of Puri in Orissa, he often led parties of his followers through the streets singing *kīrtan* songs celebrating the heroic and amorous exploits of Krishna. These wild and noisy processions were perceived as dangerous by both the Muslim magistrate and the ordinary Brahmans of the town. However, there seems to have been considerable popular support for Chaitanya's example of a direct approach to a god offering rescue, protection, and release from rebirth through personal 'loving devotion' (*prema-bhakti*). The interpretation of 'loving devotion' has been subjected to many refinements and reworkings by subsequent generations of exegetical adepts. But, however it is understood, 'loving devotion' is the core of Bengal Vaishnavism, and it is considered to be more worthy of offering to god than all the most splendid rituals put together.

The conception of a direct and personal approach to divinity, dispensing with elaborate hierarchical ritual statements, might be interpreted as a challenge to the hierarchical social order. There seems to have been a division among Chaitanya's close disciples on this issue. Some of them continued to be observant Brahmans who would not dine with persons of lower caste. Others, however, among whom one Nityananda was pre-eminent, held that the path of *bhakti* was open to all who came to it and that true devotion knew no caste distinctions. There remain representatives of both views among Bengali Vaishnavas today, but in the countryside, among all but the highest castes (i.e., Brahman, Kayastha, and Vaidya), Nityananda's position is victorious. Most Vaishnava 'brotherhoods' (*maṇḍalī*), groups of men who have taken initiation from the same preceptor, observe no distinctions among the castes of adherents. One of the favorite figures sculptured on the sides of *tulasī* pedestals shows 'Gaur-Nitai' (Gauranga, 'golden bodied', is an appellation of Chaitanya; Nitai is a shortened form of Nityananda) dancing together, hands in the air in an ecstatic posture.

In all of rural eastern Midnapur District, the Mahishya caste is much more numerous than all the other castes put together. This caste, known before the present century as Kaivartta, is anomalous in Bengali society. Though members are mainly agriculturalists, they are considered by other Hindus to lie outside the category of 'good' (*sat*) Sudras. Their rites are not performed by high-ranking Brahmans but by a group of Brahmans said to have been transformed from Kaivarttas by an utterance of the sage Vyasa (Vyasokta Brahman). Notwithstanding the low traditional position of the Mahishyas in Hindu society, the original kings of all the small kingdoms in the locality were persons of this caste. The village headmen (*grāmer mukhya, āmin*) were almost all Mahishyas, and when something is spoken of as a 'village affair', an affair of the Mahishyas is generally meant. High-ranking Brahmans and Kayasthas ordinarily hold themselves aloof from such affairs, while the other Sudra castes are pulled in or excluded according to their weight and social standing in the particular village. Bengal Vaishnavism, in its 'casteless' form, is particularly well suited to the Mahishyas, for it raises no awkward questions about their ambiguous social position. Thus, while Brahmans and Kayasthas continue the tradition of elaborate, hierarchy-maintaining worship, the Mahishya and other middle-ranking Sudras are overwhelmingly Vaishnava in dominant orientation.[3] In a Brahman or Kayastha house, a *tulasī* pedestal is often one among several shrines; in a Mahishya house, if it is not the only shrine, it is typically the most important and carefully attended of them.

Service of the *tulasī*

The kind of attention these little shrines receive varies greatly from house to house. Perhaps the most typical is the pattern in which the mistress of the house, returning from her morning bath, her clothing still wet—to ensure that she is fully purified—carries with her a small vessel of water that she pours over the earth in which the *tulasī* is planted. She bows to the *tulasī* and salutes it with hands pressed together. After this, she may begin her main work for the day, which is usually cooking the noon meal. The other usual daily observance takes place just at sunset, the ambiguous period when the day and night are joined (*sandhyā*). The mistress or another married woman sounds the conch shell in the rooms of the house to dispel any maleficent beings attracted by the growing darkness, then carries a lighted lamp to the pedestal, displays it before the *tulasī*, then bows and touches her forehead to the base of the pedestal as if laying it on the feet of Tulasi. Taking the dust from the feet of that faithful wife (*satī*) upon one's head imparts to the worshiper some of her qualities of chastity and devotion to one's husband. The solemn but auspicious sound of the conch shell and the yellow flames flickering as women bow before *tulasī* shrines in the swiftly falling evening are among the ineradicable images of a Bengali Hindu village, and Bengali poets have difficulty in avoiding them when they want to evoke serenity.

Initiated Vaishnavas, who are mostly males, must also serve (*sevā*) the *tulasī* plant. Their observances are more elaborate than those of uninitiated women, including verbal formulas (*mantra*) taught by their preceptors and recited when offering water or light to the plant. They may also offer special service, such as the observance in Vaisakha (April-May), the first and hottest month of the year, throughout which a pot with a small hole at the bottom is hung over the *tulasī* and kept filled with water so that it will drip continuously and provide the plant with a constant supply of water.

Many domestic rituals, including both life-cycle rites (*saṃskara*) and the regularly repeated worship of deities (*nitya karma*), are carried out near the *tulasī* pedestal, not because of any textual prescription, but because it is the purest and most auspicious place in or around the houses of most people. Vaishnava texts are quite eloquent on the qualities of the *tulasī* that make it so attractive. The sixteenth-century *Hari-bhakti-vilāsa* of Gopala Bhatta, an authoritative ritual manual of Bengal Vaishnavism, often refers to the *tulasī*. For example, in performing the daily worship of Vishnu,

> The worshipper should ... go to the Tulasi grove, and worship the shrub, which is Hari's darling, with perfume, flowers, and rice, bow down before it with complete prostration of the body, and pray with appropriate Mantra and Stava for its favour. A large number of Purana and other texts [cited by Gopala Bhatta] supplies exuberant and endless eulogy of the sacred Tulasi. Sometimes the laudation is extravagant, but nothing appears exaggerated to the devout mind, which even believes, among other things, that if one sits even for a single moment under the Tulasi shrub, sins of one crore [10,000,000] re-births melt away! (De 1961: 478; see also 461–517 *passim*.)

Devout Vaishnavas in rural Bengal today often cultivate entire gardens of *tulasī* plants, both to meet their ritual needs and as acts of devotion.

The elaboration of the *tulasī* pedestal

Almost every village in eastern Midnapur District possesses as common property a cluster of three or four small temples. A typical group of temples includes one for Sitala, goddess of smallpox and other diseases, who is often said to be the 'mother' of such-and-such a village; an associated shrine for Olabibi, the Muslim goddess of cholera; a Siva temple, containing a representation of this god in the phallic form; and a Hari temple. To refer to these as 'common village property' means, in most villages, that they are cared for by Mahishyas, together with representatives of other populous Hindu castes apart from the highest and lowest. High-caste landowners have often been donors of temples—usually of Siva rather than Sitala or Vishnu—and Brahmans perform the worship in all the village temples (save the Olabibi shrine, at which only a Muslim is deemed qualified to make offerings). But the money and offerings required for worship are collected by the middle-ranking Hindu castes. A group of male householders, the principal men of the village, makes the arrangements for worship and, at the beginning of the ritual, one of them undertakes, on behalf of the village, the solemn commitment (*saṃkalpa*) to conduct the worship. Thus, the fruits of the worship are thought to be returned to the village as a whole, rather than to a particular family, as is usually the case in the rituals of families of the highest castes. The lowest castes participate in these collective rituals in the same subordinate roles they play in the rites of the highest castes—as laborers, musicians, or providers of other caste-specialized goods or services.

A few Hari temples are ordinary, small, single-roomed structures containing a raised platform on which the *śālagrām* form of Vishnu is enthroned. But beginning in about the 1920s a new style of Hari temple became increasingly prevalent in this area. A typical example of this new style of temple is an oblong platform about six feet by nine feet raised two or three feet above the ground. The platform is constructed of brick covered with cement. Three or four steps lead up to the platform, which is covered by a low, four-sloped (*cārcālā*) roof. The sides are left open but there is usually a fence around the platform to keep out stray animals. Five *tulasī* pedestals are erected on the platform, four at the corners of a square, and a larger fifth one in the centre. The effect of this arrangement is reminiscent of the roof of a *pañca-ratna* style temple. The villagers refer to these structures as temples (*mandir*) despite the absence of the usual enclosed room (*garbha gṛha*, 'womb room') within which a deity is housed. After the construction of such a temple is completed, when it is ritually established (*pratiṣṭhā*), a small figure of the half-man, half-eagle Garuda, the King of Birds upon whose back Vishnu rides, kneeling, hands together in salutation, is added in front of the pillars.

It is usual for each village to offer worship in its Hari temple on the night of the full moon. The priest who is engaged to perform the ritual may be a Vyasokta Brahman, but many of them are Saktas—adherents of a goddess. Scrupulous Vaishnavas, even though they are Mahishyas, often prefer to employ locally-resident Brahmans of the Orissan order (Utkala Sreni Brahmans), most of whom are Vaishnavas, to worship Vishnu. The procedures of worship are quite simple, calling for no steps other than those prescribed for an ordinary Vishnu pūjā. Offerings consist of flowers, white sandalwood paste, water, a few cut-up plantains or other seasonal fruit, small round wafers of sugar (*bātāsā*), and a large tubfull of flattened rice (*ciṛā*) mixed with molasses (*guṛ*). This last item is a special offering, said to be an 'enjoyable feast' (*bhoga*), which is not obligatory although it is very desirable.

While the priest does the necessary ritual work of presenting the offerings to the deity, a band (*dala*) of village men sing *kīrtan* hymns about Krishna, Chaitanya, Nityananda, and repeat the names of Vishnu, while dancing before the temple. Such hymns are among the most common expressions of *bhakti* to Krishna in Bengal and bands of singers, equipped with their indispensible instruments, the *khol* drum and *karatāl* cymbals, are frequently invited to perform during other auspicious ceremonies in middle-caste households. The ground on which they dance while singing the name of Vishnu is considered to be infused with the substance of well-being, and mothers often place their infants prone upon it to transfer its qualities on to their bodies. When the priest has completed his work, the sugar wafers are thrown into the crowd of listeners, who scramble wildly after them as the 'scatterings of Vishnu' (*harir luṭ*).

Each month, by turns (*pālā*), one of the middle-caste families bears the cost of worship, of which the largest amount goes for flattened rice and molasses. The food that is left after it is offered to the deity is considered the 'favor' (*prasād*) of Vishnu. The men who organized the worship divide this food into small parcels, one of which is carried to each house in the village—including the houses of the highest and the lowest castes—so that all who are fellow villagers may share in the divine favor won through the collective worship. This sharing symbolizes the unity of otherwise decentralized and often strife-torn villages by concretely enacting it; everyone embodies some of the same divinely tainted substance.

Between 1960, when I first did fieldwork in Midnapur, and 1968, when I returned for a second period of research, the new style of temple seemed to have undergone a considerable increase in popularity. In that period a substantial number of village families had constructed such temples for their own worship, replacing the single *tulasī* pedestals they had previously venerated with the more elaborate structures.[4] Such temples are typically built by men above the age of forty who are financially successful, usually in agriculture. The cultivation of betel leaves which began, in the late 1950s, to be marketed from this locality throughout northern India, was the source of substantially increased incomes for many of the temple builders. Of course, financial means is a necessary but not a sufficient condition for the construction of one of these temples; the motivation must also be present.

The spirit of Vaishnava devotionalism is constantly accessible in

Bengali Hindu villages; mendicants wearing *tulasī* necklaces and singing the names of Vishnu daily pass from house to house begging; there are many occasions for the processional singing of *kīrtan* hymns through the villages; the graves (*samādhi*, or colloquially *samāj*) of devout Vaishnavas who are thought to have obtained release while still in their mortal bodies (*jīvana mukti*) are frequent gathering places for Vaishnava brotherhoods holding religious discussions or singing; and so on and on. Bengalis consider it natural and proper that people whose sons are grown and married should hand over to the latter the responsibility for family affairs (usually referred to as *saṃsāra*, 'mundane attachment') and turn their own thoughts and actions toward *dharma-karma*. In this environment, people from cultivator and other middle-ranking castes are overwhelmingly drawn toward Chaitanyite Vaishnavism: it is common at such a juncture to seek initiation, which often entails dietary restrictions (e.g., giving up meat and those 'heating' vegetables thought to provoke the passions), and undertaking elaborate daily, weekly, monthly, and annual cycles of worship. In the family that has the means, a commitment to construct one of the new style of Vishnu temples has in recent years become one of the obligations men undertake.

Understandings of the new temple

Enquiries about the meaning of the new-style, five-pedestalled Vishnu temple did not elicit uniform responses. Many villages had evidently given them little thought beyond the idea that if one *tulasī* pedestal was good, five were better. All sorts of auspicious substances come in groups of five. However, men who had themselves built such temples, or who were responsible for their care, seemed more sophisticated and consistently referred to them as *pañca-tattva* temples. *Pañca* means five; *tattva* means a great many things, among which are 'principle,' 'essential substance,' 'fundamental reality,' and, occasionally, just 'god.' In Bengal Vaishnavism, however, *pañca-tattva* has a special and peculiar meaning: it refers to Chaitanya and his four principal disciples as the objects most worthy of worship. This group is conventionally depicted in polychrome lithographs with Chaitanya in the center, the aged Advaitacharya (Advaita, 'non-dualist') to his right at the front, Nityananda right rear, Srivasa left front, and Gadadhara left rear. Several times, men produced such pictures to illustrate the significance of the five pedestals in the Vishnu temple.

The *pañca-tattva* interpretation of the Vishnu temple seemed quite secure, if slightly esoteric, until I interviewed an elderly Brahman of the Orissan order who, quite uncharacteristically for a high-caste person, had constructed one of these temples. He had spent his active life as a deed-writer working near the courts in the subdivisional headquarters town; he had never done priestly work. He said that '999 people in a thousand cannot say correctly what is represented by the pedestals. They will tell you *pañca-tattva* or Gauranga (Chaitanya) and his four disciples.' He explained that the temple represents the four-armed (*caturbhuja*)[5] Narayana. The central pedestal is his body, and each of the others is one of his four arms bearing his distinguishing features: the mace (*gadā*), discus (*cakra*), conch shell (*śankha*), and lotus (*padma*). He also said that this form of Vishnu temple had been created by Raja Rukmangada[6] during the Satya (i.e., Krita) Yuga; Chaitanya was responsible for making it popular in the present degraded Kali Yuga.

Despite the antiquity of the tradition invoked, it appears that this is a modern style of temple without any old precedents other than the medieval *pañca-ratna* temple roof. It is worth noting that the feminine and devotional significances of the *tulasī* plant have been submerged in the development of this more public temple with its more elaborate ritual requirements. However, such historical concerns are not the issue here. Rather, the second interpretation of the Hari temple (as well as the possibility of still others), and the apparently doctrinaire manner in which the alternative interpretations were presented opens the question of the 'social diversification' of understanding among Bengali Hindus. In Christianity, differences in religious interpretations of a scale comparable to this one have been treated as substance for conciliar deliberations and authoritative resolutions. How are such differences treated by Hindus?

Interpreting the Hari temple

Although both my Brahman informant and a good number of devout Vaishnavas of agricultural castes tried to persuade me that there is a single true and correct exegesis for the new style of temple, any attempt to impose the conceptions of orthodoxy and heterodoxy on their interpretations will lead to misunderstanding. There is a spirit of sectarianism in Bengali religion, exemplified in numerous apparently doctrinaire statements endorsing one practice and condemning another.

For example, persons who worship in their Hari temples on the eleventh days of lunar fortnights hold that their practice is superior to that of persons who worship on full moon nights: those who do the 'service (*sevā*) of Vaishnavas' (i.e., feeding five or seven initiated Vaishnavas the *prasād* of Vishnu worship) contend that this act is more meritorious than offering *prasād* to all who come, and so on. But if we try to interpret these differences as having to do with 'belief,' as this term is used in connection with Christianity, we will do some violence to the ideas of Bengali Hindus and fail to grasp what appears to me to be a fundamental feature of Hindu cultures in general.

It is common in Bengal for people to ask one another their *mat* on a particular issue, whether of religion, politics, the state of the world, or whatever. In this context, *mat* means something like 'opinion' or 'view'. A statement of one's *mat* is most likely to lead to a disagreement; Bengalis think that even wise men are invariably of different opinions (*nānā munir nānā mat*). However, they typically do not seek among a welter of differing *mats* to find one that is correct and thus to exclude contending views. It is rather that different *mats* provide different routes of action (*yato mat tato path*). Of course, some issues are more serious than others and some *mats* are worth more than those of two friends engaged in idle conversation. The ultimate sources of the interpretations of the Hari temple are various Vaishnava preceptors (*guru*), of whom there are many in the locality. When a pupil receives an opinion on a religious subject from the preceptor who initiated him, he is likely to adhere to it with the same firmness as a Hard Shell Baptist in the Tennessee Hills adheres to the King James translation of the *Bible*. But here is where the difference arises: while the Baptist is convinced that he is walking the one narrow road to salvation, the Vaishnava in rural Bengal thinks that other people are following other paths that will lead to the same goal. Thus, in the Hindu case, the issue is not whether someone has different beliefs (*viśvāsa*) or even different practices (*ācāra*), since these are bound to be different in some way or another for any two people. The question is what one *understands* oneself to be thinking and doing, and the answer to this question is a statement about the nature of the universe, of human beings, of divinities and of what kind of salvation one seeks.

A man of an agricultural caste who is responsible for the care of the Hari temple in one village provided me with a lesson on the subject of what I call understandings rather than beliefs in Hinduism. His paternal grandfather had migrated to the village in about 1890 (to take up cultivation on some land he had inherited from a childless mother's brother). During the 1920s, his father donated a small plot of land to support the village Hari temple, which is said then to have been a single *tulasī* pedestal. Other villagers contributed the money to construct a Hari temple in the new style, which was built in 1929. The man explained that it is customary for all the 'Hindu houses'—he used the term so as to include the middle-ranking, Vaishnava-oriented castes but exclude the predominantly goddess-oriented high caste—to take turns in providing the offerings for monthly worship. Then he added that the high-caste houses also contribute, but only for the special occasions of worship on the birthdays of Krishna and Radha. He explained the difference of practice by saying that the agriculturalists are of *sāttvik mat* ('inclined toward goodness'), while the high caste is of *rājasik mat*, by which he meant something like 'royalty inclined', that is, favoring the ranked relationships among persons that are brought into play in large-scale, special observances over the egalitarian relationships fostered by the simpler monthly observances in which the identity of follow villagers is emphasized.

In making this distinction my informant was calling upon the Hindu theory that human bodies are suffused with ineffable but substantial qualities (*guṇa*) that predispose them toward certain kinds of action. There are several different sets of qualities in Bengali culture; one that is very frequently referred to distinguishes 'three qualities' (*triguṇa*), *sattva*, goodness, *rajas*, action, and *tamas*, darkness. These qualities are thought to be acquired by birth (*janma*), together with 'caste' (*jāti*, 'birth group'), and to be a part of a person's own natural constitution or inherent disposition (*svabhāva*). At the same time, bodily qualities and caste are elements of a person's moral disposition or his own inherent code of conduct (*svadharma*). Thus, stated in western cultural terms, the castes and the qualities are seen in Bengali culture to be both 'natural' and 'moral' at the same time.[7] This identity between nature and morality is one expression of the postulate of non-dualism in Bengali Hindu culture.

Non-dualism does not imply a vagueness or indistinction between categories. Bengali Hindu culture includes numerous dualistic oppositions that are sharply drawn, but they are not mutually exclusive. For example, the *ātmā*, 'soul' or 'self,' may be distinguished from the *śarīra*, 'body,' in a way that appears familiar to westerners in whose cultures soul and body are treated as belonging to utterly disparate realms of existence. But in Bengali Hindu culture there is no radical distinction between the two; rather, *ātmā* and *śarīra* are treated as interdependent entities composed of the same matter, not mutually exclusive but mutually immanent.

The relationship among the three qualities in the make-up of a person's body is likewise not one of mutual exclusion but of relative balance and proportions. A person is usually considered to be dominated by one or the other of them and to exhibit the strength and proportion of his qualities in his conduct. A person dominated by *sattva* is inclined toward quietude, good actions, and simplicity in all things, including his characteristic manner of worship. While Brahmans are supposed to be naturally endowed with *sāttvik* dispositions, Vaishnavas of all castes cultivate the manifestations of *sattva* in their conduct and sometimes become known as 'Brahmans by quality' (*guṇa-brāhmaṇa*). A person dominated by *rajas* is inclined toward activity, governed by his passions, and disposed toward grandiose displays, including elaborate forms of worship. In this locality, high-caste landowners, particularly Kayasthas, are thought to have *rājasik* dispositions by their births. A person dominated by *tamas* is inclined toward disorderly action, such as drunkenness, evil conduct, and chaotic displays, including noisy worship, dancing, and the absence of devotion to the deity. The lowest castes are supposed to be innately of *tāmasik* disposition; however, rites of worship organized by young men who, regardless of caste, appear more interested in enjoying themselves than in worshiping the deity are also characterized by others as *tāmasik*.

A person's disposition to act in a particular way and his understanding of things are, in Bengali culture, both conceived of as being coded by the innate qualities in his body. Differences of *mat* among persons, whether this term be interpreted as 'disposition' or 'understanding,' are subject to strongly-worded evaluations that often fall upon the ears of a dualistically inclined westerner as statements of right or wrong, true or false, or orthodox or heterodox. However, dichotomies based upon mutual exclusion do not comprehend the simultaneous assessment of superiority/inferiority and of appropriateness that are present in the Hindu evaluation. Fürer-Haimendorf (1967: 176) has written of Hindu ethics that 'individual actions are not considered good or bad *per se*, but are evaluated according to the status of the agent.' So too in the realm of Hindu religious meanings, the understanding that a worshiper brings to his act of worship is judged by its appropriateness to a person endowed by birth with his qualities.

4. *The Village Mother in Bengal*

Mother herself is a person to be worshiped in Hindu Bengal.[1] In this, however, she is no different from the father: the honor, respect, and devotion worshipfully offered to the father are the prototypes of what one's mother should receive. Mother and father together are said to be the givers of a person's birth, body, food, knowledge, deliverance from fear, and liberation. The joint responsibility of parents for their children is but one of the many ways of stating the complementarity of the sexes that is emphasized in Hindu cultures. In this cultural scheme, the mother, as a wife, is always dependent upon her husband and is second, after him, to receive the veneration of her children. A similar relationship of complementarity with subordination often seems to prevail among Hindu divinities. The male gods are commonly depicted with their wives seated properly at their left hands. In this manner the beneficent goddess Lakshmi often accompanies Narayana, the chaste and long-suffering Sita accompanies Rama, and the beautiful daughter of the mountain, Parvati, accompanies Shiva. However, to accept a view of the feminine half of the Hindu pantheon as simply a collection of 'consorts' of the gods would be to miss something fundamental about Indian religion as well as to pass silently over a critical part of what Hindu cultures say about women.

There is a large body of Hindu myths relating the autonomous, often powerful actions of goddesses (*devī*). One of the most commonly used Sanskrit words for 'power,' Śakti, is also a name for a goddess, designating either an individual or a class of power-wielding feminine divinities. The most ancient Indian myths contain references to goddesses, but they seem to be of lesser importance than the gods and are not separately worshiped. It is not in ancient texts, the Vedas, Brahmanas, Upanishadas, or the epics, that we find the myths of powerful, independent goddesses, but rather in the Puranas and later literature, beginning about the sixth century AD. From that time onward there is a continuous tradition, extending throughout India and up to the present, of the worship of goddesses, including the discovery of new ones and the composition of new myths about them. Such goddesses are often named after their fathers or husbands by changing the gender of the name from masculine to feminine. However, even in early Puranas goddesses are sometimes identified as Ambika ('mother' or 'good woman'), as well as Chandi ('angry') or Durga ('fortress' or 'formidable'), for whom there are no equivalent male deities. Overtly maternal images—succor, nurturance, intercession, deliverance—are by no means always at the forefront in myths and rituals addressed to Indian goddesses. Underlying all such deities, there is the widely held Hindu concept that the male (*puruṣa*) is by himself incomplete and inert, and must be conjoined with an active, feminine 'nature' (*prakṛti*) in order to act in the world. Like *śakti* or 'power,' the term *prakṛti* (which is often used to mean all that is signified by 'nature' in English) may be used to designate a goddess or class of goddesses. The complementary interaction of masculine and feminine in Hindu thought is well summarized in the expression, 'Śiva without Śakti is a corpse' (*śiva śaktihīna śava*).

The cultures of the Christian West, with their single transcendent masculine divinity, whom 'no man hath seen . . . at any time' (John 1:18), finds its antithesis in the exuberant polytheistic iconolatry of Hinduism. Judaism, Christianity, and Islam have all done battle against religious systems with large pantheons, female deities, demigods, and demons. Some angels, the Blessed Virgin, a panoply of saints, and Satan and his hosts remain as minor pockets of polytheism in the Semitic religions. Islam claimed a share of India, mainly through the preaching of an inward religion and a pantheistic god. But the largest part of the South Asian population has continued over millennia to work out religious meanings through a set of understandings embodied in a very large, complexly interconnected array of myths, deities, and modes of worship. Additions are often made to the set, but deletions are rare. To call these understandings 'Hinduism' is mainly a convenience to outsiders; and indigenous Indian religion contains numerous 'isms' of its own, although these tendencies lack the exclusivity of Western sectarianism.

For centuries, Western scholars (as well as those persons for whom some aspect of Hinduism seems to offer religious meaning missing from our own tradition) have sought to make sense of Indian religion. The contribution of anthropologists to this effort consists mainly in trying to make intelligible the Indian religion of ordinary life, describing and explaining the deities, rituals and myths of people in the villages, towns, and regions accessible to personal investigation. We have been able to demonstrate that various linguistic groups and castes often show proclivities for one or another group of deities, a particular set of myths, and specific patterns of worship. However, it would be too optimistic to think that a breakdown of India by language and caste will provide *the key* to Hindu diversity. The line of analysis I pursue here might suggest such a pattern in regional religious orientations. But permutations of what I have seen in Bengal are found in the other linguistic areas of India and among other castes, involving somewhat varying groups of deities, myths, and manners of worship.

Bengal is the region around the mouths of the Ganges; its core is the 50,000-square-mile delta formed by the Ganges and the Brahmaputra. The predominant language of the region is Bengali, the easternmost of the Indo-European languages. The larger part of the area is included in Bangladesh, where about 90 percent of the population is Muslim. (Why Bengalis should turn from Hinduism to Islam is a fascinating problem in cultural history that I cannot discuss here.) The remainder of the region constitutes the Indian state of West Bengal, in which Hindus predominate. Bengali Hindus are characterized throughout the South Asian subcontinent by several distinguishing features: in religion, it is their peculiar attachment to mother goddesses (despite the fact that a detailed examination of religious preferences in West Bengal would probably show the male god Krishna to be the popular favourite). Calcutta, the capital of the state and the metropolis of eastern India, is a pilgrimage place of the goddess Kali.

The eastern part of Midnapur District, in West Bengal, is a part of the lower Ganges delta. In this area there is a cluster of eight villages, known collectively as Kelomal, which were inhabited by about 3,700 people of twenty-one different castes in 1968–69. These villages are

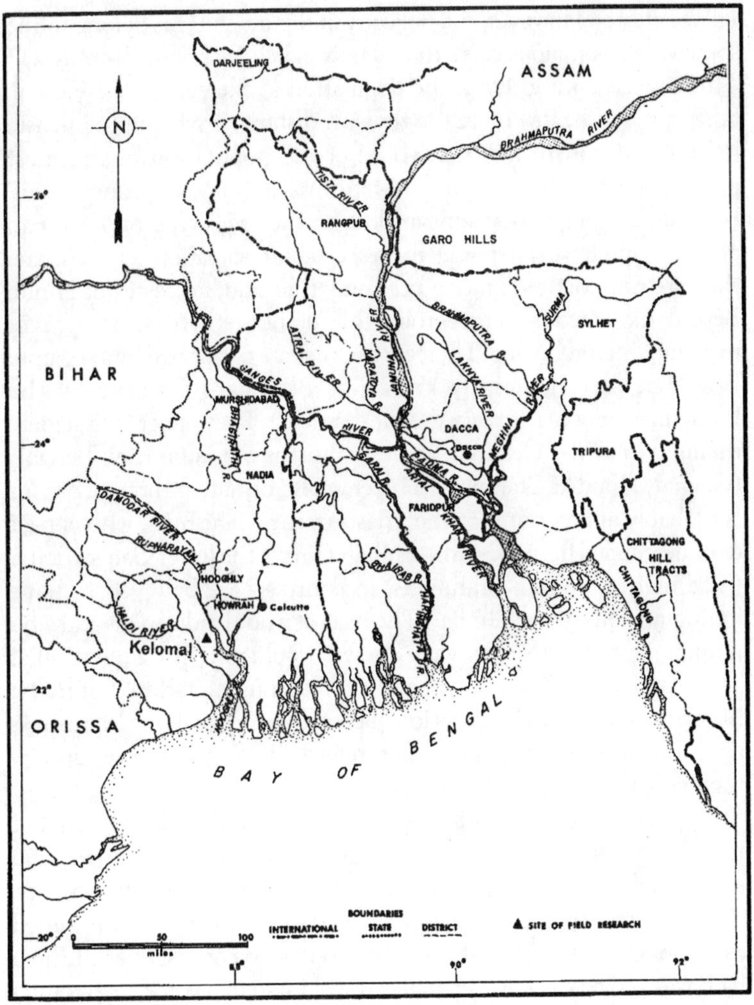

Bengal, West Bengal, and Bangladesh.

all of comparatively recent origin, having been settled during the last two hundred years. Previously, the area was too low-lying and deeply flooded during the monsoon season to permit continuous habitation. The affairs of landed estates and of several small kingdoms in the locality brought a nucleus of high castes, Kayasthas (traditionally scribes) and Brahmans (traditionally priests and teachers), into the center of this village cluster. However, the majority of the inhabitants belong to the somewhat anomalous caste that is now called Mahishya (Māhīṣya).[2] This caste is a minority of the population at the center of Kelomal, but it preponderates increasingly with distance from the high caste houses and constitutes the whole of the population of the most peripheral village. I refer to the Mahishyas as 'somewhat anomalous' because, although they appear close to the ideal type of a yeoman peasantry, preferring to pursue the respectable occupation of agriculture, they are not counted among the nine 'true Shudra' castes of Hindu Bengal. Excluded from this group, they do not receive the services of high-ranking Brahmans. Their ceremonies are performed by a separate Brahman caste generally known as Brahmans Created by the Pronouncement of the Sage Vyasa (Vyāsokta). They prefer to designate themselves as the Original Vedic Brahmans of Gaura (i.e., Bengal) (Gauṛādya Vaidika Brāhman). This emphasis on autochthonous origins is probably appropriate for the priests of the Mahishyas, who appear to be descended from the earliest inhabitants of the lower Ganges delta. (The higher-ranking Brahmans, in contrast, are believed to have immigrated from north India.) The issue of who is indigenous and who is immigrant, if the history were known, would turn into a question of 'more' and 'less' indigenous, of earlier or later immigration. But in the historical and cultural perception of people in Kelomal, the Mahishyas appear as the autochthons—often referred to by themselves and by high people as simply 'the Bengalis.'

Until the recent abolition of zamindari tenure,[3] the land was under the control of the high castes and it was Kayasṭha zamindars who exercised the predominant social and political authority over the locality. Yet at the same time the villages, as unified social entities, were regarded as belonging to the Mahishyas. Though landed control over the area by Kayasthas has recently changed, the old system has not been totally erased. Kayasthas still appear as the petty chiefs of Kelomal and symbolically enact their kingly roles in certain ways. However, the man who is 'master' (*kartā*), or 'supervisor' (*āmin*) of each village is a Mahishya. Corresponding to this cultural distinction between the petty 'kingdom' (*zamindāri, parganā, rājya*) and the 'country' (*deśa*) or 'village' (*grāma*) is a distinction between two goddesses, each of whom is addressed and venerated as a 'mother' by Bengali Hindus.

Durga the formidable, slayer of the Buffalo Demon (Mahiṣāsura), identified with Parvati, daughter of Himalaya and wife of Shiva, is foremost among the divine mothers of the Kayasthas. Her worship is held with great pomp and splendor each autumn in permanent pavilions (*maṇḍapa*) maintained in the houses of the principal Kayastha and high-ranking Brahman families of Kelomal. I cannot say much about Durga here; her personality, worship, and mythology are very complex. However, a few of her characteristics are important in understanding what follows. The central image of the goddess is made afresh each

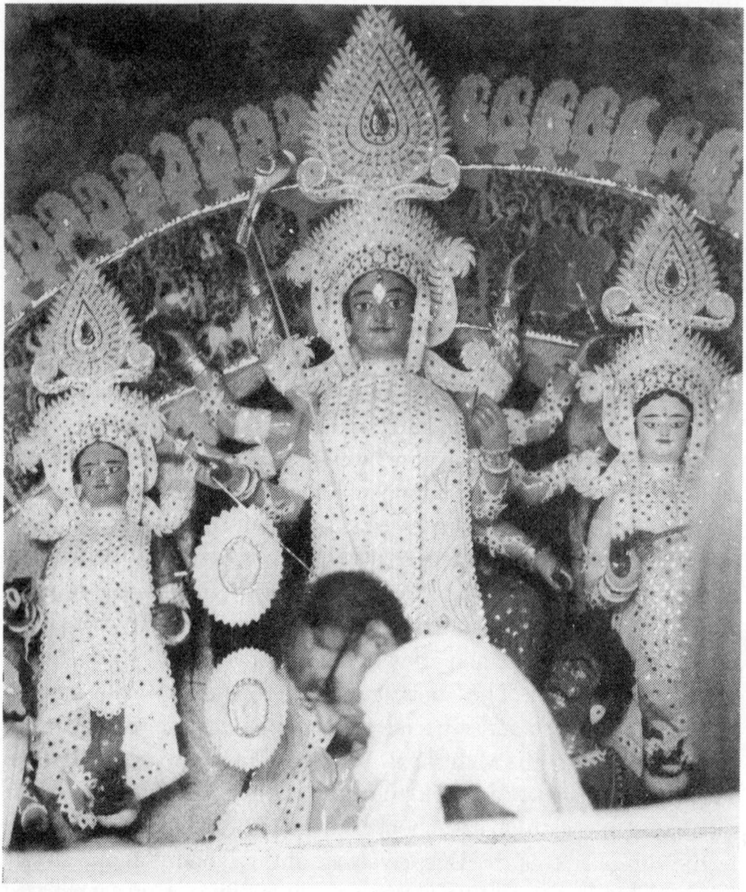

The goddess Durga receiving worship from a Brahman priest in the house of a high caste family. With Durga are her daughters, Lakshmi (*left*), goddess of prosperity, and Sarasvati (*right*), goddess of learning. The face of the Buffalo Demon, who is about to die, is visible behind the back of the priest.

year; she does not dwell permanently in the houses where she is worshiped but, rather, visits annually as a daughter coming from her husband's house, bringing her four children with her. She is invariably represented as of benign countenance, with a golden complexion that symbolizes the red principle of action (*rajaḥ-guṇa*) shining faintly through the pure white of the principle of truth (*sattva-guṇa*). At the same time, she is always shown trampling the corpse of the dying Buffalo Demon as she spears him with one of the weapons she carries in her ten hands. She is always very beautiful, with long almond eyes and a triangular face, full, high breasts, a slender, graceful waist, and appealingly rounded hips. In short, she is as sexually desirable to a man as only a greatly idealized woman could be—and, as his mother, she is sexually forbidden. Thus, the figure of Durga embodies elements of strong ambivalence. The goddess, perceived as taking several different forms, is offered many animal sacrifices during the three central days of her worship. Blood sacrifice is an emotionally charged act for Bengalis; many meanings are represented in each sacrifice, some of them unconscious. The overt, culturally coded meanings of the sacrifices are contained in a Sanskrit myth known as 'Chandi' (*Caṇḍī*) or 'The Exaltation of the Goddess' (*Devī Māhātmya*), a portion of the *Markaṇḍeya Purāṇa*. This myth provides in verbal form the overall structure of the ritual of Durga worship; in it the goddess repeatedly engages and destroys the leading demons (*asuras*) who have conquered heaven from the gods (*devas*). She is drawn into battle each time by the posturing and megalomanic boasting of demons who alternately wish to possess her, as the goddess of unmatched beauty, and to destroy her, as the sole threat to their control of heaven. Each animal sacrifice during the ritual symbolizes her destruction of a demon army or champion.[4]

Shitala (Śītalā), 'The Cool One,' as she is catachrestically named, goddess of diseases and especially of smallpox, is the pre-eminent mother goddess of the Mahishyas. Whereas Durga is worshiped in the autumn, Shitala is worshiped in the spring; whereas Durga is worshiped separately in each high caste house, Shitala is worshiped collectively by the village or 'country.' Durga is always anthropomorphic and clearly benign; Shitala is often a crude stone of dubious mien. Durga is married to Shiva and has four divine children; Shitala may be represented as a married woman, but her husband is unknown and she is childless. The splendor of Shitala's worship is strictly limited by the ability of the usually poor agricultural and laboring families to contribute in

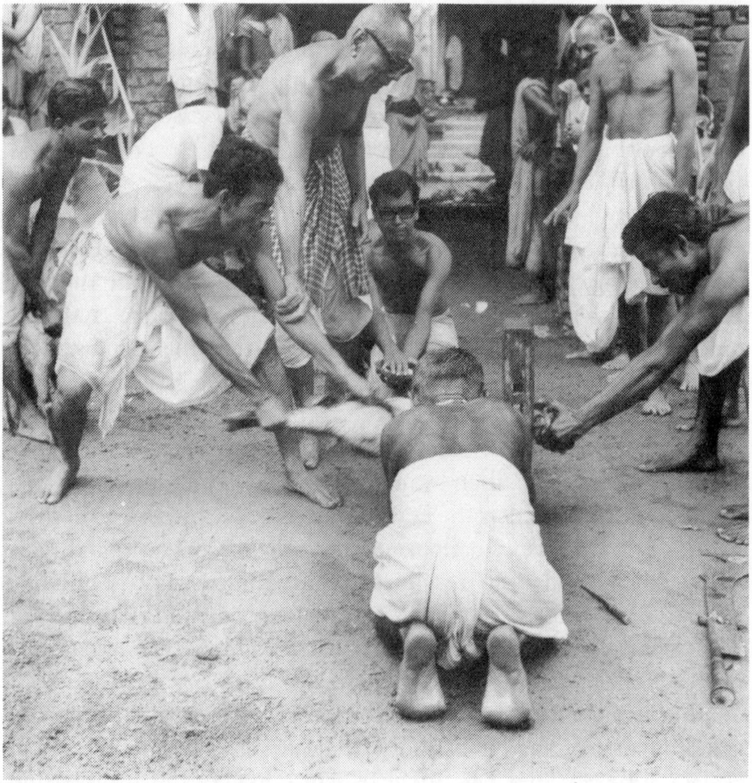

Men of a Kayastha clan sacrifice a goat to Durga. They shout *jay ma*! (Victory Mother!) as the immolator, a man of the Blacksmith caste, severs the goat's neck with a single stroke from a sacrificial blade. A second blade is visible at the lower right.

cash or kind. Moreover, cooperation is often difficult to gain where factionalism is rife and no one's motives are above suspicion. It is the goddess herself and the urgent necessity of worshiping her during the proper season that bring divided villagers together and restore lost unity. The Bengali word for spring, *basanta*, is also the most commonly used term for smallpox. Thus, behind the obligatory timing of her worship is a threat of punishment as well as the promise of common well-being.

There is a formulaic description of Shitala in Sanskrit, but most of her mythology is in the Bengali language.[5] She is described in her myths as, in true form, a very beautiful maiden, but she spends most of her time in the guise of a haggard, witchlike Brahman widow. Her principal courtier is the horrendous, triple-headed Fever Demon (Jvārasura), who goes about disguised as a young servant. She is also accompanied by a somewhat shadowy serving woman named Possessor of the Blood (Raktāvati). Whenever Shitala is worshiped collectively by a village, the Cholera Goddess, Olabibi (who is a Muslim), is also worshiped.[6]

In broad outline, the myth of Shitala that is performed in the Kelomal villages consists of six segments or 'dramas' (*pālā*).[7] In the first, she is born as a beautiful maiden from the cooled ashes of a sacrificial fire; the god Brahma names her 'The Cool One' from the circumstances of her birth. Shiva gives her the Fever Demon as a servant, and she sets off to the kingdom of the god Indra to receive her first worship. She enters the royal court disguised as an ancient crone and is arrogantly treated, first by Indra, then by many other gods. Humiliated and in a great rage, Shitala orders the Fever Demon to take possession of their bodies; after the fever, smallpox erupts on their bodies. Shiva reveals to the afflicted gods that 'this illness is caused by the wrath of Shitala.' They then understand the true nature of the goddess and worship her with devotion; at once the pain and pustules disappear. Then Shitala proceeds to obtain worship from mortals.

In the second segment, Shitala appears to the king of Virata in a terrifying dream, and offers him all that life can give, as well as final release, if he worships her. She threatens him with the annihilation of his kingdom if he does not. The king, a devotee of Shiva, refuses to worship her. Infuriated, she assembles a vast army of diseases, including a separate detachment of poxes. The poxes are disguised as so many varieties of vegetable pulses. The Fever Demon places sacks of these appealing delicacies on the backs of bullocks. With the goddess on her mount, the ass, they hasten down the road to Virata.

The third drama concerns her encounter with a greedy toll collector who helps himself to the pox pulses, which he feeds to his seven sons. They, in turn, share them with the other boys of the village. When all the toll collector's sons have died horribly of smallpox, he and his wife prepare to bury themselves with the sons' bodies on the cremation ground. Shitala reveals herself to them at the last moment and says that she will revive the sons if the toll collector will worship her, which he gladly does. In order to avoid giving away her game, the goddess turns the boys' bodies into stone to wait for revivification until she has conquered Virata.

In the fourth and dramatically central segment of the narrative, she moves swiftly to punish the kingdom, selling pox pulses to the king and to his subjects in all of his markets. The kingdom is devastated. When the king's sons die, the king and and queen prepare to follow the course of the toll collector and his wife. But Shitala again appears and revives the dead sons. The royal preceptor praises the goddess with an elaborate hymn, and she then restores life to the king's subjects. Thereafter, Shitala is worshiped throughout Virata.

In the fifth episode of the myth, a young, devoted merchant has a number of adventures while traveling to the southern Kingdom of Pakisa to bring back the golden pot originally used in the worship of Shitala. When the merchant returns to Virata, the king uses this pot in worship of Shitala.

A final, brief drama describes the obtaining of Shitala's worship in Gokul, the childhood habitation of Krishna.

The entire myth is referred to as the 'Vigil Drama' (*Jāgaraṇa Pālā*). Singers take various parts in the several episodes, and the myth is performed as a cantata. (Once I saw a full operatic form with costumes and sets.) The drama continues through the night in front of the image of the goddess. The villagers obtain Shitala's blessing by remaining awake and attentive to the entire myth and its message about this mother who oscillates so often between rage and mercy, punishment and compassion.

Although practically the same version of the myth concerning Shitala's activities in the world of mortals is performed in conjunction with her worship in each village, she does not appear in any two villages in quite the same form. In five of the eight villages there are permanent images of Shitala; these receive regular daily worship as well as the special annual collective worship in the spring. Each of these five goddesses is most often referred to by villagers in an ambiguous expression (*grāmer mā*) that may mean either 'mother of the village' or 'mother belonging to the village.' The three villages that presently lack such mothers nevertheless offer annual worship to Shitala. The following brief summary sketches the diversity of the forms and treatment of the goddess among closely linked villages.

In one village, Shitala has the form of an old, rather crude stone

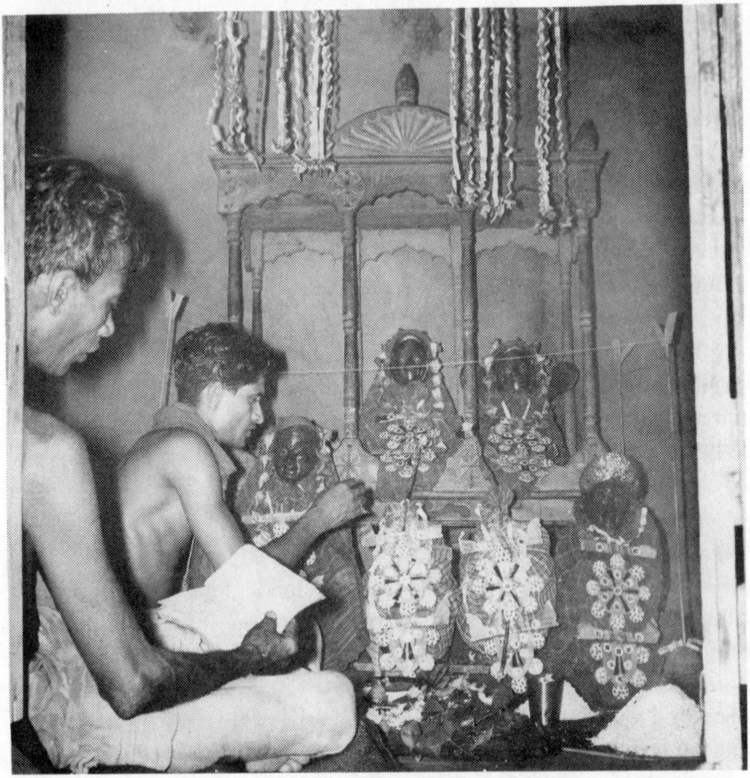

The goddess Shitala (*center*) receiving offerings during her annual worship in a village temple. At her left is Manasa, goddess of snakes, with the hood of a snake emerging from behind each shoulder. Seated on a lower level are two older images of these goddesses; Manasa wears a silver repoussé crown. Between them are the pot icons of the deities, established especially for their worship. One Brahman reads the verses of offering from a manual to insure against errors in their recitation by the second Brahman, who is making the offerings.

image, heavily coated with vermilion, that shares a temple with a ferocious form of Shiva and with the Bengali Snake Goddess (Manasā), both of whom receive worship and animal sacrifices when Shitala is worshiped. In the next village there are two images of the goddess, one a purchased modern brass figurine, and the other a stone roughly resembling a face and believed to have revealed herself in a village pond to a Vyasokta Brahman woman three generations ago. The two icons are worshiped as one and fed a cooked food offering including fresh fish curry. In a third village, which is on the southern boundary of the previous two, there are two figurines of Shitala (and two of the Snake Goddess) in a village temple. The older pottery image sits beneath a newer brass one installed by an upwardly mobile family as a means of establishing a new family name. This goddess eats a vegetarian diet.

In a fourth village the goddess has her own temple, in which pots representing the Fever Demon and the Bengali Tiger God (Dakṣiṇa Rāya) flank her brass image. She is said to accept animal sacrifices from individuals periodically during the year, but she receives only a fish in her annual collective worship. In the next village, the icon of the goddess is a pot that previously shared a temple belonging to the Snake Goddess. The temple is in disrepair and the Mahishya village headman has taken the deities' pots into his own household shrine, where they are worshiped daily by a Vyasokta Brahman who lives elsewhere. The annual village worship of Shitala is done at the Brahman's household temple. The northernmost Kelomal village has an image of the goddess, but no temple; so the goddess dwells in the temple of the Vyasokta Brahman who worships her. Families from this village send individual offerings to their goddess and there is no collective worship. The smallest of the villages has neither a temple nor a permanent image of Shitala, yet she is worshiped annually in a major collective ceremony. She and her attendants are established in the form of pots on the verandah of the Mahishya village headman's house.

The eighth village also has no permanent Shitala shrine but once came near to having one. The village headman there is not forceful and effective, and it is difficult to get villagers organized for a collective ceremony without strong leadership. Despite this problem, the annual worship of the goddess is done intermittently by the villagers. However, she receives worship every year in one household. An elderly Brahman of the Orissan order is head of a large, prosperous family in the village. He is a deed writer and is knowledgeable about land laws; he is also punctilious in ritual matters and contemptuous of the religious understandings of other villagers. It occurred to him some years ago that he might perform a social benefice by establishing a Shitala temple for the village. He planned to donate a large part of his agricultural holdings to support the worship of the goddess, thereby obtaining a remission of taxes on the land. By declaring himself servant (*sevāit*) of the temple, he would receive considerable financial benefit in addition to religious merit. As he was preparing to do this, the goddess appeared to him in a dream and told him, in effect, that she did not approve of his motivation. Although he felt thenceforth unable to establish Shitala in the village, he thought it perilous to ignore the goddess. Therefore, he established her annual worship in his own house. He is basically inclined toward Vaishnavism and does not offer her animal sacrifices. However, the goddess is fed a fish curry—made not from the inferior variety of fish offered by Mahishyas, but from a large, expensive carp.

What can be concluded from this cursory review of the village mothers of Kelomal? First, it seems obvious that accidents of history and the motives of particular individuals in specific times, places, and circumstances have played a part in establishing the various goddesses. Second, villages have probably made some effort to create collective representations, emulating other villages while at the same time distinguishing themselves from them. Insofar as the villages have succeeded in establishing and maintaining village mothers, these are clearly differentiated from one another, even though they are all identified with Shitala. Third, there are important differences between the center and the periphery of the village cluster. The personality of the goddess is most strongly marked in the villages with high caste populations, where Shitala worship is close to the Durga worship of the Kayasthas; and the elaboration of Shitala worship is greater in the central villages than in the peripheral ones. These relatively trivial generalizations aside, the fact remains that it is always a mother goddess who identifies the ordinary cultivators of each village as a unity, but why a mother rather than any other possible kind of representation?

It is not possible to achieve a full and convincing cultural explanation of this phenomenon without examining much more of the religious understanding of the Mahishyas of Kelomal. I have not said anything about Shiva, the pre-eminent father and male fertilizer in the local pantheon. (There are Shiva temples in several of these villages.) Nor have I said anything about the other very significant goddesses—particularly Kali, Lakshmi, and Sarasvati—who are worshiped as mothers by most villagers, but who are not said to be the mothers of villages. The largest omission in this discussion has been the Vaishnava pantheon, centered on Krishna, Narayana, and Vishnu. Most of the Kelomal villagers—virtually all of the Mahishyas and many of the higher and lower castes—devote most of their regular religious attention to these deities. The number of people who profess to be pre-eminently goddess worshipers (*śākta*) is very small. At a sociological level, most of these villages are unified by a system in which, once each month, it is the turn of a different household to make a food offering to the village Vishnu temple. Enough food must be provided so that everyone in the village can share in the auspicious leftover food of the god (*prasāda*), and a quantity of it is carried to every house.

It may appear that I have biased the whole issue by focusing on a small part of a total system, thereby distorting the larger pattern. But this is not the way Bengalis think about the matter, for when a particular deity is being worshipped, all of the others recede into the background; they are not ignored or forgotten, but the deity before one at a particular time and place becomes the most high. When Shitala is being worshiped, there is no doubt that she is the foremost divinity.

The most fundamental mother of all, in the Bengali scheme of things, is the earth (*pṛthivi*) or the land (*bhūmi*), which is thought of as giving birth to all the most important things in the moral world, including food and people. The earth is a very productive symbol of maternity. She is believed to menstruate for three days in the spring (*ambubācī*), during which time men are forbidden to use their plows or to dig in the earth. Following this flow, the rains begin and men should dig and plow and plant their seeds, which the goddess then rears in the womb of her fields (*kṣetra*), providing the food that nourishes men's bodies. Like many symbols in Bengali culture, the earth may be seen as progressively encompassing or as divisible yet whole. Thus, one may worship a particular image of a deity in one place and satisfy that deity wholly even while others are doing the same thing elsewhere with equivalent effect. So, too, the earth of a particular village may be regarded as whole and complete in itself, or as a part of the encompassing earth of Bengal, or even all of India. Persons born of the same mother are considered to be closely related because they shared her womb. Similarly, persons born of the same village are considered to be closely related because they share the earth of that village. Thus, the unity and common concern with one another's well-being that fellow villagers should have is expressed in the maternal symbol of the earth of their village.[8] This is a very important part of the cultural explanation of the cult of the village mothers in Bengal, but is not the whole of it.

The goddess Shitala, even though her image is often regarded as consubstantial with the earth of a particular village, does not symbolize the birth-giving aspect of motherhood; other deities are worshiped for barrenness or successful delivery. Nor does she symbolize authority and protection, as does Durga, seen as vanquisher of the demons who wrested control of heaven from the gods. On the contrary, Shitala's mythology depicts her as invariably accompanied by the grotesque Fever Demon, whom she treats with the greatest affection, as if he were her own son. She punishes virtuous kings who are worshipers of Shiva or Vishnu and destroys peaceable kingdoms whose only fault is ignorance of her worship. She tempts fallible persons, and especially mischievous children, with irresistible delicacies, which then break out on their bodies as horrifying and fatal poxes. In the end, people are able to recognize the great goddess behind these terrifying manifestations. When they worship her, she sets the kingdom right again and restores the dead to life. The myth and ritual of Shitala make it possible for people to recognize the 'grace of the Mother' (*māyer dayā*) even in their own suffering. Less explicitly, Shitala reminds Bengalis that the mother who gave them birth is also a punisher, sometimes with sudden and inexplicable rage. Petulant behavior, met on one day with indulgence, might evoke a beating and a screaming fit on the next.

Infectious disease may be an apt symbol of maternal punishment: it often seems to strike arbitrarily, laying low the righteous, ignoring sinners, and breaking out in epidemic rampages. However, it seems likely that there is also a specific historical connection between the founding of these villages, about two centuries ago, and outbreaks of contagious diseases, among which a severe form of smallpox may have been most fatal.[9] This unprecedented experience of devastating epidemics seems to have been a focus for religious creativity as well as practical action. Whereas the other Bengali mother goddesses, such as the Snake Goddess and Chandi (a much more complex and generalized mother), are well established in myths written down before the seventeenth century, the first known manuscript of a Shitala myth was not written until about AD 1690. Then there was a hiatus until about 1750 when suddenly half a dozen versions were composed within a few years. The rapid growth of interest in Shitala, evidenced by this large number of texts of her myth written in the mid-eighteenth century, was probably motivated by epidemics that swept lower deltaic western Bengal during these years. The longest, most detailed, of these texts, summarized earlier in this article, was written in a village only a few miles from Kelomal, and the others were all composed in the lower part of West Bengal. It would be a mistake, however, to think of Shitala as a localized Little Traditional goddess. She is known throughout Indo-Aryan-speaking India under the same name; and village tutelaries under various names, all associated with contagious and epidemic diseases, appear also throughout Dravidian India.[10]

Some verses from the 'Salutation of Shitala' illustrate the complex and condensed character of this maternal figure. After saluting her divinity and her resplendent beauty, the poet says:

> Whomsoever you look at, Mother, from the corner of your right eye, attains paradise merely at that hint. Whoever you look at with your left eye loses existence, and no one remains to light the lamp of his lineage.
>
> With you, your handmaiden Possessor of the Blood; you travel on your special vehicle, the ass, with the Fever Demon and all the poxes in attendance.

> Oh, Mother of the Universe, Bestower of Life, Controller of Diseases, Daughter of the Ordainer [Brahmā], remove all obstacles and destroy all enemies.[11]

Even when she is perceived as Controller of Diseases, she remains capable of deliverance as well as destruction. She is the Supreme Mother of the Universe and Bestower of Life even while she is engaged in teaching humans of her grace by giving them horrible diseases. According to the tenets of Bengali culture, punishment is also a form of parental love.

5. *Caṇḍī*

Introduction

The long Sanskrit poem usually called *Caṇḍī* by Bengalis is the foremost authority for the worship of Durgā and, at the same time, an integral part of her worship. In contemporary Bengal, the 'totalizing' form of the goddess (*devī*)—the form (*rūpa*) considered to contain all her other forms—is almost always called Durgā ('Difficult of Access') and represented as 'Killer of the Anti-god Buffalo' (Mahiṣāsura-mardinī). In the poem, the totalizing form of the goddess is most commonly visualized as Caṇḍī ('Wrathful') and called by the name Caṇḍikā, although a host of other names and epithets also appears in it.

The *Caṇḍī* is a poem of great magnificence—an efficacious power in its own right, according to Bengali Hindu views—and it is frequently read as a complete item of religious practice in itself. Much can be learned from an approach to the poem that ignores its connection with the contemporary ritual of Durgā worship. And, for purposes of historical or literary scholarship, consideration of the modern ritual is just as likely to obscure as to elucidate the ancient meaning of the text. But if the object of study is an understanding of its meaning for those living Bengalis who read it, hear it, and mull over its significance, then examination of its relationship to the ritual in which it is so centrally implicated is inescapable.

The *Caṇḍī* is received today as chapters 81–93 of the *Mārkaṇḍeya Purāṇa*, one of the early Sanskrit Purāṇas, its oldest portion dating from perhaps the third century AD.[1] It appears, from geographical references, to have been composed in western India, far from Bengal. The *Caṇḍī*, or *Devī-māhātmya* ('Glorification of the Goddess') as it is called in the Purāṇa, is a somewhat later composition, dating from the fifth or sixth century, the last three chapters probably being more recent still. However, it is safe to assume that the text was complete long before the development of the modern form of the ritual of Durgā in Bengal. The dates, the provenance, and the historical layering of the composition are not of much relevance outside of scholarly circles among Bengalis today. They usually treat the *Caṇḍī* as integral and complete in itself and, thus, read it apart from the Purāṇa; I have followed this practical authority in examining it here.[2] The thirteen chapters are customarily grouped in three units, the *caritas*, 'acts' or 'deeds' of the goddess: the *prathama*, 'first,' or *pūrva*, 'early' deeds; the *madhyama*, 'middle' deeds; and the *uttara*, 'later,' or *uttama*, 'highest' deeds.

The text begins (1.1–48) and ends (13.1–17) with a framing tale, concerning an ascetic Brāhmaṇ sage, a defeated king, and dispossessed Vaiśya, which has little to do with the central narrative but carries one of the most important moral message the Bengali audience finds in the *Caṇḍī*. The 'early deeds' of the goddess are related in the latter half (1.49–78) of the first chapter. The *madhyama-carita* is considered to include chapters 2–4, but chapter 4 is entirely devoted to an elaborate hymn of praise (*stuti*) to the goddess, chapters 2 and 3 containing all the narrative in 109 verses. Chapters 5–13 constitute the third section, which includes three praise hymns, two enumerations of the benefits of worshiping the goddess, and some other material—altogether 354 verses—besides the central narrative, which is contained in chapters 6–10. The progressive elaboration of the text from one *carita* to the next is closely paralleled in the progressive elaboration of the rites of Durgā worship during the three principal days of the pūjā.

In most of the versions of the *Caṇḍī* used in Bengal, a contemplation verse (*dhyāna-mantra*) evoking a particular form of the goddess is included before each *carita*. The 'first deeds' are preceded by the contemplation of Mahākālī, black, the embodiment of the quality of entropy (*tamaḥ-guṇa*), who is saluted as slayer of the anti-gods Madhu and Kaiṭabha. Mahālakṣmī, with a coral-colored complexion, embodying the quality of action (*rajaḥ-guṇa*), is contemplated as the slayer of the anti-god Buffalo before the *madhyama-carita*. And before the 'final acts' of the goddess, she is contemplated as Mahāsarasvatī, radiantly white, the embodiment of the quality of goodness (*sattva-guṇa*), slayer of the anti-gods Śumbha and Niśumbha. No effort is made to present these contemplations as being anything other than interpolations in the text, but they are regarded as wholly harmonious with it and as important aids to understanding the character of the goddess as she appears in each section.

Like most Sanskrit compositions about divinities, the *Caṇḍī* is considered to be both verbally and acoustically encoded. That is, its words and sentences carry a semantic load—they 'make sense' as ordinary language—as well as an intrinsic efficaciousness capable of exercising its beneficent influence on hearers whether they 'understand' it or not—they are more than ordinary language. Sanskrit scholars from outside Bengal sometimes marvel at the tenacity of this conception of the language among Bengalis, whom they regard as 'distorting' Sanskrit pronunciation to fit the phonological pattern of Bengali. The matter is quite otherwise among Bengalis, however, many of whom consider that they pronounce Bengali as if it were Sanskrit rather than vice versa. (Modern Bengali spelling is often quite faithful to the Sanskrit original, although the pronunciation is unquestionably 'prakritized.') The doctrine of the double-encoding of Sanskrit is a formidable block to translation, since anything that changes the sound of the original (*mūla*, 'root') destroys its acoustic efficaciousness. The term most commonly used for 'translation,' *anuvāda*, derived from a root meaning 'speech,' emphasizes the significance of sound itself. Thus, the reading aloud of the *Caṇḍī* (*Caṇḍī-pāṭha*) in ritual contexts—including the reading given over the Calcutta station of All-India Radio at dawn on Mahālayā day, at the beginning of the goddess's fortnight—is done in Sanskrit.

The well-known difficulty notwithstanding, many Bengali translations of the *Caṇḍī* have been reverently made over many centuries. The usual practice has been to join the translation to the original so that the sound and the sense are presented together, and this procedure has been followed in modern English renderings as well. I have had to go a step further here in preparing a condensed and abridged version intended to show its place in the worship of Durgā. This summary recounting is based upon several sources, each of which I have used for its particular strengths.[3] Some passages have been mercilessly summarized, as will be evident from the number of verses comprehended in single sentences or paragraph. However, I have given more complete translations of episodes that Bengalis consider particularly significant. Except for a few sample verses, I have omitted the praise hymns entirely; besides space, these would demand either more poetry than I can command, or more exegesis than I can afford, depending on whether I approached them constructively or destructively.

I. The Early Deeds of the Goddess

Chapter 1. The killing of the anti-gods Madhu and Kaiṭabha

In a previous age a virtuous king, Suratha ('Good-chariot'), was defeated in battle and robbed by evil ministers. He departed alone on the pretext of hunting and, in the midst of a dense forest, he came upon the peaceful hermitage of the Brāhmaṇ sage Medhas ('Wisdom'), who became his host for a time (1.1–10). The king's mind was overcome with attachment (*mamatva*) and he began to worry about the fate of his capital city, courtiers, and royal possessions (1.11–14). While thus obsessed, he encountered a Vaiśya near the hermitage, and asked, 'Who are you? Why have you come here? Why do you appear so depressed and downcast?' (1.15–16). The Vaiśya replied, 'I am Samādhi ['Accomplishment'], born of a wealthy family, and cast out by my sons, wife, and closest kin, who were greedy for my wealth. Now, I wander the forest in sadness, not knowing how they fare at home' (1.17–21). The king asked, 'Why are you so affectionately attached to those whose greed dispossessed you?' (1.22). The Vaiśya replied, 'I was wondering about that just as you asked. Yet I find that I still love those evil persons who have deprived me of my wealth. The heart is prone to love one's kinsmen even though they are worthless' (1.23–26).

Suratha and Samādhi approached the sage and asked him to explain the attachment and delusion (*moha*) they felt (1.27–33). The sage told them that, although the objects of perception approach the sense organs of different living beings in different ways, humans are not the only creatures that have sensory knowledge. The birds know what their senses tell them and feel their own hunger, yet they drop grain into the beaks of their young because of delusion. Greed (*lobha*)—expectation of return benefaction—causes humans to be attached to their children. Thus are human beings thrown into the abyss of delusion by the power of Mahāmāyā ('She of Great Transformative Power') who makes permanent the flux of worldly life (*saṃsāra*). She is the contemplation sleep (Yoga-nidrā) or Viṣṇu and by her the world is deluded. This goddess forcibly leads the minds even of the wise into delusion. She creates the entire universe, moving and unmoving. When she is gracious (*prasannā*) she bestows upon men boons conducive to their liberation (*mukti*). She is the eternal supreme knowledge, the cause of liberation, and the cause of bondage to this world. She is the ruler of all the gods (1.34–44).

The king asked the sage more about the goddess he called Mahāmāyā, her origin, activity, nature and form (1.45–46). The sage replied that she is eternal, having the form of the universe; everything is a manifestation of her. Nevertheless, she originates in many ways. When she originates to accomplish the purposes of the gods she is said to be born in the world, although she is eternal (1.47–48).

At the end of a cosmic cycle (*kalpa*) the universe was a single ocean. Viṣṇu lay in the sleep of contemplation (*yoga-nidrā*) upon the serpent Śeṣa. The terrible anti-gods (*asura*) Madhu and Kaiṭabha sprang from the dirt of Viṣṇu's ears, intent on killing Brahmā. Sitting on the lotus that grew from Viṣṇu's navel, the father of creatures Brahmā saw the two *asuras* as well as the sleep of Viṣṇu. In order to awaken him, Brahmā concentrated his thoughts upon the goddess Yoga-nidrā dwelling in his eyes. The lustrous lord Brahmā began to extol the goddess of Viṣṇu's sleep as Queen of the Universe (Viśveśvarī), Supporter of the World (Jagaddhātrī), and the cause of its maintenance and destruction (1.49–53).

[Verses 1.54–67 are Brahmā's elaborate praise of the goddess, in which he describes her universal and comprehensive qualities. Verse 1.58 is noteworthy: there she is praised as 'great goddess' (Mahādevī) and 'great anti-goddess' (Mahāsurī) at the same time.]

Thus praised, the goddess Tāmasī ('Entropy'), in order to arouse Viṣṇu so that he could kill Madhu and Kaiṭabha, came forth from his eyes, mouth, nostrils, arms, heart, and chest. Released by her, the Lord of the World arose from his resting place in the midst of the ocean and saw those two evil anti-gods, heroic and valiant, eyes red with rage, eager to kill Brahmā. Viṣṇu fought them bare-handed for 5,000 years. Intoxicated by their own great strength, and deluded by Mahāmāyā, the anti-gods exclaimed to Viṣṇu, 'Ask a boon from us!' Viṣṇu asked them to be slain by him. Thus deluded, the anti-gods asked that they be slain in a place not covered by the flood. The Lord took their heads upon his loin and split them with his discus. Thus did the goddess originate when she was praised by Brahmā (1.68–78).

II. The Middle Deeds of the Goddess

Chapter 2. The killing of the armies of the anti-god Mahiṣa

Long ago there was a war between the gods, with Indra as their leader, and the anti-gods, led by Mahiṣa ('Buffalo'), which lasted a hundred years. The heroic anti-gods were victorious and Mahiṣāsura became Indra (i.e., ruler of heaven). The gods, making Brahmā their leader, went to Śiva and Viṣṇu and described their defeat, and Mahiṣa's usurpation of the authority of all the gods. Now compelled to wander the earth like mortals, the gods besought Śiva and Viṣṇu to find a way to kill Mahiṣa (2.1–7).

Viṣṇu and Śiva were angered by what they heard; their brows furrowed with rage. Great radiant energy (*tejas*) sprang from the face of Viṣṇu, and from those of Śiva and Brahmā as well. Energy sprang from the bodies of Indra and the other gods, and it united into one. It was like a blazing mountain, illuminating all the quarters, pervading the three worlds; then the energy from the bodies of all the gods was concentrated at a single place and transformed into a female. The energy of each god constituted a different part of her body: Śiva's her face, Yama's (Death) her hair, Viṣṇu's her arms, the Moon's her breasts, Indra's her waist, Varuṇa's (Water) her calves and thighs, the Earth's her hips, Brahmā's her feet, Surya's (Sun) her toes, the Vasus' (Bright Ones) her fingers, Kubera's (Wealth) her nose, Prajāpati's (Lord of Creatures) her teeth, Agni's (Fire) her three eyes, the two Sandhyas' (Sunrise and Sunset) her eyebrows, Vāyu's (Wind) her ears, and the energy of all the other gods became an auspicious goddess (*śivā*). The oppressed gods were overjoyed at the sight of her (2.8–18).

The gods drew weapons forth from their own and gave them to her: Śiva a trident, Viṣṇu a discus, Varuṇa a conch-shell trumpet, Agni a spear, Māruta (Wind) a bow and two quivers full of arrows, Indra a thunderbolt (*vajra*) and a bell from his elephant Airāvata, Yama a rod from his rod of time (*kāla-daṇḍa*), and Varuṇa a noose. Brahmā gave her a string of beads and a water pot, Sūrya put his rays into the pores of her skin, Kāla (Time) gave her a sword and shield, and the Milk Ocean provided a pair of undecaying garments and many excellent jewelled ornaments. Viśvakarmā (Maker of the Universe) gave her an ax, impenetrable armor, and various weapons; the Ocean decorated her with lotuses; Himālaya gave her a lion as a conveyance, as well as jewels; Kubera gave her a drinking vessel ever filled with liquor; and the great serpent Śeṣa, who supports the earth, gave her a bejewelled serpent necklace (2.19–31).

Thus honored by the gods, the goddess began to laugh with a ceaseless, horrifying roar, until the universe echoed with her terrifying sound. The joyous gods cried out 'Victory!' to the lion-rider (Siṃhavāhinī), and the sages bowed in devotion (2.32–34).

The anti-god armies rallied when the three worlds began to shake, and when Mahiṣa saw the goddess in her pervasive splendor, the earth sinking beneath her feet, her crown scraping the sky, the twang of her bowstring shaking the lower world, and filling the universe with her thousand arms, he rushed toward her. In that battle all the quarters were illuminated by the flash of weapons. Cikṣura was general of Mahiṣa's army, and Cāmara commanded an army of four parts. Udagra ('Fierce') had 60,000 chariots and Mahāhanu ('Big-jaw') battled with ten million; Asiloma ('Sword-haired') had fifteen million, and Bāṣkala six million. Parivārita joined the battle with thousands of horses and elephants, and surrounded by ten million chariots. The anti-god Biḍāla ('Cat') fought surrounded by five billion chariots and Kāla ('Time') had five million. There were innumerable other *asuras*, with their chariots, horses and elephants, engaged in that battle with the goddess. Mahiṣāsura himself was surrounded by many billions of chariots, horses, and elephants. They fought against the goddess with javelins, slings, maces, swords, axes, and halberds. Some hurled spears, others nooses; some tried to kill her with swordstrokes (2.35–48).

The goddess Caṇḍikā, as if in play, cut their weapons to pieces with her own. Her face serene, she pierced the bodies of the *asuras*. Her lion, shaking its mane, moved through the enemy army like fire through a forest. Her troops were born by the hundreds of thousands from the breaths Ambikā (Mother) exhaled during the battle. They fought with axes, slings, swords, and javelins; sustained by the power of the goddess (*devī-śakti*), they slew the anti-gods and played martial drums and blew conch-shell trumpets (2.49–54).

The goddess, using all her numerous weapons, slaughtered anti-gods by the hundreds. The battlefield became a grisly sight, thick with severed limbs, cloven corpses, bodies so thick with arrows they looked like porcupines, headless torsos trying to carry on the battle, and freshly severed heads still shouting at the goddess. Piles of fallen bodies and rivers of blood quickly made the ground impassable. The lion searched out the remaining life breaths among the bodies. After that battle the gods praised the goddess, showering down flowers (2.55–68).

Chapter 3. The killing of the anti-god Mahiṣa

The great generals and valiant heroes of the *asura* army, beginning with Cikṣura, came forward to do battle with the goddess; Bhadrakālī (Benign Black Goddess) slew them one by one (3.1–19). Seeing his army thus destroyed, Mahiṣāsura assumed his own buffalo form and destroyed the goddess's troops. When he turned upon her lion, she became enraged. The mighty anti-god pounded the earth, tossed mountains from his horns, and lashed the ocean into a flood with his tail (3.20–26).

When she saw the great *asura* swollen with rage, the goddess's fury became sufficient to destroy him. When she threw her noose over him, he abandoned his buffalo form and became a lion. She decapitated the lion and immediately he appeared as a man with a sword. She cut him to pieces and he became a huge elephant, pulling at the goddess's lion with his trunk. When she cut off his trunk, he resumed his buffalo form, shaking the three worlds (3.27–32).

Caṇḍikā, mother of the world (*jaganmātā*), enraged, drank repeated draughts of the supreme liquor, and began to laugh as her eyes became red. The anti-god, drunk with his own strength and valor, hurled mountains at Caṇḍikā with his horns. She pulverized these with a shower of arrows and spoke to him in tangled words, her face flushed with liquor, 'Roar, roar, O fool, for a moment while I drink this liquor! Soon the gods will roar when I have killed you here' (3.33–36).

She leapt upon the great *asura*, pressed her foot down on his throat, and pierced him with her spear. Trampled by her foot, and enveloped by the valor of the goddess, the anti-god came halfway out of his own mouth. Thus half-revealed, the *asura* continued to fight until the goddess struck off his head with her sword, and he fell. So, crying sorrowfully, did the whole army of the anti-gods perish; the hosts of the gods were jubilant. The gods and sages praised the goddess, while the celestial musicians sang and danced (3.37–41).

Chapter 4. Praise of the goddess by the gods beginning with Indra

[Verses 4.1–28 contain an elaborate praise of the goddess by the gods, identifying her with the entire universe. Although it emphasizes her desirable qualities, it also notes some important ambiguities in her character, e.g., 'You are Lakṣmī (Śrī, 'Good Fortune') in the houses of the virtuous and Alakṣmī ('Ill Fortune') in the houses of the evil . . .' (4.4), 'The three qualities are yours, as are the defects (*dośa*) . . .' (4.6), and, 'Your lovely face, golden, like the full moon. . . . Your wrathful face, red, like the rising moon' (4.11–1).

Pleased with their praise, the goddess asked the gods what boon she might grant them. The gods replied, 'Nothing remains to be done since the adorable goddess has slain Mahiṣāsura. If you will give us a boon, O Maheśvarī (Great Queen), destroy our calamities when we think of you. O mother of spotless countenance, whatever mortal shall praise you with this hymn, graciously grant him prosperity in wealth, wife, and children. Give us increase, O propitious mother' (4.29–32).

Then the sage (narrator) told the king that the goddess Bhadrakālī said, 'Be it so,' and vanished from their sight. 'I have told you how the goddess, who desires the well-being of the three worlds, was born from the bodies of the gods. Again she was born with the body of Gaurī ('Golden,' here meaning Pārvatī) to slay the wicked anti-gods and Śumbha and Niśumbha, to preserve the world, as benefactress of the gods. Listen as I relate how this happened' (4.33–36).

III. The Final Deeds of the Goddess

Chapter 5. The conversation of the goddess with the messenger of the anti-gods Śumbha and Niśumbha

Long ago Śumbha and Niśumbha took the three worlds from Indra and deprived him of his share of the sacrifice. They assumed the powers of all the gods. Bereft of authority, the gods remembered the invincible (*aparājitā*) goddess who had promised them relief from calamities. They went to the Himālaya and began to extol the goddess Viṣṇu-māyā (5.1).

[Verses 5.7–36 are a hymn of praise saluting the numerous appellations and qualities of the goddess.]

While the gods were engaged in praise, Pārvatī (Mountain-dweller) came there to bathe in the Ganges. She asked the gods whom they were praising so. An auspicious goddess (*śivā*) sprang forth from her bodily sheath (*śarīra-kośa*) and replied, 'I am praised by the assembled gods who were vanquished by the anti-god Śumbha and defeated by Niśumbha.' Because she was sprung from the bodily sheath of Pārvatī, that mother is celebrated as Kauśikī in all the worlds. After she had come forth, Pārvatī became dark and dwelt in the Himālaya celebrated as Kālikā (Respected Black Goddess) (5.37–41).

Caṇḍa and Muṇḍa, servants of Śumbha and Niśumbha, saw Kauśikī, that mother of supreme beauty, and told Śumbha that he who already possessed every other divine treasure should possess her as well (5.42–5). Śumbha dispatched the *asura* Sugrīva ('Handsome-neck') as his messenger to the goddess, charging him to address her sweetly so that she would come to him in love. The messenger told the goddess of the conquests of the anti-god king, and of his great wealth. He entreated her to choose either Śumbha or Niśumbha as a husband and make this wealth hers (5.54–65).

The auspicious goddess Durgā replied to the messenger, saying that he had spoken truthfully but that she had once vowed to have as husband only one who defeated her in battle, removed her pride, and was her equal in strength. So she urged that Śumbha or Niśumbha come to defeat her without delay. The messenger said that it was arrogant for a lone female to stand against one whom all the gods could not defeat, and she would end up being dragged away by the hair, her dignity lost. The goddess replied that she could not break her vow. She asked the messenger to tell the *asura* king exactly what she had said, and to 'let him then do whatever is proper' (5.66–76).

Chapter 6. The killing of the anti-god general Dhūmra-locana

When the anti-god king heard the report of his indignant messenger, he angrily dispatched the chieftain Dhūmra-locana ('Smoky-eyed') with his army to bring back the impudent woman by force, dragging her by the hair, and killing anyone who interfered. When he saw the goddess seated on the mountain, the anti-god chieftain shouted at her to come before Śumbha and Niśumbha or he would take her there by the hair. She replied that he was quite strong and had a large army, so if he chose to take her by force, what could she do? (6.1–8).

When Dhūmra-locana rushed at the goddess, she reduced him to ashes with the utterance of her mighty sound 'HŨ!' The anti-god army quickly joined the attack with all its weapons, and the goddess's lion, its mane shaking in rage, destroyed them all (6.9–15).

When Śumbha heard of this defeat, he wrathfully ordered Caṇḍa ('Cruel') and Muṇḍa ('Shaved-head') to go with a still greater force, bind her, and drag her back by the hair. If there was any doubt about success, they were to order the army to attack, wound her, and kill the lion (6.16–20).

Chapter 7. The killing of the anti-gods Caṇḍa and Muṇḍa

The *asura* army, with Caṇḍa and Muṇḍa at its head, found the goddess, smiling slightly, seated on her lion atop a mountain peak. Some made excited efforts to capture her, while others approached, bows bent and swords drawn (7.1–3).

Then Ambikā became enraged against her enemies, and her face grew black as ink. Suddenly, from between her eyebrows, issued forth Kālī of terrible countenance, armed with a sword and a noose. She carried a bizarre skull-topped staff and wore a garland of human heads for ornaments; clad in a tiger skin, she was horrifyingly emaciated. Her vast mouth agape, tongue lolling out terribly, and deep-sunken bloodshot eyes, she filled all of space with a roar. She fell frenzied upon the great anti-god army, slaughtering them and devouring them by batallions (7.4–8). Elephants, together with their rear guards, drivers, warriors, and bells, she flung into her mouth with a single hand. Likewise horses and their riders, chariots and their drivers, and ground them between her teeth. One she seized by the hair, another by the neck; she crushed one underfoot and another against her chest. The great weapons hurled against her she caught in her mouth and crunched in her teeth. She destroyed the entire army of evil anti-gods, battering some, devouring others; some she slew by the sword, some by a blow from her skull-topped staff, and still others died horribly between her sharp-pointed teeth (7.9–14).

When he saw the destruction of the entire *asura* army, Caṇḍa rushed against the horrendous Kālī. Caṇḍa loosed a shower of arrows and Muṇḍa discuses by the thousands, covering the terrible-eyed goddess. The innumerable discuses disappeared into her mouth like so many glowing suns into a dark cloud. Kālī howled and laughed terrifyingly in a fury, her fangs glinting in her dreadful mouth. Astride her great lion, she rushed at Caṇḍa, grasped him by the hair, and beheaded him with her sword. When he saw Caṇḍa killed, Muṇḍa rushed toward her and she felled him with an angry swordstroke. Seeing the mighty Caṇḍa and Muṇḍa fallen, the remainder of the army fled terrified in all directions (7.15–21).

Carrying the heads of Caṇḍa and Muṇḍa, Kālī approached Caṇḍikā; her words mingled with wild laughter as she said, 'I offer you Caṇḍa and Muṇḍa, the great beasts given in the sacrifice of battle. Now you will kill Śumbha and Niśumbha yourself.' Seeing the two great *asuras* brought to her, Caṇḍikā said with gracious good humor, 'Since you have caught Caṇḍa and Muṇḍa and brought them to me, O goddess, you shall be famous in the world as Cāmuṇḍā' (7.22–25).

Chapter 8. The killing of the anti-god Rakta-bīja

With Caṇḍa and Muṇḍa dead, and most of his forces destroyed, the angry Śumbha ordered forth all the anti-god army. The remaining *asura* clans, surrounded by thousands of troops, marched into battle (8.1–6). Caṇḍikā filled the space between heaven and earth with the sound of her twanging bowstring; her lion gave an exceedingly loud roar, which Ambika magnified with the clanging of her bell. Her mouth expanded to fill the four quarters, Kālī drowned them all out with her 'HŨ!' sound. When they heard that roar, the enraged *asura* army surrounded the goddess, the lion, and Kālī (8.7–10).

At that moment, in order to annihilate the enemies of the gods, and for their welfare, the strong and vigorous Śaktis (feminine, energetic forms) issued forth from the bodies of Brahmā, Śiva, Kārtikeya, Viṣṇu, and Indra, each with the form and conveyance of the god. Thus came Brahmāṇī, Maheśvarī (Śakti of Śiva), Kaumārī (Śakti of Kārtikeya), Vaiṣṇavī, Vārāhī (Śakti or Viṣṇu's Boar *avatāra*), Nārasiṃhī (Śakti of Viṣṇu's Man-lion *avatāra*), and Aindrī (Śakti of Indra) (8.11–20).

Śiva said to Caṇḍikā, who was surrounded by the Śaktis, 'For my sake, let the *asuras* be killed straightaway.' From the body of the goddess issued the Śakti of Caṇḍikā, howling like a hundred jackals. This invincible goddess asked Śiva to go as emissary (*dūta*) to Śumbha, Niśumbha, and the other anti-gods. He was to tell them to relinquish the divine prerogatives and dwell in the nether world, or prepare to feed their flesh to her jackals. Because she engaged Śiva as emissary, she became renowned as Śiva-dūtī (8.21–27).

When they received the message, the outraged *asuras* rushed to where the goddess stood and began showering her with weapons, which she playfully cut to pieces with her arrows. Kālī stalked in front, bashing some with her skull-topped staff and spearing others. Brahmāṇī deprived many of their vitality by sprinkling them with water from her pot. Maheśvarī slew them with her trident, Vaiṣṇavī with her discus, Kaumārī with her javelin, and Aindrī with her thunderbolt. Vārāhī used her snout, tusks, and discus, and Nārasiṃhī roared through the battlefield, tearing great *asuras* with her claws and devouring them. They fell demoralized by the wild laughter of Śiva-dūtī and she devoured them where they lay (8.28–37).

The enemy troops began to take flight before the band of Matṛs (Mothers). Then the great and wrathful *asura* Rakta-bīja ('Blood-seed') came forth to do battle with them. Whenever a drop of blood fell upon the earth from his body another *asura* of equal size was immediately produced from it. As the Matṛs struck him with their weapons and his blood poured out, hundreds of those great beings were born, filling the universe and terrifying the gods (8.38–51).

Seeing the gods so discountenanced, Caṇḍikā laughed and said to Kālī, 'O Cāmuṇḍā, open your wide mouth and swallow the drops of blood that fall when my weapons strike and the *asuras* produced by those drops, then others will not be born.' The goddess struck Rakta-bīja with her spear and Kālī drank the blood. He struck the goddess with his mace, but caused her no pain. When the goddess struck him with her mace the blood poured out and Cāmuṇḍā devoured it, together with the anti-gods produced from it. The goddess struck Rakta-bīja with spear, thunderbolt, arrows, sword, and javelin, while Cāmuṇḍā drank the blood. Stricken with so many weapons and bloodless, Rakta-bīja fell. The gods were overjoyed, while the Matṛs born from them danced, drunk with blood (8.52–62).

Chapter 9. The killing of the anti-god Niśumbha

The king, entranced by the sage's narration of the goddess's exploits, asked him what Śumbha and Niśumbha did after the death of Rakta-bīja (9.1–2).

The sage said: Śumbha and Niśumbha were in a great rage after the slaying of Rakta-bīja and the other anti-gods. They ran toward the goddess, each surrounded by the best *asura* forces, with a rain of arrows pouring down from each side. Armed with a sharp sword and shining shield, Niśumbha struck the goddess's lion on the head. She quickly cut his sword and shield to pieces with a bladed arrow. He hurled a spear at her, and she severed it with a discus; his javelin she pulverized with her fist, and his mace she reduced to ashes with her trident. As that heroic anti-god advanced toward her with a battle-ax, the goddess struck him down with a multitude of arrows (9.3–14).

Angered by the sight of his mighty brother fallen, the splendorous Śumbha rode forward in his chariot, a weapon in the hand of each of his eight long arms. The goddess blew her conch-shell trumpet and twanged her bowstring, creating an intolerable sound. The ringing of her bell filling all the directions deprived the anti-god troops of their strength. The roar of her lion stopped rutting elephants in their tracks. Kālī leapt into the sky and slapped the earth with both her hands, creating a sound that submerged all the others. Then Śiva-dūtī emitted a peal of ominous laughter, terrifying the *asuras* and enraging Śumbha. As Ambikā shouted, 'Halt! Halt! You evil one,' the gods cried out 'Victory!' from the sky (9.15–22).

Śumbha brandished a brilliantly flaming spear but when he hurled it she neutralized it with a great meteor. His lion-like roar filled the three worlds, but it was silenced by a thunder-clap. Each of them released arrows by the hundreds of thousands that cut one another apart. Angered, Caṇḍikā struck him with a spear and he fell wounded (9.23–26).

Niśumbha regained consciousness and took up a bow; he struck the goddess, Kālī, and the lion with arrows. He greatly multiplied the number of his arms and threw myriad discuses at Caṇḍikā. Then the enraged Bhagavatī Durgā, destroyer of difficulties and afflictions, shattered his discuses and arrows with her own arrows. Niśumbha, surrounded by anti-god forces, seized a mace and rushed at Caṇḍikā to slay her. She split his mace with a sword and, as that tormentor of the immortals advanced with a spear in hand, she pierced his heart with a swiftly thrown spear. Another person of great strength and valor issued forth from the pierced heart, shouting 'Halt!' The goddess laughed loudly and beheaded that person as he emerged. He fell to the ground (9.27–33).

The lion devoured those *asuras* whose necks he had broken with his fierce teeth; Kālī and Śiva-dūtī devoured others. Some of the great anti-gods perished pierced by the spear of Kaumārī, others by the aspersion of water containing the *mantra* of Brahmāṇī. Some were felled by the trident of Maheśvarī, others pulverized by the snout of Vārāhī. Some were torn asunder by the discus of Vaiṣṇavī, and others by the thunderbolt of Aindrī. Some of the *asuras* died, some fled, and some were devoured by Kālī, Śiva-dūtī, and the lion (9.34–39).

Chapter 10. The killing of the anti-god Śumbha

Infuriated at the death of his own dear brother and the slaughter of his army, Śumbha said, 'O Durgā, you are proud of your strength. But where is pride in fighting with the strength of others?' The goddess said, 'I am alone in the world. Who else is there besides me? O vile one, these others are but my powers entering into me.' Then all those goddesses, Brahmāṇī and the rest, were merged into her body and Ambikā alone remained. 'Through my power I stood here in many forms, but now I have withdrawn them. I stand here alone. Be you steadfast in combat!' (10.1–5).

Then began a dreadful battle between the goddess and Śumbha, with all the other gods and anti-gods as onlookers. They released great volleys of weapons upon one another. The *asura* broke the goddess's missiles with his own, while she playfully destroyed his with her terrible sound of 'HŨ!' and the like. When the *asura* discharged hundreds of arrows at the goddess, she angrily split his bow with her arrows. When he grasped his spear, she split it with a discus. When he ran at the goddess with his brilliant sword and shield, she split them with a sharp arrow. He rushed at her with his fist and struck her in the heart; with the palm of her hand she hit him on the chest, knocking him to the ground. He jumped up, seized the goddess, and leapt high into the sky. There, with no means of support, they battled hand-to-hand. Then the goddess picked him up, whirled him around, and flung him onto the earth. Yet he raised his fist and, in his evil nature wishing to kill Caṇḍikā, rushed at her again. The goddess speared him in the heart and threw him dead to the ground, shaking the whole earth (10.6–23).

When the evil-natured one was slain, the world became happy and regained perfect well-being; the sky became clear. The ill-omened clouds and inauspicious falling stars became tranquil, and the rivers began to follow their courses when Śumbha was killed. The minds of the gods became happy, and the celestial musicians began to play, sing, and dance. Favorable winds began to blow and the sun shone with brilliance. The sacrificial fires began to burn in peace and tranquillity, and the strange sounds that filled the quarters became peaceful (10.24–27).

Chapter 11. Praise of the goddess Nārāyaṇī

When the great lord of the anti-gods was slain by the goddess, Indra and the other gods, led by Agni, their desire fulfilled and their faces shining, praised her, Kātyāyanī (11.1).

[Verses 11.2–35 are a eulogy of the goddess which, again, identifies her with the entire universe, emphasizing her beneficence but mentioning ambiguous qualities as well. Verses 11.7–23 end with the half-line Nārāyaṇī *namostu te*, 'Nārāyaṇī, Obeisance to you,' which gives the reading a well-known punctuation. The various forms she took in doing battle with the *asuras* are all identified with her as the Śakti of Nārāyaṇa (i.e., Viṣṇu), and the entire hymn—which is sometimes read separately from the rest of the text—is thus named 'Praise of Nārāyaṇī.' The concluding verses of the eulogy, 11.31–35, implore her to save other beings from all the dangers and enemies of the world.]

The goddess heard the prayer of the gods and agreed to grant them a boon for the welfare of the world. The gods asked her to destroy all their enemies and the afflictions of the three worlds (11.36–37).

The goddess made these promises: (1) When another pair of great anti-gods named Śumbha and Niśumbha were born, she would be born in the womb of Yaśodā in the house of the cowherd Nanda to slay them. (2) She would be incarnate in a terrible form to slay the *asuras* descended from Vipra-citti, and she would be known as Rakta-dantikā ('Bloody-toothed') because her teeth would become as red as pomegranate flowers. (3) When the rains failed for hundred years, she would be born on earth, though not from a womb, and celebrated as Śatākṣī ('Hundred-eyed'); then she would sustain the world with vegetables born from her body, for which she would be known as Śākambharī ('Vegetable-nourishing'); and then she would also slay the *asura* Durgamā, for which she would be called Durgā-devī ('Goddess Difficult of Access'). (4) She would be born in a terrible form on a Himālayan mountain to destroy the *rākṣasas* (anthropophagous demons) for the protection of the sages, for which she would be celebrated as Bhīmā-devī ('Terrible Goddess'). (5) She would appear in the form of innumerable bees (*bhrāmara*) to slay the anti-god Aruṇa, for which she would be praised as Bhrāmarī. And (6) whenever there was trouble caused by anti-gods, she would become embodied and destroy the enemies (11.38–51).

Chapter 12. The results of hearing the *Devī-māhātmya*

[In verses 12.1–28 the goddess enumerates the benefits she will provide to those who hear this glorification of her, who perform her worship, and who make sacrifices to her.]

Having thus spoken, the adorable Caṇḍikā of fierce prowess vanished from the spot before the eyes of the gods. Their enemies killed, the gods were free from fear, and they returned to enjoying their shares of the sacrifice and to performing their previous duties. With Śumbha and Niśumbha dead, together with many other *asuras*, the remaining anti-gods went to the netherworld. Thus does the goddess, although eternal, take birth again and again to protect the world. By her is the universe deluded—the universe to which she gives birth (*prasūyat*), she gives knowledge when entreated, and prosperity when satisfied. The entire cosmos is pervaded by her, and at the end of time she is Mahākālī, the great destroyer. She is the great destroyer at one moment; at another, she, the unborn, gives birth to all creation, and throughout time she is the eternal preserver of all beings. She is Lakṣmī who brings prosperity to the homes of men in good times; in bad times, she becomes Alakṣmī who brings ruin. When she is worshiped with flowers, incense, perfumes, and other offerings, she bestows wealth and sons, a mind fixed on dharma, and an auspicious life (12.29–3).

Chapter 13. The granting of boons to Suratha and the Vaiśya

The sage said, 'O king, I have now recited to you the excellent *Devīmāhātmya*. The goddess possesses such power that she supports the world. She is the giver of knowledge and the transformative power of Viṣṇu. You, this Vaiśya, and other men of discernment are deluded into worldly attachment by her, as were others in the past, and as others will be in the future. Take refuge in this supreme goddess, O great king. She gives enjoyment, heaven, and final release to men who worship her' (13.1–3).

When he heard this, the king prostrated himself before that sage of austere vows. He who had become despondent because of excessive attachment and the loss of his kingdom went to perform austerities, as did the Vaiśya. The king and the Vaiśya sat on a sandy river bank where they undertook demanding ascetic practices and recited the Vedic hymn to the goddess, in order to obtain a vision of her. They made an earthen image of her on the sand and worshiped her with flowers, incense, fire, and libations of water. Sometimes they fasted and at other times they restricted their food, fixing their minds on her with concentration, and they offered her sacrifices sprinkled with blood drawn from their own bodies (13.4–8).

When they had worshiped her with minds subdued for three years,

Caṇḍikā, supporter of the world, was pleased and spoke to them in visible form, 'What you desire, O king, and you, pride of your clan, I shall grant, for I am well pleased.' The king requested a kingdom, imperishable even in another life, and in this life his own kingdom from which the force of his enemies was utterly extirpated. The wise Vaiśya, his mind now indifferent to the world, requested that knowledge which removed the attachment of 'mine' and 'I' (13.9–12).

The goddess said, 'O king, within a few days you will recover your kingdom, and, when your foes are destroyed, it will endure with you. After your death, the god Vivasvāt (the Sun) will give you another earthly birth as the *manu* Sāvarṇi. O best of Vaiśyas, I grant you the boon you request: you shall have the knowledge for your perfection' (13.13–15).

Having granted each of them his desire, the goddess disappeared while they extolled her with devotion. As a result of that boon from the goddess, Suratha, the foremost of Kṣatriyas, shall be born again by Sūrya as the manu Sāvarṇi (13.16–17).

Analysis

The *Caṇḍī*, like myths from many other cultures, relies on a degree of grandiosity that is otherwise uncommon in the public life of adults. With a distinctively Hindu particularism, this myth specifies when the events it recounts took place, but that was some hundreds of billions of years ago, so it comes as close to being 'timeless' as Hindu cosmology permits. It is extraordinarily redundant, with its triple repetition of the annihilation of the anti-gods, signaling the presence of some higher-order communication within the overt narrative. Like other myths well known among Hindus, the *Caṇḍī* has been frequently used by commentators as a vehicle for demonstrating the priority, validity, and comprehensiveness of certain philosophical-religious-cosmological positions; a full exegesis from only the most important of these positions—that of Sāṃkhya philosophy—would be impossibly long, not to say tedious, and in the end would not illuminate some of the reasons this text has such central importance in the contemporary worship of Durgā in Bengal. This analysis, then, is selective and incomplete from a Bengali point of view. But readers who are not Bengalis are more likely to be troubled by what may appear to be my methodologically haphazard approach; I hope that the consideration of the ritual that follows will lay this criticism at rest. For the present, what I am mainly concerned to show is that the sequential relationship of elements in this narration—particularly the building up of scale and detail after the 'climactic' death of Mahiṣāsura—contributes something to human understanding that is not found in its atemporal structure. The setting and circumstances of its reading, the temporally ordered unfolding of its elements amidst human beings and in the presence of the goddess, contribute still more to understanding (and intelligibility), that becomes clear in the ritual.

The Framing Tale

Much of the sociological content of the *Caṇḍī* is found in the thin envelope of verses concerning Suratha, Samādhi, and Medhas. There is an explicit existential problem raised by the attachment living beings feel to the people and things of the world, and by the difficult conceptions of *māyā and moha*, which are often glossed as 'illusion' and 'delusion.' There are three actors, the ascetic Brāhmaṇ sage Medhas, whose name means 'Wisdom,' the good Kṣatriya king Suratha, whose name means 'Good-chariot,' connecting him to the royal duty of warfare as well as to Sūrya, the Sun-god and great celestial charioteer, and the good Vaiśya householder (*gṛhastha*) Samādhi, 'Accomplishment,' whose name portends his achievement at the conclusion of the narrative.

At the outset a relationship is established that can be understood simultaneously as, in caste terms, Brāhmaṇ-Kṣatriya-Vaiśya, and, in terms of personal status, ascetic-king-householder. Veena Das (1977: 18–56) has analyzed a Gujarati myth that includes this double set of relationships, and I have largely relied on her exhaustive consideration of their structural logic, most particularly her conception of the Brāhmaṇ as intermediary between the social 'man-in-the-world' and the asocial 'renouncer,' participating in some characteristics of each (pp. 46–47). Medhas is a forest-dwelling hermit (*vānaprastha*), intermediate between householder and renouncer (*sannyāsī*), able to give hospitality to the dispossessed and depressed king and householder without accepting anything from them, and able to give them the wisdom they need to free themselves from bondage to the world, which is the substance of the *Caṇḍī* narrative.

Suratha lost his kingdom due to powerful enemies abroad and evil ministers at home. His attachment is to the accoutrements of royalty, and he becomes anguished by continually thinking of them.

Samādhi was cast out of his house by his greedy wife, sons, and kinsmen (*svajana*), and yet it is to these people that he feels attached. Medhas begins his explanation of attachment by mentioning the goddess under the name of Mahāmāyā, a name often translated 'Great Illusion,' but which is apt to suggest the wrong things in this form. *Māyā* is a specific divine power, the power to make what is in reality one appear as manifold, the power to create a universe of differentiated things out of the uncreated ground of existence (*brahma*). This power is possessed by the god Viṣṇu, the 'preserver,' and is attributed to him in the *Caṇḍī* as well as numerous other authoritative sources. During the intervals between creation, when the universe is an oceanic void, Viṣṇu sleeps. While he sleeps he supports the intrinsically inert Brahmā, the divine personification of uncreated reality, upon a lotus that grows from his navel. This is the condition of the universe described at the beginning of the central narrative (1.49). But in the *Caṇḍī*, *māyā* is also represented as personified; she is a goddess who dwells within Viṣṇu, his *śakti* or feminine, enérgetic constituent. However, during episodes of universal dissolution (*pralaya*) she is in her entropic (*tāmasika*) form of Yoganidrā, 'Slumber of Contemplation,' so there is no activity in the universe. When she begins to move, so does the flux of worldly life (*saṃsāra*), of which the attachment of persons and things to one another—the links holding together a differentiated universe—are intrinsic and unavoidable parts. The people and things that make up this differentiation must be created (*sṛṣṭi*) before they can be maintained (*sthiti*), but creation is not the object of the *Caṇḍī* myth or the Durgā pūjā rites (and belongs to the Gājan rites in Kelomal), so it is largely ignored. This goddess is the mother who gave birth to the created world (*jagat-jananī*), and it is by her that persons are bound to it and set free from it.

This matricentric conception of the universe, which is harmonious with views widely held by Bengali Hindus, is contained primarily in the non-narrative sections of the *Caṇḍī*. The king and the Vaiśya induce it into the narrative at the conclusion when, together, they undertake their ascetic ordeals with the hope of seeing her, who is the universe, in her own form. Although their effort to please her, which is successful, is a joint one, their objectives turn out to be quite different from one another. The king asks for an enduring kingdom, while the Vaiśya, who had achieved indifference to the world, asks for the knowledge (*prājña*) conducive to final release from it. The king is told that he shall obtain his kingdom, which will continue in this life and the next, after the killing (*hatyā*) of his foes (*ripu*). The code for conduct of Hindu kings (*rāja-dharma*) enjoins the use of force in the selfless maintenance of the well-being of the kingdom, and the goddess's slaughter of the anti-gods who had displaced Indra as king of heaven is a noisy reminder to rulers of their duty. The king, bound by *rāja-dharma*, is not free to seek release from the world. But the householder who has fulfilled his *gṛhastha-dharma* by raising a son to maturity and seeing to the well-being of his kinsmen, may seek release, although he must be capable of extinguishing the attachment represented by 'I' and 'mine' in order to do so.

The goddess who causes attachment can also give release from it, and a counterpoint to the element of *rāja-dhārmika* violence throughout the narrative is the repeated 'delusion' (*moha*) of the anti-gods, caused by the goddess; the gods, by contrast, give fulsome recognition to her supreme power. Thus, the *Caṇḍī* carries significant messages for both the king and the householder, although the royal one is more lavishly treated. The Vaiśya is transformed into a renouncer at the end of the narrative, while the king is simply restored to his *dharma*. The wise Brāhmaṇ ascetic, in whom the characteristics of both the social and asocial men meet, is structurally intermediary between them. He is also narratively intermediary, since the unitary knowledge he imparts to them enables each to obtain a distinctly different goal.

Rulership, householding, and Brāhmaṇhood are strongly marked elements in the Durgā pūjā rites. Community as a social form is subordinated to the conception of a hierarchical transmission of well-being from goddess to ruler to subjects. At the same time, proper and harmonious relations within the household are strongly emphasized. The Brāhmaṇs who perform the ritual are bound by particularly severe restrictions that make them half-ascetics throughout the duration of Durgā worship. The place of renunciation in the scheme enacted by the rites is, however, not clearly prefigured in the myth. The framing tale offers both a restoration of right relations and a rightful transformation of them; the ritual makes overt use of the idea of restoration but the transformative action of renunciation is concealed with the sacrifices that are offered to the goddess.

The Principal Narrative

The knowledge the Brāhmaṇ imparts to the king and the Vaiśya is contained in the three *caritas* of the goddess, the meanings of which are by no means as evident as those of the framing tale. The first deeds of the goddess are quite simple: when praised by Brahmā, she withdraws her entropic presence from within Viṣṇu's body, causing him to awaken to do battle with the anti-gods born from the dirt (*mala*) of his ears. Although the fight lasts for long, the description does not; at the end of 5,000 years of weaponless combat, the *asuras*, deluded by the goddess, agree to their own deaths at the hands of Viṣṇu, the pre-eminent slayer of anti-gods.

In the second *carita*, both the appearance of the goddess and her deeds are much more distinctly marked. She is created from the *tejas* or 'radiant energy' from the bodies, first of Viṣṇu and Śiva, here seen as superior to the other gods, second, from Brahmā, treated as the leader of the other gods (completing the Hindu triad of Creator, Preserver, and Destroyer), and finally, from the other gods, including important Vedic deities. This is a goddess of gigantic proportions and enormous might who bears the weapons and equipment of all the gods when she goes to do battle. In addition to the generic term *devī*, 'goddess,' she is in this *carita* designated Ambikā, Caṇḍikā, and Bhadrakālī, pointing to her wrathful and dangerous qualities as well as her beneficent and maternal ones. She does not transform herself into other goddesses here. She generates myriad warriors (*gaṇa*) from her deep breaths and sustains them with her energy (*śakti*), and she intoxicates herself with liquor before the final battle with Mahiṣāsura, but she retains a single form throughout the *carita*.

Both contemporary Bengali iconography and numerous images from most parts of India over the last 1500 years dwell overwhelmingly on the goddess's slaughter of Mahiṣa. On the face of it, the culminating moment of the narrative appears to be the goddess's killing of the anti-god king Śumbha, but this episode is not iconographically attested, whereas the goddess as Mahiṣāsura-mardinī is a very familiar figure, and it is in this form that she is represented in Hindu Bengal during the foremost of the autumnal rites. As will be seen, at the dramatic peak of the Durgā pūjā the goddess is contemplated as Kālī and invoked as Cāmuṇḍā, vanquisher of Caṇḍa and Muṇḍa, an episode from the third *carita*, but one that appears preliminary to the destruction of Niśumbha and, finally, Śumbha. If the narrative is complete at the end of the second *carita*, as the iconographic conventions suggest, then the third *carita* seems otiose. Yet it is almost half again as long as the first two taken together. Allowing for some redundancy to insure complete communication at the level of the most general significance of the myth, there appears to be something further contained in the third *carita* beyond the already well-established killing of the enemies of the gods. In other words, although the third *carita* multiplies the forces of the anti-gods and the number of battles to the death, the goddess's killing of Mahiṣāsura has already set the capstone on this syntagmatic structure.

What the third *carita* makes explicit, and what remains indistinct in the earlier ones, is the multiplicity of identities of the goddess and their fundamental unity. The framing tale is based on the king's request that the sage explain the nature of the goddess he called Mahāmāyā, 'She of Great Transformative Power.' As I noted earlier, *māyā* is a particular power of Hindu deities, thus, it has no simple equivalents in English; in Bengali (and Sanskrit), however, it is sometimes equivalent to *moha* and *mamatva*. That is to say, words that are often simply rendered as 'illusion,' 'delusion,' and 'attachment,' are all in a significant sense the same thing. What is that 'thing'? The Bengali dictionary of J.M. Das (*s.v.*, *māyā*) offers two unattributed quotations, the first in Bengali and the second (most uncharacteristically) in English: 'The *prakṛti* ("nature") of Sāṃkhya is the *māyā* of the Vedānta,' and, '*Māyā* does not mean illusion, as some scholars think; but it is that power which produces time, space, and causation, as also the phenomenal appearances which exist on the relative plane.' The natural world of ordinary human experience is an 'illusion' in the sense that it conceals the uncreated, undifferentiated ground of reality, and in this sense, when Viṣṇu is regarded as 'preserver' of this world, it is his *māyā*—his power to make things appear other than the ultimate *brahmā* substance that they all are—that sustains it. Looked at from the perspective of the *Caṇḍī*, the *māyā* of Viṣṇu is nothing other than the *devī* Caṇḍikā herself. It is as Viṣṇu-māyā that she is extolled at the beginning of the final *carita*; this is the episode about *māyā*, revealed in the forms and transformations of the goddess.

For the most part, the gods control *māyā* throughout the narrative. However, the anti-gods also have a share of this power, as Mahiṣāsura shows in his repeated transformations of himself during his battle with the goddess. His capacity to go from buffalo to lion to elephant to buffalo and finally to human is the greatest display of *māyā* among the anti-gods, and is an assertion of his pre-eminence among his kind in the myth. Niśumbha manifests a comparable power, but he manages only a single transformation of himself. (The awesome power of Rakta-bīja to propagate himself is stated in terms of reproduction rather than transformation.)

That the anti-gods too possess *māyā* is an indication that they are not altogether different from the gods. They are the enemies of the gods and when they reign disorder prevails throughout the entire cosmos. But they are described as 'great in heroism' (*mahā-vīrya*) or in 'heroism, strength, and courage' (*vīrya-bala-vikrama*). It is only their intrinsically evil selves (*durātman*) that decisively differentiates them from the gods. If the anti-gods are not opposed to the gods in every characteristic, then it is not surprising to find some malign features among the gods as well. What is perhaps surprising is to find the goddess described as *both* the great goddess (Mahādevī) and the great anti-goddess (Mahāsurī) at the same time. When she appears as serene, luminous, and utterly beautiful, granting boons to the oppressed, it is not difficult to acknowledge her as a proper sort of divinity. Some ambiguity creeps in when she goes heavily armed into combat, and her heavy drinking before doing battle with the anti-god Buffalo is very difficult to understand. But ambiguity seems to give way to paradox in the third *carita*, where she appears as 'violent,' 'terrifying' (*dāruṇā*), and 'exceedingly horrible' (*atibhīṣanā*).

Because of the multiplication of names as well as of identities of the goddess in the third *carita*, it is sometimes difficult to keep track of their parts in the narrative. She first appears as Pārvatī, who is the daughter of the mountain lord Himālaya. When the radiantly beautiful goddess Kauśikī springs forth from her bodily sheath, she leaves behind her 'dark half' as Kālikā. It is Kauśikī—variously denominated as Caṇḍikā, Ambikā, and Durgā—whose beauty tempts the anti-gods, introducing *kāma*, sexual desire, into the narrative in a significantly understated way. Kauśikī is the form of the goddess who enters the battle in chapter 6, but she there employs only her acoustic power; the lion, her conveyance, does the bloodletting and devouring of the enemies. In chapter 7, Kauśikī (Ambikā) inverts her relationship with Pārvatī by emitting the dark form of Kālī from her forehead. Kālī undertakes the slaughter of the anti-gods herself, using all the weapons at her disposal but leaning strongly in favor of devouring them. However, she does not consume Caṇḍa and Muṇḍa, but, in an act of symbolic emasculation, decapitates them and worshipfully presents their severed heads to Kauśikī (Caṇḍikā) as metonyms of the great beasts of the 'sacrifice of war' (*yuddha-yajña*). For this offering, Caṇḍikā graciously bestows the name Cāmuṇḍā upon Kālī. Thus, chapters 6 and 7 present split images of the goddess, one serene, fair, and beautiful, whose aggressiveness is muted, and the other frenzied, black, and horrifying, whose aggressiveness is her most marked character trait. Although strongly opposed in many obvious ways, Caṇḍikā and Kālī are envisioned as complementary to one another, and Kālī, as the part, is subordinated to Caṇḍikā, as the whole.

Caṇḍikā, Kālī, and the lion, which had served them both in the preceding chapters, face the *asura* armies together in chapter 8. They are joined by seven additional females, described as the Śaktis, or energetic feminine constituents, of the bodies of the gods. (Śakti is a somewhat different conception from *tejas*, the 'radiant energy' which the gods emitted to form the goddess in the second *carita*; one of the meanings of Śakti is 'goddess,' and from it is derived the term Śākta, used to describe a votary of a goddess.) This group of seven Śaktis, represented as feminine counterparts of the male gods from whose bodies they were emitted, are referred to as the 'troop of mothers' (*matṛ-gaṇa*). Caṇḍikā emits her own Śakti to participate in this battle, and she becomes known as Śiva-dūtī for her use of Śiva as an emissary (*dūta*) to the anti-gods. The principal combat in chapter 8 is with Rakta-bīja ('Blood-seed'), from whose blood dropped onto the earth new anti-gods equal to the original are produced. He is defeated by the complementary action of Śiva-dūtī, who uses her weapons to wound him, and Kālī (Cāmuṇḍā), who devours blood and *asuras* as quickly as they are produced.

Chapter 8 is the pivot of the narrative in the third *carita*, lying in its center. It is the longest chapter in this narrative and the most elaborate with respect to the variety of goddesses. Rakta-bīja is a more formidable foe than any of his predecessors, witnessed in the anxiety displayed by the gods at his self-multiplication. What remains to be done after he is dead, the killing of Niśumbha and Śumbha, is obvious and the outcome is certain. The main significance of this episode does not lie in the final destruction of the anti-gods, for the goddess goes on to reveal that others will be born in the future and she will be born again to combat them.

In chapter 9, Śumbha and Niśumbha enter the battle against Śiva-dūtī, Kālī, and the seven Matṛs. The Matṛs figure only peripherally in the episode of Niśumbha, and it is Śiva-dūtī who slaughters him and decapitates the vigorous warrior who springs from his pierced heart.

Then Śiva-dūtī's Kālī-like devouring of *asuras* is explicitly mentioned, and repeated again as if once were not enough, pointing out the underlying identity between these 'opposed' forms.

The goddess is not often referred to as Durgā in the *Caṇḍī*, although that is the most popular of her names in Bengal. However, this name does arise once in chapter 9 (v. 29). And it is the name used by Śumbha to address the goddess at the beginning of chapter 10, the conclusion of the narrative, where he challenges her for fighting with the strength of others. The goddess responds to the *asura's* taunt by withdrawing all of the other goddesses (*devī*) into herself, asserting that they are all her powers (*vibhūti*) and at the same time demonstrating vividly their relationship to her as the whole. Earlier I said that in Bengali Hinduism Durgā is treated as the 'totalizing' form of the goddess, the one in whom all the other goddesses or mothers are contained. Here, in the last episode of the narrative, that conception is dramatically spelled out. It is under the name of Durgā that she absorbs all the other goddesses and this is the name used in Bengal to represent the most comprehensive form of the goddess.

The relationship between the 'totalizing' form of the goddess and her subordinate manifestations is here conceived in the same way as the relationship between a Hindu king (*rājā*) and his subjects (*prajā*). The term *prajā* means 'born of,' that is, the 'offspring' or 'creature' of another. Thus, the classical conception of Hindu kingship is based on the idea that the subjects are bodily products of the king, but he is not a bodily product of his subjects. The relationship is hierarchical and asymmetrical: the subjects share in the king's body, but he does not share in theirs, he encompasses them. Durgā is produced from the collective energies of the bodies of the gods and, thus, she 'belongs' to them, but she is greater than any of them. The creatures that she produces from her body and the powers of the individual gods are all her subordinate parts, as she shows by absorbing them into herself. This example is an important reason for the continued vitality of the conception of Hindu kingship in rural Bengal long after the extinction of Hindu kings, and it is central to the hierarchial structure of society that is symbolically enacted and annually rehabilitated in the Durgā pūjā.

As with the other narrative chapters, chapter 10 concludes on the slaughter of an anti-god. Śumbha is a valiant, if 'evil-selfed' (*duṣṭātma*) foe, and he wages a fierce fight, although there is not a moment in which the goddess's final victory seems in doubt, as occurred in the Rakta-bīja incident. Thus, the chief function of the episode, and of the third *carita*, is to show that the many names and forms of the goddess represent a single, powerful, invincible, grandiose, female divinity, who is mother of the universe. Something further about the character of this goddess is revealed in the identity of the anti-gods as it is established in the ritual.

In the contemporary rites of Durgā worship, the *asuras* are represented by animals sacrificed to the goddess. The symbolism of these sacrifices is complex, and I shall consider it fully in analyzing the ritual. But I shall anticipate that discussion here by briefly mentioning one strand of exegesis that is commonly offered for the sacrifices. (For an elaborate consideration of the character of the *asuras* in Hindu myths see O'Flaherty [1976: 57–93]). Among the high-caste and usually well-educated people who perform Durgā pūjā, the blood sacrifices represent the *asura*, the enemies (*ripu*) of the gods, slain by the goddess. At the same time, they represent the 'six enemies' (*ṣaṛ-ripu*) 'established in the body' (*śarīrastha*) of a human being: *kāma*, 'desire,' *krodha*, 'anger,' *lobha*, 'greed,' *moha*, 'attachment,' *mada*, 'vanity,' and *mātsarya*, 'envy.' It is not difficult to understand how the goddess Mahāmāyā might be conceived as the author of these impulses, how they might be experienced as personal enemies in the contexts of Hindu family and society, and how one might try to renounce them in an act of ascetic sacrifice. However, the myth does not lay extensive groundwork for this interpretation, and insofar as it does so at all, it is in the framing tale rather than the main narrative. To understand the *asuras* as the 'enemies within' it will be necessary to see them in the ritual and its social setting as well as in the myth. Only then will it be clear what kind of 'mother' this goddess is thought to be.

6. *The Fever Demon and the Census Commissioner: Śītalā Mythology in Eighteenth and Nineteenth Century Bengal*

With Aditi Nath Sarkar

Disease appears not to be a religious problem for most Americans in the last quarter of the twentieth century. Our culture defines malaria, cholera, tuberculosis, and smallpox as the natural results of infection by particular species of protozoa, bacilli, and viruses. It is easy to forget the recency of empirical knowledge about micro-organisms and their role in illness. Well educated Westerners who are otherwise sensitive to cultural differences often become impatient when presented with explanations of disease that do not correspond to the 'facts' as we know them. It seems that so much meaningless and needless suffering could be eliminated if poor and uneducated people would but take a naturalistic view of infection and illness. Yet understandings of affliction that give meaning beyond bare empirical explanation to disease and suffering abound in Western tradition. Consider the second chapter of Job, where Satan challenges God, 'Skin for skin, yea, all that a man hath will he give for his life.' The righteous Job is put to the test:

> So went Satan forth from the presence of the Lord, and smote Job with sore boils from the sole of his foot unto his crown. And he took himself a potsherd to scrape himself withal; and he sat down among the ashes.
>
> Then said his wife unto him, Dost thou still retain thine integrity? curse God and die (Job II: 7–9).

The issue is not whether to join Job's wife and curse God or to join Job and bless him, but rather that however much we may understand about micro-organisms and the effective medical treatment of boils, there is always a residual question: 'Why me?' And if the answer is 'God only knows!', then it is clear that the religious problem remains. Americans and Western Europeans nowadays get the best medical care the world has ever had to offer, yet great and unexpected suffering from disease persists and constitutes for many a source of religious awe and discovery. People continue to pray to God for relief from illness, especially when medicine seems to fail, and to accept suffering as a manifestation of God's will and wisdom.

The religious setting of Bengal in the eighteenth and nineteenth centuries was quite different from that of the West in the late twentieth century. There is no reason to speak in the past tense about Bengal, where religious beliefs and practices of earlier centuries are still current. Bengali Hinduism partitions off deities according to their functions in much the same way that caste distinguishes among persons. Among deities, it is the Goddess Śītalā, 'The Cool One,' who is *Vyādhi-pati*, 'Master of Illnesses,' *Roga-rājā*, 'Ruler of Diseases,' and *Basanta-rāy*, 'Ruler of Poxes.' Her constant companion and advisor is Jvarāsur, 'The Fever Demon.' Behind them like an army are arrayed numerous diseases ranked in corps according to both Ayurvedic and folk systems of classification.

Suffering from disease has been a part of the common human experience in Bengal for centuries. It is not only that almost everyone suffers from serious afflictions of his own, but also that everyone has suffered from the agony and death of those whom he loved. The history of disease in Bengal has not yet been written. However, we get a glimpse of the great epidemics of the past in W.W. Hunter's recounting of the sixteenth century plague that destroyed the capital city of Gaur: 'Thousands died daily writes the historian of Bengal.'

> The living, wearied with burying the dead, threw their bodies into the river. This created a stench which only increased the disease. The governor was carried off by the plague. The city was at once depopulated, and from that day to this it has been abandoned. At the time of its destruction it has existed two thousand years. . . . In one year it was humbled to the dust, and now it is the abode only of tigers and monkeys.[1]

Four centuries later Bengal remains one of the few world areas from which smallpox has not been completely eliminated. It was only during the 1960s that systematic DDT spraying dramatically reduced the population of Anopheles mosquitos and broke the transmission cycle of malaria. The quality of the drinking water supply has been improved throughout the region, but cholera and other severe gastrointestinal infections remain endemic. The disfiguring symptoms of leprosy and filariasis are sufficiently common to serve as a constant reminder of these diseases. Diptheria and poliomyelitis, quickly forgotten in the West, continue to afflict Bengali youngsters. The weakening and wasting effects of hepatitis and typhoid fever are known to all Bengalis.

Our concern here is not so much with the experience of suffering and disease but rather with one way in which this experience is dealt with in Bengali religion. The evidence we have examined suggests that there is a connection between concrete historical events, the particular experience of suffering from disease, and the abstract, 'timeless' belief system expressed in religious texts. Western medicine explains disease by reference to micro-organismic infection and cellular and chemical dysfunctions; Ayurvedic medicine explains disease by reference to imbalances among the three basic bodily humors. However, the Bengali belief system concerning Śītalā explains disease, within a different framework of meaning than either of these, by reference to who controls it. Actual suffering is thus experienced by millions of ordinary Bengali Hindus as an expression of a divine will. The myths that we deal with here acknowledge the fact that human beings afflicted by disease often fail to recognize in their suffering the action of divinity. These texts seek to insure that illness will be experienced as *māyer dayā*, 'the grace of the Mother.' We cannot know just how long a belief in a Goddess of Disease, together with an oral mythology, may have existed in Bengal. However, written texts of the *maṅgal kāvya*[2] type praising Śītalā and describing her exploits and the establishment of her worship on Earth appear to cluster in the middle of the eighteenth century.

Thc *Śītalā Maṅgal* of Kavi Kṛṣṇarām Dās, which seems to have been written about 1690, stands out as peculiar, being the only seventeenth century text of which we have any knowledge. The editor of Kṛṣṇarām's works, Satyanārāyaṇ Bhaṭṭācārya, says that the text is known from only one nineteenth century copy, a manuscript of poor quality that lacks a conclusion and contains no information about its composition and copying.[3] The relative importance of pustular diseases as against fevers in this text suggests that it predates the eighteenth century efflorescence of *Śītalā Maṅgal* composition. It appears that Kṛṣṇarām, who has given us texts of five different *maṅgal kāvyas*, may have been particularly devoted to copying down material from the oral tradition.

After Kṛṣṇarām there seems to be a hiatus of 60 to 70 years, following which five and possibly six written versions of the *Śītalā Maṅgal* appear in rapid succession. In about 1750 Dvija Harideva, of Jhorhāṭ village (in present Howrah District, near Shankrail Station), composed a *Śītalā Maṅgal* of which we know two parts: *Śitalār Sārigān* and a *Jāgaraṇ Pālā* that concludes with an *Aṣṭa Maṅgala.*[4] Kavi Jagannāth, a courtier of Rājā Kamalnārāyaṇ of Tamluk (ruled 1752–1756) in present-day Midnapur District, composed a *Śītalā Maṅgal* of which we have only one fragmentary manuscript containing most of a *Bardhamān Pālā.*[5] Māṇikram Gāngulī, who is well known for his large *Dharma Maṅgal,* lived in village Beldihā (or Belṭā), which is now in Goghāṭ Thana, Arambagh Subdivision, of Hooghly District; he composed his *Śītalā Maṅgal* sometime after 1750. The fragments available contain a *Lava-Kuśa Pālā* and part of a *Gokul Pālā.*[6] Śrī Kavivallabh Devakinandan was probably another eighteenth century poet. He was from village Bandipur (or Baidyapur) in Māndaran Parganā, now in Khānākul Thana of Arambagh, Hooghly District. His composition is known from two manuscripts, an incomplete *Candraketu Pālā* and a complete *Virāṭa Pālā.*[7]

Nityānanda Cakravartī is by all odds the foremost composer of poems to Śītalā.[8] He was a courtier of Rājā Rājnārāyaṇ (ruled 1756–1770) of Kāśījoṛā Paraganā in what is now Midnapur District. We know his work from two *baṭtala* editions and not from any manuscript sources.[9] The earlier printed versions (which we shall refer to as 'Text B'), published in Calcutta in 1878 under the title of *Śītalār Jāgaraṇ Pālā*, is 91 pages of solid type, much longer than any of the manuscripts of which we have knowledge.[10] This book makes several interesting claims that suggest there was competition over the right to publish Nityānanda's text during the 1870s. The title page says:

In metric verse, *Śītalā's Jāgaraṇ Pālā,* that is, the narration of Śītalā Devī's glory in Matsya Deśa. . . . Written by Dvija Nityānda [sic], translated by Śrī Śivnārayāṇ Siṃha into metric verse from [the language of] Orissa. Corrected by Śrī Tinkaṛi Biśvās. Printed and published by Śrī Trailokyanāth Datta.

The final page of the book is a 'publisher's statement' which says:

The *Jāgaraṇ Pālā of Śītalā* was in broken pieces (*bhaṇgabhāy*) and was nowhere in good order. Witnessing the desire [for it] of many, and thinking it over, [I] asked for and obtained manuscript(s) from Orissa. Dvijā Nityānanda had written it in Oriyā, framing it in various kinds of verse. Seeing this, I was content to spend money to give it out to be translated into Bengali. Śivnārāyaṇ Siṃha is skilled in Oriyā. He composed the manuscript in verse. He who feels the desire in his mind to read it may do so carefully by buying the book (*pũthi*, literally 'manuscript'). If anyone were to seek to defraud, and taking the sense of this book, composes another good work (*suracanā*), and I were to find one or two words from this in that, I will cause him legal trouble. Let Mother Śītalā not leave an heir to light the lamp of the lineage of him who seeks to get this, my book, by fraud. She will punish him with blood eruptions (*rakta-cāmdal*), [while] we shall worship the Mother with [sacrifices of] sheep and goats. Trailokya, my name, is well known in the three worlds (*trailokye*), famous on earth. I have never done anyone harm. Why do others harm me?—that is what I ask, Oh my brother. Evidently such a person is not his father's son, since he is not ashamed to address someone else's father as *bāp*! This time around I will strip him of his reputation, and we will see what clan (*kula*) he is born in, and his manhood amounts to.[11]

The second printed version ('Text A'), which is still currently available from pavement booksellers in Calcutta, is called *Bṛhat Śītalā Maṅgal bā Śītalār Jāgaraṇ Pālā*, published by Tārācā̃d Dās and Sons. It was in its twelfth printing in 1968 and contains the following publication data on the back of the title page:

Special Notice

Prior to publication this book was purchased by the Māṇik Library from its publisher of 1285 (1878–79), Śrīyukta Binodbihāri Śīl; we now hold exclusive rights. Damages must be paid for the copying of this book according to the notice of 28th July 1931. 1339 *sāl* (1932–33).

The main difference between the two versions consists of seven pages of 'introductory' material that appears in Text A but not in the earlier Text B. This introduction consists of an account of the birth of Śītalā and of her lieutenant Jvarāsur, and of their activities before they descend to the mortal world. This section contains no signature lines (*bhanita*) and is paginated separately from the body of the work. Remarkably enough, the only other printed text we have is the *Śītalā Maṅgal* of Rāmnārāyan Bhaṭṭācāryya, published in Calcutta by Trailokyanāth Dās De in 1874.[12] This text, which was put into *payār* verse by Maheścandra Dās De, deals primarily with the births of

Śītalā and Jvarāsur and with their doings in the immortal world. It concludes with a *Vṛndāvana Pālā* and a short *stava*. Although this text, 32 pages in length, is more detailed than the introduction to Text A, the incidents and often the language of the two correspond very closely.

It is evident that there was competition among *baṭtalā* publishers in Calcutta over the right to print Nityānanda's *Śītalā Maṅgal*. The afterword to Text B is clearly inveighing against such publications as the original edition of Text A and that of Maheścandra Dās De. The publishers of Text A, even at this late date, are still concerned with establishing the legitimacy of their claim.

The questions to which we are seeking answers here are: (1) Why was there so much concern about the publication of Nityānanda's *Śītalā Maṅgal* in the 1870s? And, no less interesting, (2) Why was so much creative activity directed toward the composition of *Śītalā Maṅgal Kāvyas* in the mid-eighteenth century? While we are dealing with some religious and mythological problems of the *Śītalā Maṅgal*, we do so from a special historical angle.

Some surprises in the first census

It is not surprising that before the first census in 1872 the British had a very uncertain idea about the size of the population of the province of Bengal, which they had now ruled, in effect, for over a century. As the Report of that census put it: 'The fact is, population figures in Bengal have hitherto been treated as mere estimates, and so little importance has been attached to them, that it has never appeared worthwhile to see that they were even correctly quoted.'[13] Ironically, at the very time that 'the reproach of ignorance on this important subject [was being] wiped away,'[14] the population that this enlightened efficiency was enumerating was declining due to causes that pre-existed the advent of the English, but which they had complicated and even triggered into action. British public works had stimulated, in the second half of the nineteenth century, a malaria epidemic, known successively as 'Rangpur Fever' and 'Hooghly Fever' as it coursed over Bengal, but most notoriously as 'Burdwan Fever' for its prolonged virulence in that District.[15]

Perhaps because of the absence of firm earlier data on which comparisons could be based, the documents of the first census are remarkably silent about the epidemic that had been raging already for a decade and that was to be the single most important demographic influence in large areas of central and western Bengal in the decades to come. It is not that mention of this vast loss and change of population is totally absent. But such statements as 'diminutions . . . such as may well be ascribed to the ravages made by the epidemic fever which had pervaded Burdwan for several years'[16] or 'the deserted remains of ruined houses . . . the havoc the fever has committed . . . whole households have been swept away'[17] are surprising for their rarity. The picture of an epidemic that had lasted ten years and had carried off a third of the population in the areas it afflicted has to be constructed from bits and pieces.

There is a definite feeling that the first census presents its figures with an awareness of the vast size of the population recently transferred to the direct rule of the British crown, and with wonder and disbelief. Many a civil servant had now been shown to control the destiny of more 'souls' in his district than several European monarchs. Bengal (excluding the Sunderbans) was more densely populated than England and Wales, which were only a third its size.[18] But such populations and densities were possible 'where the diet of the people consists almost entirely of rice . . . [and] where almost the whole soil is capable of giving at least one crop of grain in the year.' Moreover, the people 'inculcate in the strongest manner the duty of women to propagate the species, and . . . the injunction is complied with, as far as human nature will admit.'[19] What checks there are, are natural: 'famine and pestilence—the scourges of oriental countries—[that] doubtless periodically thinned the population, and kept it stationary, the losses of one decade being repaired in the next.'[20] Surely the imposition of British rule could only have brought stability, freedom from calamities, establishment of peace and order, extension of cultivation, development of trade—and a corresponding increase in this rural population.

Yet the officers of the 1872 census had good reason to suspect that the population in the districts of north and central Bengal had remained stationary or diminished in the preceding sixty years,[21] and that of districts in western Bengal appeared to be in the active process of shrinking at that time. Metcalfe, the Magistrate of Burdwan, wrote:

> All medical officers for several years have remarked on the severity of the fever in and around the Sudder Station. Gopalpore, once a flourishing village is now reduced to a small population, 2,000 people have disappeared from Khojanarbear. The deserted remains of ruined houses depict the havoc the fever has committed. . . . Dr. Jackson the Sanitary Commissioner, in his tour

in March remarked on the depopulated condition [of Culnah]. The Cutwah subdivision too has suffered from fever; so have the thanas of Selimabad, Roynah, Jehanabad, and the Munglekote. In some villages death has been noted at 24%. . . . [In Selimabad] the mortality from fever has been frightful. Whole households have been swept away.[22]

Pellew, the District Magistrate, reported that 'the population of Hooghly was increasing before 1860, and but for the fever would be an increasing population still, but that owing to this cause, its population is now less than it was in 1860, and much less than it would have been but for fever.'[23] Were the 'scourges of oriental countries' not signs of the misrule of oriental despots? Was enlightened British rule to be as ineffective against them as previous regimes?

Much of the official silence may be explained by the absence of base figures for comparison and the lack of universal mortality registration. But it needs to be remembered that it was only in 1880 that the malaria parasite was identified (in Algeria) and 1898 that the role of the Anopheles mosquito as the carrier fully understood. In the absence of such knowledge, the census would have had to admit openly the presence of a wholly irreducible difficulty.[24] So the first census chose, more often than not, to ignore the phenomenon, mention it as 'a further obstacle [that] threatened at the time to jeopardize the completion of the undertaking,' or pretend that it had been corrected by efficient sanitary measures. It is as if the new rulers took their first scrutiny of their 'rich possessions,' but the subject revealed its true nature so strongly as to disconcert the scrutinizer. Beverley, the Inspector General of Registration, Bengal, saw, in 1872, not as yet clearly, but through an obscuring darkness, the hazy form of Jvarāsur striding across the land. It was sufficient to set him and his colleagues puzzling over the mysterious disappearance of population.

Beverley argued that 'the Census figures must be accepted or condemned on their own merits, and not by comparison with figures which have no pretensions to accuracy whatever.[25] So it is appropriate that one set of its own figures caused great concern:

In the Burdwan and Presidency Divisions, the proportions of children appear to be abnormally low for India. . . . In Hughli and Burdwan Districts, where the epidemic fever has been raging, the proportion of children in the population is not more than 29.2 and 29.4 per cent, respectively. . . . In Bancoorah, where there has been no fever at all, 33.6. These results corroborate to a remarkable degree what the medical authorities tell us regarding this fever. They say that one of its characteristics is that those who are attacked by it are enervated to such an extent as to be unable to propagate the species.[26]

Moreover, malaria struck most fearsomely at young children and pregnant women. Here indeed is one of the bases of the *pālā* ('drama') of children that is part of the *Śītalā Maṅgal* cycles. To the first census it was a sign of a population vanishing before its eyes.

The first census suspected all prior large-scale estimates of the population of Bengal 'to be very inaccurate . . . hardly . . . more than a mere guess,' this being the precise reason for its lack of a base figure for comparison. 'The one exception is the attempt made by Dr. Buchanan, between 1807 and 1814,'[27] to compute the figures for Rungpore, Dinagepore, Purneah, Bhagalpore, Patna-Behar and Shahabad. It could not 'enter upon a study of the people of Bengal without confessing the extent to which [it] is indebted to Dr. Buchanan's writings,'[28] since the latter too accepted the principle that 'an Indian population indeed would seem to be limited only by the extent of cultivable land in each district.'[29] When confronted with the first census figures it appeared that the tract had lost thirteen persons per square mile, or a total of 516,000 people, three to four percent of the whole, in the intervening 60 years. This was a disturbing fact since

it is remarkable that the districts which a comparison with Dr. Buchanan's estimates . . . show to have largely decreased in population, namely the conterminous districts of Dinagepore, Maldah, and Purneah, are precisely those which a glance at the census maps shows to be among the districts of the Gangetic plain abnormally low in population.[30]

Of Purneah, which reflected the whole tract in having gained in area but lost in the number of inhabitants, Buchanan had already observed, 'the population seems in some places to be diminishing. . . . The extreme timidity and listlessness of the people [which has] in some parts prevented them from being able to repel the encroachments of wild beasts'[31] being given as reasons. The Vernacular Education Report prepared by Adams in 1838, another reliable earlier set of data, when contrasted with the 1872 figures, indicated that, in the Kalna Thana of Burdwan, for example, the population had remained stagnant for 30 years and, though the number of houses had increased, average occupancy had diminished from 5 to 3.7.[32]

Burdwan, chief town in the Company's original eighteenth century grant from the Nawab, steadily lost population, at an accelerating rate

TABLE I. PROPORTION OF CHILDREN UNDER 12 YEARS, 1872

Bengal	34.5%
Burdwan Division	30.9
Hooghly District	29.2
Burdwan District	29.4
Beerbhoom District	31.4
Midnapore District	32.3
Bancurah District	33.6
Presidency Division	30.8
Calcutta	14.8
24 Paraganas District	28.3
Jessore District	32.1
Nuddea District	32.9
Rajshaye Division	34.0
Dacca Division	35.5
Chittagong Division	37.9

Source: H. Beverley, *Report of the Census of Bengal, 1872*, p. 145, Paragraph 396.

TABLE II. CHANGES IN POPULATION IN DISTRICTS SURVEYED BY BUCHANAN

District	*Buchanan 1807–14*		*Census 1871–72*	
	Area (sq. mi.)	*Population*	*Area (sq. mi.)*	*Population*
Rungpore	7400	2,735.000	7811 +	2,970,625 +
Dinagepore	5374	3,000,000	5022 –	1,747,635 –
Purneah	6340	2,904,380	6409 +	2,324,705 –
Bhaugulpore	8225	2,019,900	8573 +	2,990,692 +
Patna & Behar	5358	3,364,420	5225 –	3,168,706 –
Shahabad	4087	1,419,520	4385 +	1,723,974 +
Total	36,784	15,443,220	37,425 +	14,926,337 –

Source: H. Beverley, *Report of the Census of Bengal, 1872*, p. 82, fn.

between 1869 and 1872, unusually virulent fever years. W. Butterworth Bayley, Judge and Magistrate of Burdwan, had made a careful attempt at estimating the population of the town and the district in 1813. He fixed the population of the town at 53,927.[33] It had shrunk in 1869 to

46,121 and in 1871 to 32,321. It is finally when comparing Bayley's figures with those of 1871 that the first census makes some connection between disease and depopulation of extensive tracts. The comparison established this result:

> While the number of houses has largely increased, the average per house has fallen. . . . When we take into account the mortality which has been raging in Burdwan for the past three or four years, this result is probably just what might have been expected. The 300,000 souls, by which the population falls short . . . may represent approximately the numbers which have been carried off by the epidemic fever. . . . In the southern thannahs it would not be an exaggeration to say that two-thirds of the people have fallen victims.[34]

Finally, and inevitably, the census comes to be haunted by the ruins of Gaur, located in the heart of the abnormally underpopulated tract of Dinajpur, Maldah, and Purnea, which 'testify that in some places at any rate, disease has worked a great depopulation . . . . The census report but too clearly points to the evidence of a serious effect on the population of the Burdwan district caused by the disease.'[35] Gaur of the magnificent palaces was reduced to being the haunt of tiger and wolf; its 'beautiful artificial lakes . . . were the refuge of fierce alligators,'[36] because of human powerlessness in the face of disease in 1560. Were large tracts of their own 'rich possessions' to follow this inevitable fate of oriental empires? It is the same question in a changed form that Bīrsiṃha, Rājā of Burdwan, asks of the Goddess Śītalā in Jagannāth's poem:

> 'May you increase in wealth and progeny, Oh King. May your years be long. This pauper woman . . . will dwell in your Bardhamān ultimately. From today there will be no fear of my disease. You will be the King and I the subject,' thus said Śītalā.
>
> Said the King: 'Be the ruler of this land. Revive the subjects and let me die. If You wish me to be the King of the land—my subjects have all died. Of what shall I be King?'[37]

Jvarāsur on the march

Jvarāsur, the Fever Demon, had raged in Bengal for almost two whole decades when the second census was taken in 1881; and his trail could be observed, by then, as the demographic calamity that it was. However, the epidemic's violence was not as fatal in the decade preceding the second census as it had been in that preceding the first. By 1857 it was already in epidemic form in Nadia and 24 Parganas, and the second census is careful to point out that no notice of the fever was taken by the authorities until the end of 1861.[38] In any case, the spread of the epidemic from the east, westward is described thus: 'Like the waves of a flowing tide it touched a place one year and receded, reached it again next year with greater force and again receded, repeating this process till the country was wholly submerged and the tide passed further on.' The epidemic apparently first showed itself in Muhammadpur in Jessore in 1836, among a body of five- to seven-hundred prisoners engaged, ironically, in one of the British modernizing operations, constructing the Dacca-Jessore Road.[39] In the next seven years 'the total desolation of the place ensued.' It caused many deaths in Jessore in 1847–48. After a respite it broke out there again in 1854–56, and in the last year moved into Nadia and devastated Krishnagar.[40] It moved ever westward and culminated in epidemic form in the 24 Parganas from 1857 to 1864, being most violent by the end of 1856. Finally, its ravages in Barasat subdivision and northern 24 Parganas caused it to be 'observed' by the authorities in 1861.

Its greatest severity in the Presidency Division was felt in the rainy seasons and winters of 1860 to 1862–63, and there was an abatement in 1864–65. Meanwhile, it had crossed the Hooghly River and the first cases were reported in 1862 from the Katwa and Purbasthali thanas that abut on the river. In 1863 it moved southward into northern Hooghly District. In 1864 and 1865 it moved west in Hooghly and Burdwan and reached Howrah in the south. In 1868 and 1869 the epidemic made a great leap, taking Burdwan town, and expanding north, west, and south. In 1870 there was no further westward move but in the north it invaded Birbhum and extended itself along the northern bank of the Ajay River. An unprecedented advance took place in 1871, further west in Burdwan, north and northwest in Birbhum, and over a large tract of northern Midnapore. In 1872 the fever reached its maximum westward extension in Burdwan, the highland at the Burdwan-Bankura border arresting its progress; but Birbhum was devastated further north and in Midnapore 'a great southern extension' took place, enveloping the north-east of the district. It abated slightly in Hooghly and Birbhum during 1872; but in Midnapore and Howrah mortality was twice that of the preceding year. The last year of the epidemic in the Burdwan Division was 1874 and what fever there was in 1875 had the characteristics of an ordinary seasonal malarious fever. It had already abated in 1873 on the eastern bank of the Hooghly, where it had first been 'observed.'[41]

Thus did Jvarāsur, the Fever Demon, marshal the forces of disease in a grand campaign over the face of Bengal in the 1860s and 1870s. The first printed text of the *Śītalā Maṅgal* that we have encountered, that of Maheścandra Dās De, dates from 1874, and the competition to print the text of Nityānanda Cakravartī took place in 1878.

The statistics of mortality from this epidemic are staggering. Burdwan, a Division that had been famous for its salubrity, showed a loss in overall population from the previous census; the Presidency (+6.01%) and Rajshahi (+4.78%) Divisions showing only small increases.[42] Though the sterner blows had fallen before the decennium preceding it, especially with reference to the Burdwan Division, the second census observes that, even then,

> the ravages of the disease have not yet been repaired, the ruined villages have not yet been rebuilt, jungle still flourishes where populous hamlets once stood, and while many of those who fled before the fever have returned, the impaired powers of the survivors have not been sufficient to fill the smiling land with a new population.[43]

Assuming conservatively, that the normal population increase over these nine years would have been about ten percent, based on statistics from the non-malarial districts, it can well be seen why the Bengal epidemic was especially identified with Burdwan. The Sanitary Commissioner calculated that in the twelve years that the fever raged in Burdwan District, it 'carried off in that time not less than *three quarters of a million persons*' (italics in the original). Equally detailed reports were not available for the other districts, however it is clear that Hooghly lost as much as Burdwan; Midnapore and Birbhum somewhat less; Howrah not as much; and Bankura, where the highlands had stopped the advance of the fever, comparatively little. The Commissioner estimated that the Division had lost above two million people in twelve years.[44]

By 1881, the second census reported that 'Rungpore fever has passed into a proverb in Bengal;'[45] this was the same fever that, in Buchanan's words, 'annually sweeps away immense numbers.' It displayed greater virulence in 1872 than in previous years. The extensive damage caused by fever and indicated by splenomegaly was already noted in the Civil Surgeon's Report of 1874: '80% of the population were anaemic, or

TABLE III. CHANGES IN THE POPULATION OF BURDWAN DIVISION, 1872–1881

	Increase/ Decrease	Percent Variation
Burdwan	– 210,707	– 2.7
Burdwan District	– 92,027	– 6.2
Bankura District	+ 73,155	+ 7.5
Birbhum District	– 59,357	– 6.9
Midnapore District	– 27,377	– 1.1
Hooghly District	– 144,617 [sic]	– 12.4
Howrah District	+ 39.516	+ 6.6

Source: J.A. Boudillon, *Report on the Census of Bengal 1881*, Vol. 2, Appendix B.
Note: Since the second census was much more thorough than the first, actual disparities are larger than they appear here.

suffered from enlarged spleens or were laid up with illness, while of the 20% found healthy one half could not be considered so in the European sense of the word.'[46] Interestingly, the same paragraph continued that, 'Lastly, the opening of the Northern Bengal Railway through the Sudder and northern sub-division of the district has had a direct effect upon the population of the thannahs through which it passes,' these two subdivisions having lost about 6% of their population over the preceding decade. The second census also showed a gain over the decade of only 0.82% for Dinajpur, and this perhaps wholly attributable to more efficient enumeration.

This pitiable result is due only to the ravages of malarious fever for which this district has as evil a reputation as its neighbouring Rungpore. In 1872 the reported deaths from fever in Dinagepore were higher than any other district of the [Rajshahi] Division. The four following years showed little improvement.... In 1877, ... the most unhealthy year in this district within living memory, ... over 30,000 deaths were reported from this cause alone.[47]

Fifteen out of the seventeen European administrators had to be evacuated and official business almost stopped. Investigations revealed constant sickness, a very high death rate, and nearly 75% of a sample of 1,000 individuals examined were found to be in bad health, 53% suffering from splenomegaly. A slight remission followed in 1879, but it returned with renewed virulence in 1880.[48]

In these tracts, where Buchanan early in the century had noted 'fever makes such ample havoc, that little room seems to be left for other diseases,' malarial fever would remain the most prevalent and fatal malady.[49] For example, for the decade 1893–1902 the deaths from fever were 33.30 per thousand as compared to 3.24 for all other causes.[50] If we consider that by 1940 seventeen out of twenty-eight districts, and 60,000 out of 86,000 villages of Bengal were regularly afflicted by malaria, which took an annual toll of 350,000 lives,[51] the long-term menace becomes more clear. From the accounts of the last quarter of the nineteenth century and the first decade of the present century, the complexity of 'fever' and its totally exhausting enmity to man is evident. In Rangpur, 'It is a slow lingering fever, usually attended by spleen and liver complications, and leading in the damp cold of the winter months to dropsy, pthisis, and other pulmonary affliction.'[52] Besides the malignant quotidian and tertian forms, the Civil Surgeon in 1908 noted 'also a very deadly form of fever that, clinically, is marked by a double daily rise in temperature and is associated with enlarged liver and spleen, progressive anaemia and weakness, and bowel complaints of a dysenteric nature.'[53] In Dinajpur, 'The fevers are often of the remitting kind and terminate fatally in a few days; but more commonly they terminate in agues, or commence under that form, and are accompanied by enlargements of the spleen and dropsical swellings, which carry off the sufferer after long confinement.'[54] In Maldah, malarious fevers 'alternate in a most perplexing way' with cholera.[55] The specific fevers to be met with in Murshidabad, in one list, are: malignant tertian malarial, including comatose, algide and hyperpyrexial forms; typical intermittent—quotidian, tertian, quartan, double tertian malarial; cachectic (Leishman-Donovan); enteric; filarial; 'and, more doubtfully, a continued fever, neither enteric, nor malarial . . . which is as yet the subject of much discussion.'[56] It is not very surprising that the following classification, 'neither complete, nor altogether scientific,' prepared in 1910 by the Civil Surgeon of Burdwan for his district, should remind us so strongly of earlier lists in the *Śītalā Maṅgal* texts:

1. Intermittent fever: a) quotidian, b) double quotidian, c) tertian, & d) quartan.
2. Remittent fever: a) bilious remittent ('Bilious remittent fever is a true malarial fever, and is associated with gastro hepatitic complications, with slight jaundice, and enlargement of the spleen.'), & b) typho-malarial fever.

3. Pernicious malarial fever.
4. Unclassified fever.
5. Pernicious cachectic fever.
6. Typhoid fever.
7. Kala azar.[57]

At a more local level, it is instructive here to note the losses sustained by the areas where a hundred years previously two of the poets of the *Śītalā Maṅgal* had lived and worked,[58] where it is still performed today, and where it was, in all likelihood, performed in the 1870s.[59]

Contai remained almost free of fever, although Ghatal and Tamluk were neighboring areas, illustrating how the violence of the fever epidemic could vary with apparent arbitrariness from place to place.

As if the fever epidemic were not enough, an unprecedented series of calamities visited Midnapore District in the immediately preceding years. In October 1864 occurred 'the most important feature in the recent meteorological history of Midnapur . . . the cyclone of 1864. In the southern and eastern part of Midnapur . . . the effects were most disastrous.'[60] At Tamluk the Rupnarayan River rose over thirteen feet, and the flood-waters reached Pargana Kāśījoṛā.[61]

The loss of life and property was very great. . . . The number drowned or killed in the storm, however, by no means represents the total loss of life caused by the cyclone. The immediate losses were equalled, if not exceeded, by the deaths caused by the famine and pestilence (cholera, dysentery, and small pox), in a great measure the consequence of the inundation.[62]

TABLE IV. SOME POPULATION CHANGES IN MIDNAPORE DISTRICT 1872–1881

	Increase/ Decrease	*Percent Variation*
Midnapore Sudder Sub-division	– 20,254	– 1.6
Ghatal Subdivision	– 58,248	– 16.9
Tamluk Subdivision	+ 11,401	+ 2.4
Panskura Thana	– 21,834	– 13.4
Contai Subdivision	+ 39,724	+ 9.0

Source: *India Census 1881: Bengal*, Vol. 3, Appendix C, p. 653. Table 23: 'Statement Showing Increase or Decrease of the Population of Each Thannah,' Part 4, 'Midnapore District.'

Hard upon this, in 1866, partly as a consequence of the cyclone, partly because the rains ceased unusually early in 1865, came

> the worst famine [in British times] of which there is detailed information, . . . the great Orissa famine, from which Midnapore suffered more than any district in Bengal outside Orissa. [It was] estimated that in the western part of the district from ten to fifteen percent of the population died of starvation and diseases induced by it, and that in the central portion of Contai subdivision from two to three percent and in Tamluk a half percent perished.[63]

When the epidemic struck, then, there were ample portents of an impending cataclysm.

Western Bengal in the mid-eighteenth century

We do not know as much about disease in Bengal in the middle of the eighteenth century, when most of the *Śītalā Maṅgal* texts were being composed, as we know about the 1870s, when the competition over the printing of the *Maṅgal* was underway. However, there is some historical information with indirect bearing upon the disease situation that is worth reviewing here. This information relates to political and economic conditions in the middle of the eighteenth century, and to changes in rivers and drainage in western Bengal during this period.

Given the cataclysmic events that were taking place around the time of the efflorescence of *Śītalā Maṅgal* composition, it is remarkable that the texts contain no reference to particular historical happenings. This should serve as a reminder that we are dealing with mythology and that myths speak in timeless and metaphorical terms about persistent human problems. We do not want to suggest a mechanical connection between historical contingencies and myth-making; what we are examining is the process of endowing a disaster with cultural significance.

When Nādir Shāh raided Delhi in 1739, the Mughal Empire was in decline and the Province of Bengal was to a considerable extent autonomous. Between 1742 and 1751, Maratha horsemen repeatedly swept over western Bengal, the area in which these texts were composed, sacking villages and capitals of important kings, looting, raping, and laying waste.[64] In 1757 Nawāb Sirāj-ud-daulā was defeated at Plassey by a combination of treachery and British force. The British helped Mir Jāfar, who was installed as Nawab in 1757, and he made the grant of the 24 Parganas to the East India Company. There was a severe financial crisis between 1757 and 1760; many of the Bengali zamindārs refused or were unable to pay their revenues to the treasury in Murshidabad, and Mir Jāfar was unable to pay large amounts of damages due the British for the Black Hole incident. In 1760 Mir Jāfar was replaced by Mir Qāsim, who ceded the Districts of Burdwan and Midnapur (from which most of our texts come) as well as Chittagong to the East India Company to make good the Company's claims on his court. In 1765 the Company was made Diwan of Bengal.[65]

In the period between 1760 and 1770 the zamindārs of Bengal were progressively impoverished. History does not relate the experience of the ordinary people—the cultivators and artisans of the villages—during this period. However, it is most probable that the zamindārs increased their revenue demands on the villagers in every way possible, so that times became hard throughout the countryside. As seems to happen so often in Bengal, the uncontrollable forces of nature put the seal on this calamatous period. As N.K. Sinha relates the events:

> The Famine of 1770 was caused by an uncommon drought. There was a partial failure of December crop of 1768 and September crop of 1769. From the middle of August 1769 there was no rain till the beginning of January 1770 and then it lasted a few hours and came too late to be of general benefit. There was therefore a complete failure of the December crop of 1769. Thus came the great Famine which raged in all severity throughout 1770. Pestilence came in the wake of Famine. . . . About ten millions of people must have perished in Bengal and Bihar. But the collection of revenue was not permitted to be affected. Assessment was made on the surviving ryots to make up for the loss by death or desertion.[66]

In summary, then, the period between about 1740 and 1770, to which we can date most of the *Śītalā Maṅgal* texts, was a time of great trouble in Bengal, much of it due to human agency, the remainder due to famine and disease.

There was another kind of difficulty besetting western Bengal in the mid-eighteenth century, less easily understood by contemporary observers but of greater long-term importance for the well-being of the people of the region. This is the decay of the river system in the western part of the delta, a decay that was hastened by the construction of roads and embankments in the nineteenth century, but that was already underway due to natural causes in the eighteenth. It is not our aim here to provide a sketch of the ecology of the Bengal delta, interesting as it is, but rather to look at some of the human problems to which Bengalis have found religious answers. Therefore, we may be forgiven for compacting and simplifying what we have to say about the decline of the western Bengal rivers.

The central part of the Bengal region, and its cultural nucleus, is a very large delta built up mainly by the deposits of silt brought down to the sea by the Ganges and Brahmaputra rivers. These are enormous rivers and they carry staggering quantities of suspended material. When they reach the delta, which is extremely flat, their velocities decline abruptly, and they deposit much of their suspended material quickly. The volumes of water and silt that they carry during the monsoon season is much greater than at other times of the year and, on a landscape unaffected by human habitation, they would spill out of their courses and deposit much of their loads on the land, building it gradually to higher and higher elevations. During the drier parts of the year they deposit silt on their own stream-beds. These deposits along and within a river course have a self-damming effect and, frequently during the floods, major distributaries of the Ganges and Brahmaputra desert one course and excavate a new channel through lower-lying areas. Thus, unhindered by manmade embankments, a deltaic river tends to wander in different courses over the land, raising land elevations a few inches along one route, then shifting its channel to a lower area. Settled agriculturists find living in such circumstances precarious; when technology, manpower, and social organization have made it possible, they have tried to train rivers to particular courses. Interference with the processes of delta-building bring certain unintended consequences, which we shall examine, and there are limits to the ability of man to restrain the mighty rivers of the delta.

The principal outfall of the Ganges to the sea in the seventeenth century was the Bhagirathi-Hooghly course, which begins in Murshidabad District and passes Calcutta on its way to the Bay of Bengal. The Ganges already favored its more easterly course in the middle of the eighteenth century. The lower reaches of the Bhagirathi-Hooghly channel were kept open by the addition of the waters of the Damodar, flowing out of Choṭa Nagpur and, at that time, falling into the Bhagirathi just south of Nadia. In 1770 the Damodar shifted its outfall into the Hooghly 80 miles to the south, just north of the Rupnarayan confluence and the Hooghly estuary. Rivers such as these, silting up and deserting their courses, have a profound effect upon the agricultural prosperity of the areas they once watered and drained—water supply and drainage being critical in rice agriculture, and the annual deposits of fresh silt constituting natural fertilizer for the crops. Moreover, these shifting rivers leave behind them stagnant marshes in which mosquito larvae can develop in large numbers, creating the possibility of increased rates of transmission of malaria and other mosquito-borne diseases.[67]

The Kansai or Kansabati—the principal river of Midnapur District like the Damodar, flows out of the Chota Nagpur plateau. In the mid-eighteenth century it flowed south of Midnapur town, then looped back northward to fall into the Rupnarayan about twenty-five miles north of Tamluk. It followed this course at the time when the poets Jagannāth in Tamluk and Nityānanda in Kāśījoṛā were composing their *Śītalā Maṅgals* and was evidently a source of grief for these two paraganas, which were separated by it. Rājā Kamalnārayaṇ of Tamluk (ruled 1752–1756), a patron of Jagannāth, defaulted in the payment of his revenue; and the Faujdar of Hijli, Masnad Muhammad Khan, made his favourite eunuch (*khojā*), Mirzā Didār Āli Beg, Manager of the pargana. Didār Āli erected an embankment on the eastern side of the Kansai to prevent it from flooding Tamluk, presumably by forcing all of the flood waters into Kāśījoṛā. The embankment stands today and is still known as *Khojār bheṛi* (or *bā̃dh*), but the river has long since deserted that course. It is difficult to say what the environmental effects of the embankment may have been, but it seems likely that it created some substantial silting of the stream-bed and, in Kāśījoṛā, left stagnant marshes where mosquitos bred. Stream traces suggest that the Kansai next sought a more southerly course that brought it through the embankment and into the Rupnarayan just north of Tamluk; this happened some time after Rennell's survey was completed in 1773. Still later, the Kansai moved further south, and it now flows directly into the Hooghly estuary through the Haldi river course.[68]

To summarize this indirect evidence bearing upon disease in mid-eighteenth century western Bengal, there are numerous reasons to think that during this period, the disease situation might have been becoming more severe than previously. Mughals, British, and Marathas all increased their efforts to extract wealth from the peasantry. The declining river system made agriculture more difficult and less productive, so that, on the average, the quality of the diet of the ordinary people is likely to have declined. Malnourished people are more apt than well-fed ones to fall victim to any infection that happens to be around. Moreover, the conditions for the spread of malaria were exacerbated by the declining river system. We cannot be sure about an increased incidence of pustular diseases, with which *Śītalā* is so strongly associated, for we have only such vague references as those to the 'plague' that devastated Gaur in the sixteenth century and the 'pestilence' that followed the famine of 1770. However, there is one interesting bit of negative evidence to be considered in conclusion. The events, both natural and human, that we have discussed affected primarily western Bengal. This was the area that concerned the British at that time and the locality of the Maratha raids. It was a region of dying rives, deserted by the main stream of the Ganges. Eastern Bengal, meanwhile, was prospering in relative freedom from human depredation and with the benefit of an active river system. Cultivators moved from the western areas into the active deltaic districts of the east. All of the *Śītalā Maṅgals* that we know of are from deltaic western Bengal. This does not prove anything, but it suggests a greatly heightened concern with the Goddess and her companions in the declining delta.

Sanitation versus submission

If there are major similarities between the growth of the literature of Śītalā in the mid-eighteenth century and the late nineteenth century, the one prime difference is this: The circumstances of the earlier period led to a variety of attempts at individual and autonomous creation, as attested by the number of *Śītalā Maṅgals* that survive from that time; whereas in the later period the activity is characterized by a mere bickering over rights to the act of mechanical reproduction. It is true that we have, in Maheścandra Dās De's little book, a second work, but, as pointed out earlier, it served only to fill in a blank, which, once the later editions of Text A maneuvered around it, seems to have disappeared. Somewhere between 1750 and 1850, Nityānanda's *Maṅgal* had risen to a paramount position, probably because of its completeness and other virtues, so much so that he had come to acquire the reputation of being the *ādi kavi*, or 'original poet,' of *Śītalā Maṅgal*, a totally spurious distinction and one which, in Indian literature, often means no more than 'the best.'[69] Indeed, the publisher's afterword to Text B of Nityānanda's *Maṅgal* is based on this reputation.[70] Once picked up by the first publisher and transformed by the medium of printing, it gained miles (twelve impressions, to be more precise) on the competition.

The picture must then have changed substantially from one of variant myths enjoying limited local popularity to that of one version of the myth dwarfing all others, and thus laying claims to orthodoxy.[71] Variety had disappeared and, with it, the possibility of the interfertilization among the variants, which we suspect may have been the case in the earlier period, especially given the tradition of manuscript 'collation' by singer-performers. As far as we can ascertain, no other versions saw print. It is not surprising, therefore, that when Nilkānta Bandopādhyāy[72] sought materials from which to compose a 'quality' poem on Śītalā in 1922 the *pālā* he picked up from the singers of Śītalā's myth should be the standardized *Virāṭa Pālā*, which by then had apparently been widely adopted.

Through all of the versions, manuscript and printed, the supremacy of Śītalā and Her special relationship to the poxes remains constant. However, if we compare the later texts with that of Kṛṣṇarām, the only seventeenth century version that we have, there is a distinct difference in the importance of Jvarāsur. In Kṛṣṇarām's text, Basantarāy, 'Ruler of Poxes,' is the Goddess's lieutenant, while Jvarā (here named Jvarabān) is one of her five attendants, although the most active one. But in all[73] of the eighteenth century texts, Jvarā is Her marshal and chamberlain, speaking to Her at times almost as an equal. It is obvious that fever has an important role to play during the first 72 hours of smallpox, when it seizes the victim before the pustules appear and make diagnosis possible. However, the Fever Demon who appears in the Introduction provided in the nineteenth century to Nityānanda's text is much more than a prelude to pox. His capacities are formidable—newly born from the perspiration of Siva's brow, he declaims:

Why, Lord, have you created me? Speak of what work I should do.

Should I suck the ocean dry, or consume the fire? Or should I take the earth between these teeth and chew it up? Or should I devour both sun and moon?[74]

Nityānanda describes graphically the etiology of smallpox, with fever preceding the outbreak of pustules. However, he goes on to discuss at great length the symptoms of malarial and enteric fevers not necessarily connected to any pustular manifestation. For example:

Kālandi is a quotidian (*ekayā*) fever; it seizes one at the end of the day and makes even the greatest of heroes into helpless beasts. At a glance from cerebral fever (*śirajvar*, possibly cerebral malaria), I send one to the house of death, having scorched him with 'co-wife fever' (*dosatīnājvar*, i.e., when one ceases, the other takes hold).

The terrible, tiger-felling tertian (*pāli*) [fever] makes the bones and flesh into soot, and sucks blood with angry vigour. It obeys no medicine and enjoys the patient at will; having seized him, it abandons him for two days, then returns.[75]

We are not postulating a cause-and-effect relationship in which the increased incidence of malaria somehow induces a change in the myth. What we see, however, is a cultural transformation of the immediate experience of malaria into yet another culturally mediated form of universal destruction (*nipāt*) by disease. As Nityānanda recounts the vision of the King of Viraṭa:

A hundred and twenty diseases spread all over and, assuming terrible form, devastated the King in the dream. There were uncountable [inauspicious] shooting stars, [and] rivers flowing with blood, while the diseases sucked blood.

Seeing this, the King shuddered in terror. Śītalā, seated at his head, [said], 'Listen with a calm mind, Oh King! It is my grace (*dayā*) to extend my *māyā* to you; I am the master of all disease.'[76]

It appears that the particular historical event registers itself on and adds to the timeless structure of the myth after it has been transformed into a statement that is consonant with that structure of meanings. In the case of *maṅgal kāvya* myths, signed by their composers, it seems possible to identify certain persons as the agents of the change. But what is striking is the homogeneity of the transformations wrought by different composers, suggesting that it is cultural rather than idiosyncratic creative processes that are at work.

The approach to the death and destruction of disease taken by British authorities appears initially to be quite different from that taken in the *Śītalā Maṅgal*. However, while the new embankments, roads, and railways disorganized the natural drainage, contributed to reducing the fertility of the soil by changing the patterns of silt deposit, prevented the drainage of surface water, clogged the subsoil, and contributed to the death of rivers until many turned into breeding ponds for Anopheles mosquitos that brought on the epidemic, British officials went around administering relief measures and compulsively promulgating their belief in sanitation, yet ignorant beyond various theories regarding the causes of 'morbidific marlarious poison.' Faced with a diseases of such suddenness of onset, such severity of symptoms, and such calamatous magnitude, the British turned to their faith in sanitation:

The sanitary condition of the villages, it is needless to say, is deplorably bad in every respect. Buried in jungle studded with filthy tanks, houses crowded together and surrounded by all kinds of filth, are the most common characteristics of the villages of the District. The water supply is contaminated, and the atmosphere laden with gaseous products of rotting vegetation and the excreta of inhabitants. . . . Every village that I have ever visited is pervaded by odours more or less offensive. Utterly regardless of every law that conduces to health, the villagers remain on year after year surrounded by all those oft described sources of nuisance with which we are only too familiar. . . .[77]

Another Sanitary Commissioner while acknowledging that 'filthy conditions of themselves will not always produce intermittent fever' goes on to say 'that the accumulation of house refuse is . . . [not] of necessity a source of malarious fever, nor that excrementatious matter is capable under all circumstances of generating pestilence. . . . [But we] well know that heat and moisture, reacting on each other may afford an atmosphere most suitable for the production of disease. What then can we think of all the filth and vegetable decay of Bengal villages, but that it is a source of danger, and that it ought to be removed and treated in such a manner as experience teaches to be most safe.[78]

If these complaints seem rather vague and uncertain, it is worth recalling the state of medical knowledge about malaria in the 1870s and 1880s. The connection between marshy areas, enlarged spleens, and various intermittent and remittent fevers had been established by Hippocrates, who correlated the consumption of marsh water with splenomegaly, lean physiques, and long quartan fevers and fatal dropsies.[79] The insalubrity of the Pontine marshes since ancient times led many Romans to speculate on malaria. Varro (116–27 BC) thought marshes produced minute animals borne by the air and which, entering through the nose and mouth, caused disease.[80] Columella, a contemporary of Nero, said that marshes should not be permitted near habitations and roads, both because of their noxious vapors and because they produced swarms of stinging insects that caused obscure illnesses.[81] There was an eighteenth century revival of these speculations from classical antiquity that culminated in a theory of miasms and effluvia. As late as 1886, G.M. Sternberg, who appears to have been an authoritative malariologist of the period, rejected the theory that the disease was caused by particulate poisons or living micro-organisms.[82] It was Columella's conception of noxious vapors rather than his prescient suggestion of a role for insects in the transmission of malaria that held sway in Western medicine during the 1880s. W.W. Hunter's list of causes for the Hooghly Fever reads like a direct paraphrase of Sternberg's catalog of causes for malaria generally: 'use of bad water,' 'proximity to marshes,' 'vegetable decomposition,' 'defective conservancy and general insanitation,' and finally, most important in Hunter's eyes, 'defective drainage.'[83] Thus, the British officials in Bengal merely reflected the state of the science when they insisted that cleanliness is next to godliness. But the people they ruled, who were persuaded that nothing was equal to Goddess Śītalā, chose to put their faith elsewhere.

To Western eyes, the grace (*dayā*) of Śītalā is one of the most opaque of religious conceptions. Her grace is manifest not only in the absence of disease but also—and most clearly and explicitly—in the body of a smallpox sufferer. In Christianity the gift of God's grace is 'charisma,' derived from the Greek *charizesthai*, 'to favor,' from *charis*, 'grace.' While Christians readily admit that God works in mysterious ways, a sufferer from disease is most likely to regard himself as not favored in the sight of the Lord, and often, like Job, as being in the hands of Satan. The recipient of charisma is uniquely favored; it is the apostolic gift and may even carry with it the power to heal. In the extensive non-theological literature on this concept, Max Weber's analysis of the authority conveyed by charisma remains commonly accepted as seminal: he sets it off from both traditional and bureaucratic forms of authority as 'the great revolutionary force.'[84] The charismatic leader often finds himself at the head of a movement directed toward overturning established forms of authority, traditional or bureaucratic, sacred or secular. In cultures affected by Jewish, Christian, or Muslim traditions of prophecy and eschatology, such movements have historically had a millennial character, foreseeing a complete end to temporal authority and the establishment of a divinely ruled kingdom on earth.

Many students of millennial movements have commented on their absence from Hindu India. In situations of widespread distress, such as deadly epidemics, and particularly where there is general social disorder, such as existed in the latter half of eighteenth and in nineteenth century Bengal, large numbers of people have responded to the visions of millennial dreamers with a kind of total enthusiasm unprecedented in their own experience. Bengali Hindus (and Hindus in general) have not had millennial visions nor the kind of sweeping enthusiasms characteristic of movements in other parts of the world. There are many approaches to the explanation of the absence of millennialism from India, but they all come down to a single point: integral to Hinduism is a non-eschatological conception of the universe. 'Movement,' in Western thought, is a characteristic of things in time, conceived of as continuously 'moving forward.' *Andolan*, the currently used Bengali term for such things as 'political movements,' contains a very different sense of time than does the English 'movement.'[85] *Andolan* means 'oscillation' and carries with it a conception of a single but continuously varying form.

Millennial movements take place within time and the heralded millennium itself is a period of time. The Old Testament prophets appeared at times of crisis, and the charismatic leaders of the Christian era have been as much creatures of their times—when 'nation shall rise up against nation, and kingdom against kingdom: and there shall be famines, and pestilences, and earthquakes in divers places' (Matthew 24: 7)—as of their particular gifts. Time seems always to be present in Judaism, Christianity, and Islām, and charisma is not evenly distributed through it. The anticipation of the end of time conditions the interpretation of all events, and each moment in the temporal flux is regarded as unique and idiosyncratic.

It is a commonplace of Indian studies that Hindus conceive of time as ordered in large cycles. However, in these texts we do not find much concern with such cycles; rather, it is taken for granted that human beings are trapped in the degraded Kali Yuga, where ignorance is the perpetual condition of human minds, which know little, forget much, and often wish to avoid knowing. Śītalā chooses appropriate means of revealing Herself to persons of such a severely limited capacity for perception and these means, alas, are often the ones that leave people wiser but sadder. Such searing revelations appear to the sufferers as historical cataclysms, but they are properly to be understood as nothing more than an oscillation from the implicit to the epidemic form of the grace of the Mother, a grace that is perpetual and timeless but usually unstated, only becoming explicit as the occasional *līlā* of the Goddess. What is important for mortals is to understand the unity of the two. A Hindu millennium would be no different from what is here and now, correctly perceived and properly understood. There is no difference between a 'spiritual' other-worldly realm and a 'temporal' this-worldly one.

In the development of social scientific thought in the West, the notion of 'synchronic analysis,' descriptions of things and their relations to one another as if outside time, has played an important part because it allows accounts of 'structure.' However, synchrony has generally been thought of as requiring the analyst to ignore a time dimension that is 'naturally' a part of the relations within a structure. In the kind of Hindu thought that appears in these *maṅgal kāvya* myths, relations are illusory. However, human beings, going about their daily, weekly, monthly, and annual routines, experience only diachronic relationships. They experience the onset, development and conclusion of disease, and they may even recognize it as the grace of Śītalā. However, they fail to recognize her grace equally in the absence of disease. Mother's grace is eternally present; like the Goddess Herself, it is timeless. The *maṅgal* teaches people about this timeless relationship in the midst of the existential problems of the concrete particularities of history. People are helped to realize that, literally, 'what you are able to see is what you get,' and those who insist on seeing suffering will suffer, abandoned, while those who are able to see the grace of the Mother will experience that grace.

The purpose of the *Śītalā Maṅgal* is not primarily the avoidance of disease, whether smallpox, malaria, or any other. The *maṅgal*, the 'well-being,' the 'auspiciousness,' or the 'beneficence' of the text lies in its capacity to enlighten and instruct. Stated in oversimplified terms, *bhakti*, an attitude of religious love, places the worshiper in a wholly dependent and child-like attitude toward the deity. The composition or publishing of a *maṅgal* text is an act of *bhakti* and also a means of enlightening and instructing others by explaining the divine to people so that they too can have proper *bhakti*.

Job's affliction is a result of the contention between God and Satan; it is quite otherwise for a Bengali. According to Bengali belief, a person may be free from disease but ignorant of the Goddess. The enlightened person may be free from the disease and know that it is due to the grace of the Mother. Primary enlightenment and instruction in this matter is received when that grace appears in the form of pustules on one's body. There is a disconcerting ambivalence about the revelation of the Goddess in this form; Bengalis greatly prefer to be enlightened through the secondary method—listening to the performance of Her myth in the context of Her worship, letting Her know that Her self-revelation has been received through a fitting attitude of *bhakti*. But the preference for this less taxing instruction should not blind us to the fact that both the presence and absence of disease are manifestations of the grace of the Mother.

Our discovery of a piece of the history of Bengal during the eighteenth and nineteenth centuries concealed in the Śītalā mythology has important implications for the understanding of *maṅgal kāvya* texts more generally.

Earlier *maṅgals* may be analyzed with this aim of uncovering the social history of Bengal in more obscure periods. Inden[86] and Dimock[87] have used *maṅgal kāvyas* as sources for structural accounts of kingdoms and cities in medieval Bengal. With reliable dating of the composition and copying of texts and biographical information about their composers, some of the facts of the diachronic history of the ordinary people of the countryside can also be gleaned from them. But *maṅgals* are not poor man's history; they are 'blessedness,' 'auspiciousness,' and 'well-being.' Like the deities they eulogize, they stand outside time, even though they register the transitory events of history. The principal message of a *maṅgal* myth is its religious one. Human beings are enlightened and instructed so that they can recognize the unity underlying the events of life, the permanent manifestation (*rupa*) of the grace of the Mother.

Śītalā Maṅgal Bardhamān Pālā of Kavi Jagannāth

Introduction

The following version of the myth of Śītalā is of particular importance since neither it nor its composer has previously received any notice in the history of Bengali literature. The manuscript was collected in 1970 from a village near Tamluk by Śrī Nirañjan Adhikāri. It consists of twelve leaves of hand-made paper, each 14" x 10", folded in half, giving a page of 14" x 5", and written on only one side. The first page contains only the title *Śītalāmaṅgalbadāmanpālā* and the information that there are 16 leaves. The leaves are numbered, and numbers IX–XI and XVI are missing. (We indicate leaf numbers at the side of the translation.) In addition, the side of the leaf bearing the number is labeled in the upper left *Śītalāmaṅgalbadyamān*, i.e., *Śītalā Maṇgal Bardhamān* [*Pālā*]. The composer and/or copyist has divided the text into sections by the use of signature lines (*bhanitā*) and floral ornaments (*puṣpika*). The beginning of a new section in the translation is indicated by the capitalized word 'ONE,' 'TWO,' 'THREE,' etc. Because of the numerous breaks in the text, it has not been possible for us to indicate verse divisions. The pages contain 9 (5 pp.), 10 (15 pp.), and 11 (2 pp.) lines each, except for Leaf

VIII, Side b, which contains 12 lines and may be in a different hand. The manuscript is badly damaged, particularly at the beginning and end. We are grateful to Messrs Robert Rosenthal and Sidney Huttner of the Department of Special Collections in The University of Chicago Library for their help in restoring the manuscript. Where the translation is based upon substantial reconstruction it is enclosed in square brackets. Where we have supplied words or phrases to make the sense clear, these are also enclosed in square brackets and italicized.

Kavi Jagannāth tells us that he was a courtier of Rājā Kamalnārāyaṇ. Kamalnārāyaṇ was King of Tamluk from 1752 until 1756, thus dating the text quite closely. The King was a Kaivartta and, like most of that caste, the family is devoutly Vaiṣṇava even now. Jagannāth describes the kingdom as *Viṣṇukṣetra*, 'Field of Viṣṇu,' which serves to underscore the peculiar importance of the very non-Vaiṣṇava cult of Śītalā in the region during the mid-eighteenth century.

Śītalā Maṇgal Bardhamān Pālā of Kavi Jagannāth

ONE. *Tripadī*

Leaf I. Side b. Here is written the book (*pustak*) [*Śītalā*] *Maṇgal*. Ruler of Poxes (Basantarāy), salutations. Daughter of Brahmā, descend from Mount Kailāsa, come to the mortal world. [Remove obstacles from the way] of Your protagonist (*nāyak*). How great is Your glory, Oh Mother [of the world]. Descend from Mount Kailāsa, come down to the mortal world, and abide in Your own pot. You are gracious (*dayābān*) to those who take refuge in You (*śaraṇāgatajane*). The time and place of Your birth have been propitious, at the *Brahma-yajña*. Brahmā, Viṣṇu, Maheśvara, Varuṇa, King Śurapati (Indra) of Heaven, Yama, all of the Gods have worshiped You, sounding conches and ululating. A King [?] has worshiped You on earth, and You have been named Mother of Disease (*Roger Jananī*). Now come down to the performance (*āsar*), see it and hear it, supervise the structure (*gā̃thani*) of the songs.

You wear a silken sari (*paṭṭaśāṛī*), golden *makara*-faced bangles, and a silken sari [?]. A long moon-garland (*cā̃dmālā*)[88] of diamonds, sapphires, pearls, and coral hangs from Your neck; You have fragrant *campaka* flowers on your body. [Descend, You who are so beautiful to behold], with eyes that shame the *khañjana* birds.

Leaf II. Side a. The matted locks on Your head surpass the yak-tail fly-whisk. On your forehead there is a vermilion mark. [? moon.] Your limbs are adorned with many ornaments. I salute You, Devī Śītalā, and worship Your feet. Wearing royal garments (*rāṭbastra*), yet You are space-clad (*digambarī*, i.e., nude). In Your right hand a broom [?], in the crook of Your left arm a water-pot (? *bāri*); You have with You pox-incense (*basanter dhup*). A golden broom in Your hand, a golden pot on Your left side. Come, Ruler of Disease (*Roger Rājā*), accept the worship that is rightfully Yours, and offer salvation through Your unique quality. I know neither rhythm nor measure and the Goddess has given me a great weight to carry. What You instruct, I will speak—the fault and the quality are all Yours.

King Kamalnārāyaṇ, son of King Naranārāyaṇ, being enlightened of mind, established the song of Kavi Jagannāth in the Viṣṇu-field of Tamolipta (Tamluk).

TWO. *Tripadī*

Seated one day with her courtier Jvarāsur, in great good humor, the Goddess Basantarāy (Ruler of Pox) said: 'Listen Jvarā, I say to you! we will all go invited to the earth. But tell me, which folk will worship Me? My birth was at a propitious moment, at a propitious place—in the sacrifice of Brahmā. My name is Goddess Basantarāy. All the Gods have worshiped My feet ululating and sounding conches. Brahmā, Viṣṇu, Maheśvara, Varuṇa in the waters, Śurapati King of Heaven, the terrible Yama, all have worshiped Me. But let me tell you of my great craving—

Leaf II. Side b. In whose house on earth will I receive worship? Tell me what methods I should use. How should I go?'

Upon hearing Devī's words, Jvarāsur said: 'Listen, Devī, attentively. Take my advice,[89] Mother, and go as a female ascetic to the country of Bardhamān. There is King Bīrsiṃha. Ask him in a dream to worship You. If he refuses, calamity will befall him. There, I have given my advice (*upadeś*).'

Receiving the advice of Jvarā, Śītalā [joyfully went] to the City of Bardhamān. She entered into the place where the King was lying. [Appearing] in a dream to ask for her worship, Śītalā said to the King: 'Perform my worship! I am the Goddess Śītalā. I will be compassionate to your house. Worship, and let me grant you boons.'

On hearing Her words, shouting 'Rāma!' the King jumped up and covered his ears. Abusing the Brāhmaṇī and remembering God Jagannāth, he breathed heavily and said: 'Hear me! From infancy I have worshipped the feet of Viṣṇu. Can I leave that now and worship you, old crone? That is as good as going to hell (*naraka*). Listen, go seek worship in some other house. Why come here to meet your end?

Leaf III. Side a. 'you speak, I will send my Chief Constable (*koṭāl*) to arrest you [?].'

The Goddess became incensed (*gosā bhar* [*h*]*aila*), and came to Jvarā. [Śītalā told him] all the words of the King. 'Bīrsiṃha will not worship me.'

Jvarā said, 'Mother, if you want to receive worship, summon all the diseases.'

At Śītalā's feet, Jagannāth says, keep Dulāl (? his own son, or 'precious child') in well-being.

THREE-A. *Payār*

At the Goddess's command (*ādeś*), all the diseases rushed forth. 'We will go to the country (*deś*) of Bardhamān in grand panoply.'

At Jvarā's advice (*ādeś*), the Mother of the World called out their names. Śītalāi roared out their names and the diseases were startled with delight. At Her command they stood ready in the presence of the Goddess one by one. There came Fever (*Jar*) and Headache (*Māthābyātha*) who seize the luckless. Mixed acidity and Biliousness (*do rasā Ambal-pitta*) came quickly. The brothers Phlegm Fever (*Āmjara*), Wind Fever (*Bātjarā*), and Bile Fever (*Pittajarā*), and Mixed Acidity and Biliousness came to the seat of Śītalā. *Pittaśel* (? a Bile Missile) and *Śvābāt* (? Rabies) arrived with dignity. Mad Enteric Fever (*Hauṛā Sannipāt*) came before the Goddess. The two brothers Wind Disorder and Fever (*Bāt-Jvarā*) came running. Many kinds of poisonous Fevers (*Biṣ Jvarā*) came to the seat of Śītalā. *Bāghnyā* and *Pānisāṛidhā*, these two arrived. Before the Goddess appeared *Hāṛāpani*.

Leaf III. Side b. Migraine (*Ādkapali*, *Ardhakapāli*) and Headache (*Māthābyātha*) came running. With *Sāmyājhākā* and *Saṇḍābār* came *Nāikathā*; *Koṭbirā*, and *Lok Kolā* went forth. *Galā Hāiyā*, *Danta Kaṛā*, and Cataract of the eye (*Chāni*), one and all came. Wind of the Waist (i.e., Rheumatism, *Kamarbat*), Wind of the Abdomen (Cramps, *Peṭbāt*),

Stomach Rumbling (? *Guhuriyā*), *Caurangiyā*, *Khācuniyā*, *Dhathakiyā* went forth. Acid Vomiting (*Ām Uṭhā*), Bile Vomiting (*Pitta Uṭhā*) *Gṛhini-sañcar* (? from *grahani*, an imaginary organ, locus of the 'interior fire' of digestion) one and all arrived. Convulsions (*Dhanuṣṭaṅkār*) came with a great show of strength: 'Whose father can save him whom I seize?'

Hearing this, Her joy increasing, Devī Śītalā said, 'On to Bardhamān!'

Jvarā said, 'Hear, Oh Mother Devī Śītalāi! All of these diseases will not get You worship. The Gods churned the ocean, and thereupon Dhanvantari (the heavenly physician) was born. If you go to him with these diseases, he has medicines for all of them. If people take medicine, the fever disappears and they become well, and they will not give You worship. If You are to receive worship at Bīrsiṃha's seat, then call those diseases for which there is no cure.'

Having heard [the advice] of Jvarā, the Goddess [summoned] the poxes [by name]. Receiving the command of the Goddess, *Leaf IV. Side a.* the poxes came. Kavi Jagannāth sings the *Śītalāmaṅgal*.

THREE-B.[90] *Payār*

The poxes [appeared before] the Goddess. Seeing them, Devī Śītalā was delighted. *Bāicā* (Jujube-like), *Masuryā* (Small-pox, from *masur*, a variety of pulse), and *Tilā* (Sesamum-like), came running; *Kāl-cimṭi* (the Black Pinch) and *Dhungryā-cāṭi* appeared. *Pālā-niyā* (? Intermittent *niyā*) *Ban-khurā*, and *Phuṭakiyā* (the Dotter) came running. *Kāṭhaliyā* (Jack-fruit-like), *Kākhori* (? Boils of the Armpit), and *Nāreṅgiyā* (Orange Scabs) rushed forth. *Rakta-cirā* (Chronic blood disease) and *Kāl-cirā*, the two brothers came running. *Māṃsadal* (Eruptions of the flesh) and *Cāmdal* (Eruptions of the skin) [came to] the seat of Śītilā. *Khos* (Scabies), *Karunya*, and *Minminā* (Measles) danced around. The Goddess Śītalā smiled to see them. *Padmaphulyā* (the Lotus-blossom) and *Bounyā*, these two came running. *Biṣ-phoṛa* (Poisonous boils) appeared before the Goddess. At the end came the Pox *Jagaddal* (the Earth-crushing), under whose weight everything (*taru meru*) goes to perdition.

At Śītalā's word came the cohorts of the poxes. 'Who has what qualities? Speak one by one. In Bardhamān Bīrsiṃha will not worship me. Who among you can kill human beings and in how many days?

We will destroy (*nipātiyā*) his country and kill all in it. Then, having received his just deserts, the King will do worship.'

The two brothers *Bāicā* and *Masuryā* said, 'Hear, Oh Śītalāi, of our qualities! The person whose body we two brothers seize—after three nights we send him to the house of Death.' Said *Māṃsadal* and *Cāmdal*, the two, 'The person we seize—his death is near. To a precise calculation

Leaf IV. Side b. a night and a half (or one and a half watches of the night) after seizing him, we come back with him.'

The trio *Khos*, *Kāṛunya* and *Minminā* said, 'He whom we possess has constant complaints (*sadāi gingina*).' Said *Padmaphulā*, 'I go and place myself on the back of the person who has *nibandha* (? a urinary dysfunction). He cannot see it, but his flesh rots and he dies bit by bit. His lineage does not not survive.' *Biṣ-phoṛā* said, 'Listen to my qualities. He whom I possess is truly unfortunate. When I seize someone, with it comes temperature. I do not kill him, but he calls out aloud for his father.'

Kavi Jagannāth sings the *Śītalāmaṅgal*. Show mercy to Dulāl when you punish.

FOUR. *Payār*

The Goddess thereupon gave [them] *pān*.[91] 'We will go to the country of Bardhamān for worship.'

As all of the poxes were rushing off at the Goddess's command, the courtier Jvarāsur reasoned with Her: 'Why such a panoply, Oh Mother? It seems to be the battle of a *gāraṛ* (ram) with a *meṇduk* (frog). What is the cause for such a show [of Garuda . . . with . . .]? If you go to Bardhamān dressed thus, you yourself will destroy the mortal world. [If Your . . . fill . . .] Take the poxes and other maladies, as pulses. If You meet people on the road, give them the pulses of Your own accord. [They will carry them off] and die at home.'

Leaf V. Side a. At this, the Goddess took thought and sprinkled charmed water on the poxes and they became pulses by the Goddess's mercy (*kṛpā*)—*mug*, *masuri*, *ārahar*, *māskalāi*, *biricanā*. Thus Śītalā transformed the poxes into pulses. She arranged them in two loads, there. Then Śītalā called Jvarā and asked him, 'Give me a plan. Who will carry the poxes now turned into pulses?'

Jvarāsur said, 'Mother let me tell You. Tāl and Betāl, there are these two in the city of Yama (Death). Summon them to carry your load. Then onward to Bardhamān as a peddler.'

Having heard this, the Goddess went to the abode of Yama. The Son of the Sun, exceedingly happy, hurriedly left his throne and saluted her feet a thousand times. Yama said, 'Why have You come again, oh Daughter of Brahmā? You have already destroyed my city once.'[92]

The Goddess Śītalā, laughing, said, 'You need have no fear. This time I have come on business of my own. In Bardhamān Bīrsiṃha will not worship me. So I shall go before him outfitted with diseases. Give me Tāl and Betāl to accompany me as porters. I shall go to Bardhamān as a peddler.'

King Yama's happiness increased when he heard this and happily gave Tāl and Betāl over to the Goddess. Yama said, 'Tāl-Betāl, you will go with the Goddess.

Leaf V. Side b. Wherever she sends you, you are to bring back [*your prey*].'

Tāl-Betāl said, 'Goddess, command us! Varuṇa lives in the waters; we will bind and deliver him. The two of us can bind up the Moon and the Sun. Likewise for all the Gods seated in Heaven.'

'Fine! Fine!' said Śītalā on hearing all this, and with the two She returned to Jvarā. Tāl-Betāl with Her as porters, as a peddler She went to Bardhamān. All this the Gods in Heaven saw: Dressed like an old Brāhmaṇī, all in white, Devī Śītalā went to Bardhamān. With a porter before, another behind, Herself in the middle, Śītalāi goes to Bardhamān to sell pulses.

Jagannāth speaks the song of the *Śītalāmaṅgal*. He entrusts the song to Gopi as amanuensis.

FIVE. *Payār*

Seeking worship, Śītalāi, with a happy face, made in one day the journey of fourteen. Leaving Mālatibardhan *pāṛā* (neighborhood) on the left, she entered [the kingdom of] Bardhamān, going first to Bardā village with her loads. She encountered the toll-taker (*jāgāti*) Cauraṅgi [on the road]. That Jāgāti had no fear on the road,

Leaf VI. Side a. and shouted at them to turn back on the road. The Jāgāti said, 'Where are you from [old crone]? I am the King's toll-taker. There is no fear in my breast.'

Said Śītalā, 'Child, what is this you say? I did not know there were toll-takers in [Bardha]mān.'

[*The toll-taker said*]: 'Who knows how many times you have already skipped the toll. This time you are stuck with me, and I won't let you go. If you want to take your load into the country of Bardhamān, then count out one *kāhan* (= 1280) of cowries for each load and two *kāhans* for the two brothers. First count that out, then go.'

[Said] the Brāhmaṇī, 'I think naturally of your well-being. With my blessing, you will be fortunate.'

The Jāgāti said: 'First, give me my cowries and keep your blessings to yourself. How many indeed are the Brāhmaṇīs who pass on this road! None quarrel with me about the toll.'

Said Jvarāsur, 'Mother, by what error does this Jāgāti with his lineage rush down the road [*to doom*].'

Śītalā said to the toll-taker: 'Jāgāti, I do not have the cowries for your fee with me. My precious pulses I take to the King. Why do you stop me on the road? When I return from selling the pulses I will give you your toll.'

The Jāgāti said, 'Old crone, so you say. What if you escape by some other route?'

Śītalā said, 'If I go by another road

Leaf VI. Side b. I swear by *dharma* you will [still] get your toll.'

Hearing this, the Jāgāti said, 'Good, good. Sun, Moon, and Varuṇa bear witness.' Then he said, 'Old woman, after selling the pulses, you come and give me my cowries if you do not have them now. But first, measure out some pulses for me.'

The toll-taker sat down with the edge of his garment spread out. Veiling Her face with Her garment, Śītalā laughed. She said, 'It is not fated for you to enjoy [*them*]. It is no fault of mine; you have dragged the diseases to yourself.' No grace (*dayā*) arose in the Goddess's mind and she gave the *māskalāi* (pulses) of *Jagaddal* (Earth-crushing pox) to the Jāgāti. Quite according to the nature of the race of toll-takers, upon seeing the pulses the *Jāgāti* behaved like a pauper who had lost a precious jewel and found it again. Repeatedly the Jāgāti clasped the Goddess's feet and asked for plenty of pulses so that all could eat. Said

Śītalā, 'I will not forbid you that. Thus will my name remain declared in age after age.' She gave him another three double cupped-hands full. Then she arranged her loads and set off. Looking back, she said, 'Toll-taker [. . .] out of my grace (*dayā*), I gave you pulses

Leaf VII. Side a. as an advance. Know that grace (*dayā*)[93] has not deserted this poor old hag. [The toll-taker said 'If I find the pulses] sweet, on your return, I will waive four *pans* (= 320) of cowries.'

Thereupon he tied up and stored the wonderful pulses in his house. When sundown came, the toll-taker went home and distributed them to his kinsfolk; they all ate them together. *Kālajvar* (Black or Deadly Fever) and Headaches attacked their bodies. Some had headaches, some had fever. Some had their bodies seized by all of the poxes. *Dhungṛyā* and *Cātyā* on some, *Phuṭakīyā* on others. *Kāl-cimṭi* on some, *Kā̃ṭhāliya* on others. *Raktacirā* on the bodies of some, *Jagadal* on others. The severity of the burning pressed them toward perdition. The father's younger brothers (*khuṛā*) and father's older brothers (*jeṭhā*) of some were dying, while the brothers of others died. The mother's sisters' husbands (*māṣā*) and father's sisters' husbands (*pīsā*) of some, the brothers of others. The fathers and mothers of some, while the sons of others were dying. The Jāgāti himself died, bereft of [*the Goddess's*] mercy (*nāi māyā moha*). Thus the Jāgātis, whose lineage had once thrived, eating the Goddess's pulses, all died.

Śītalā Devī learned of this in Her meditation, and turned to Her courtier Jvarāsur. Said Śītalā to Jvarā, 'The Jāgāti is dead.' Thus your reputation is maintained, says Jagannāth.

SIX. *Payār*

Then the courtier Jvarāsur said to Śītalā: 'Let me speak unto you, Mother. In Bardhamān dwells the physician (*kavirāj*) Hirādhar. If you send disease, he will supply medicines.

Leaf VII. Side b. If men and women are cured, who will give worship? First, Oh Basantarāy, slay the physician [then] Bīrsiṃha will worship you in the golden pot (*hemghaṭ*).'

Said Śītalā: 'What is this you speak dear child (*bāchan*)? How can I destroy the physician? A Vaidya is Nārāyaṇ-Hari, it says in the Purāṇas. I fear to go the house of the physician.'

Śītalā turned over the thought of slaying the *Kavirāj* in Her mind. [But] when Jvarā said, 'Then let us all go home, for how can we ever receive worship,' She changed Her mind about killing the physician.

Wearing tattered and soiled rags, her hair ripe, in color like the sun, her body but skin and bones, a cane in hand, swayed from side to side by the wind while walking, a basket in the crook of Her arm, thus She went and appeared in the neighborhood of the physicians. In a high voice, the crone cried, 'Who wants pulses? Who wants pulses?'

Hearing this, the physician came to her and asked, 'Now, honestly, old woman, how many cowries per *seer* are these pulses?'

Said Śītalā: 'Dear boy (*bāchan*), whatever do you say? The price of my pulses? It is a gem beyond price. In the world of Gods, or in the world of mortal men, no one knows its worth. Kārtik and Ganeś do know a little bit about the price.[94] If you do not wish to take any from me, out of mercy I will leave some [pulses and I will take no price]. In Bardhamān you dwell, physician.

Leaf VIII. Side a. My task in accomplished if you eat the pulses.'

Hearing all this, [the physician was pleasantly intrigued,] like a fly trapped by greed in molasses. Thus the physician reasoned in his mind, 'Who passes up anything to be had for free?' As soon as he spread the edge of his garment to receive it, shouting 'Bring it on!', the crone measured out the pulses from her basket. Having given the wonderful pulses to the physician, she went to Jvarā. The physician and all his kinfolk together ate the pulses. Everyone had poxes on their bodies and all died.

Thus the *Kavirāj* died with his lineage. Says Jagannāth, the Goddess learned of this in her meditation.

SEVEN. *Payār*

Śītalā said, 'Jvarā, the physician is dead.'

Said Jvarā, 'Your task in Bardhamān is as good as done (*siddha*). Hear, Oh Śītalāi, if now the physician is dead, then You can sell pulses in the bazar without fear. From some You will take payment, to others you will give them free, so that they take Your pulses and go home and die!'

Śītalāi considered what She had heard. Taking Tāl-Betāl with Her,

She entered the market. Goddess Basantarāy went to the middle of the market and displayed Her wares. The market-place of Bardhamān shone brightly but the Goddess's pulses were even brighter. Tāl-Betāl sat on the left and Śītalāi in the middle.

Leaf VIII. Side b. All morning they sold pulses there; some bought them with cowries, others grabbed and ate. Putting Her garment to Her face, Śītalāi laughed. She did not, on Her own, demand payment, and to those who had no cowries, She Herself called out and gave them free pulses. Thus, all the people in the market saw these unprecedentedly wonderful pulses, and each got some. Finally, only a single load remained, and the Goddess went to Jvarā: 'Listen, Jvarāsur, to my statement. How will Bīrsiṃha [*come to*] worship me? I cannot disregard your words. [*Should*] I go and set out my wares and leave my pulses at his court?'

Said Jvarā: 'How many people came to the market? To how many have You given pulses? How will You be able to obtain worship from Bīrsiṃha? There are nine *lakhs* (900,000) homesteads (*deś-ghar*) in Bardhamān. Go from door to door and distribute Your pulses for free. [*Then*] Bīrsiṃha will offer worship in the golden pot.'

At Jvarā's words, the Goddess's joy increased. A basket of pulses she took in the crook of her arm. A torn and soiled rag for clothing, her hair ripe, the color of conch-shell, her body but skin and bones, a cane in her hand—thus auspiciously the old woman started her journey to the town.

Jagannāth sings the song of *Śītalāmaṅgal*. The Mother arrived in Bardā in the guise of a Keulāni.[95]

EIGHT. *Payār*

When She arrived in a town, She shouted at the top of her lungs, 'Come get pulses! Come get pulses!'

All the men and women of the town came running. The pulses of unprecedented beauty filled the eyes of all. Some paid with cowries, some got them merely by asking for them. The Goddess Śītalāi laughed, Her garment to Her face. From some She counted the cowries in payment. She pressed them on those who had no cowries. Some said, 'Old woman, I fancy some pulses. . . . [*The manuscript breaks off here and the next three leaves are missing.*]

NINE. *Payār*

Leaf XII. Side a. [*The manuscript resumes in the dying speech of the Prince of Bardhamān. The first three lines are badly damaged.*]

['. . . If youthful vigor [*tarunatā*] remains, . . . if the sexes remain, there will be descendants.] People from all over town go to the market to buy. He whose money runs out first is the earliest to return home. My market is over, by the decree of Fate (Vidhātā). So I go home early. Why do you weep, mother? Give me leave to depart from this birth. If I come back to be reborn, please grant me refuge in your womb.'

Hearing this, the Queen Regnant (*pāṭrānī*) struck her forehead. 'Oh, please let me hear you say 'mother' once. You are the pupils of this luckless one's two eyes. Clutching you on my lap I lie, my mind lost. On my throne you were to have been King. Folk would have called me the Queen Mother. And now you speak in this way, ruining my all (*mor māthā khāiyā*). Gazing at whose countenance [*in expectation of what*], will this unfortunate one keep on living?'

Jagannāth sings the song of *Śītalāmaṅgal*. The royal Queen bewails the loss of her son.

TEN. *Payār*

The King and Queen wept, clutching their son. Their raiment, their hair in disarray, all undone. Thrashing from side to side, the two wept, their golden complexions tarnished. Holding the neck of his royal father with his arms, his face pressed to his, the little child consoled his father: 'Birth on this earth leads to death, ultimately (*nidān*). There is no escaping the clutches of Yama the terrible. The venerable Khaṭṭāṅga, the Lord of Raghu (i.e., Rāma), and Bhāgiratha, all the heroes, Yayāti, Sāntanu, Bha[rata],[96]

Leaf XII. Side b. all these kings, assuming mortal form, had to die. Weep no more dear father—I depart. King Daśaratha, sending Rāma and Lakṣmaṇa to the forest, renounced life. Seeing Bharata crowned as King, he yet [forgot all and] died calling 'Rāma, Rāma!'

[*Ms. broken, not clear who speaks here.*] ['. . . There is no second on my lap.] Whose face will I kiss in your place?'

Then the Queen wept, her son on her lap, '[. . .] Call out 'Mother.' I long to hear it.'

'Die, son of the King!' said Śītalāi, 'for if you die, I receive the worship of King and Queen [. . .] Yield up your life and come to my lap. Let's see what those two say then.'

Then the Goddess's words proved to be not in vain. The child toppled over on the lap of the Queen Regnant. The Queen said, 'Your majesty, Fate is adverse. Both of us holding him, yet we have lost our treasure.' At this, the King fell to the ground and rolled in the dust.

[*It was*] dark as the night of the new moon—as the firmament bereft of the moon. Beside themselves in grief, then wept the King and Queen, crying out like a tigress who has lost her cub.[97]

Jagannāth sings the *Śītalāmaṅgal.* [There is no suffering like the grief for a lost son.]

ELEVEN. *Payār*

['My dear child Rāma has gone on the road, rendering Ayodhyā dark.'[98] So the King lamented with his dead son in his arms. 'Who has stolen my treasure?]

Leaf XIII. Side a. Who will [hold] my royal sceptre and my throne? [Without my son] my world is dark.'

The Queen Regnant wept [with her serving women], as Mother Śacī wept, 'My Nimāi [Śrī Caitanya] has taken *sannyāsa* (ascetic vows).' ['For what fault is fate so terribly adverse?'] She [wept] as Kauśalya having lost Rāma. 'Raise your charming body again, dear child, and sit upon my lap. Let everyone else die instead of you. [Who is it that was childless and] so stole away my boy? Whom will you now go to and call "mother," you with your lovely moon-like face? Who will now rush [to me] with rapid footsteps? Who will now laughingly call me "mother"? Whose face will I now kiss, morning and evening? Whom can I now look at, dear child, to forget my grief for you?'

Said the Queen, 'You servant girls and maids in waiting, what do you stare at? Bring a golden necklace for my darling one. I will place my son in a hamper and store him in the rafters. Whenever my mind remembers, I will open it and look at him. Where does my little charmer now dwell content? Oh, take me with you, dear child, this luckless one calls out.'

It was as if Nanda and Yaśodā wept, striking their foreheads. Saying 'Hari! Hari!' they wept, and responded to no one.

Her courtier said: 'Śī[talāi], show grace (*dayā*) to the King. Bīrsiṃha will worship You in the golden pot. Go in the guise of an astrologer to the King. Reveal everything and revive his heir.'

Hearing this, grace arose in Śītalā and, donning an astrologer's garb, she rapidly went forth. Wearing a coarse *dhuti*,

Leaf XIII. Side b. a sacred thread over the shoulder, an almanac in the left hand, a sacred thread over the shoulder [sic.],[99] [she went] to where the King and Queen were going to die, and bade them pause for a moment.

Jagannāth sings the song of the *Śītalāmaṅgal*. The Mother came to Bardā in a dream.

TWELVE. *Payār*

The Mahārājā turned and looked back, and beheld verily the form of a Brāhmaṇ. Seeing a Brāhmaṇ, the king did obeisance. Said Śītalā, 'May you have well-being (*kalyāṇa*).'

The Queen said, 'Of what use is well-being any longer to me, now that I have lost my son?'

Hearing this, Śītalā turned Her face downward; grace (*dayā*) arose in her; Her eyes filled with tears.

Said the King: 'In my former life, I [*must have*] begged for this, that you appear before me at the hour of death. He who gives gifts to a Brāhmaṇ at the hour of his death, him, certainly, Lord Bhagavān receives into Vaikuṇṭha. Handing over my fame (*mān*), my wealth (*daulat*), my royal umbrella (*chatra*), and my throne (*pāṭ*) to you, I will cast myself tied [*to a weight*] into the water.'

Śītalā said, 'Why should you drown yourself? Let me find by my calculations why your son died.'

Hearing this much, the King fell down and clutched Her feet. [Goddess] Basantarāy extended her illusion (*māyā*) and chalked out the diagram [*needed for an astrological calculation*].

Said Śītalā: 'Listen attentively, Oh King! The cause will I unravel by my calculations. Goddess Basantarāy is ruler (*rājā*) of the sixty-four diseases. She is [adverse] toward [you]. In the guise of [a female ascetic] she appeared at your head while you slept.

Leaf XIV. Side a. [In a dream] She asked worship of you. [. . .] You did not worship Her. Finally She slew [. . . Heed my words. You will get back] your lost son. All that has died in Bardhamān [will revive. . . .] But you must worship Her in the golden pot.'

The King said, 'If my darling child receives the gift of life, I will worship Goddess Basantarāy without fail.'

Said Śītalā, 'If you will give worship, come then, let's see. Bring your son and let me hold him on my lap.'

Hearing this, the Queen, weeping all the while, handed over that child, who was like a golden doll (*kanak putuli*). His body was golden, like the Sun [*and from him*] it was as if moonbeams poured forth; it seemed as if the dead son's body shone. Seeing this, the Goddess was swept away by tears; in Her own tears the Goddess was drenched. 'Come,' She said, as She took the prince on her lap. Looking at him, Śītalā called out, 'Your father and mother are about to die. Why don't you rise? Raise your limbs, Oh Son of the King, gain consciousness. Having found My lap, you now turn your mind to slumber.'

She passed both Her hands over the prince's body. All of the poxes on his body disappeared into his body (*aṅgete lukāy*). 'Come to life! Come to life! (*prāṇ pāo*!)' Śītalā cried out. From the Goddess's mercy (*kṛpa*), the child received the gift of life. Having received the gift of life, he sat

Leaf XIV. Side b. on Śītalā's lap. The King and Queen fell at Her feet.

Kavi Jagannāth sings, meditating (*dhiyāiyā*) on the Goddess. Says Gopi, Give the shade of your feet to Dulāl.

THIRTEEN. *Payār*

Seeing their dear child, the King and Queen fell prostrate at Śītalā's feet. 'With my sinful eyes I am unable to recognize You. Reveal Your identity. Who may You be? I am the lowliest of men (*narādham*) foolish (*muḍhamati*) and at the very limits of ignorance. With mercy (*kṛpa*), break the shackles of my mind. A luckless King am I, and luckless my Queen. By your intrinsic quality, be gracious (*dayā karo*) to us, Oh great lady (*ṭhākurāṇī*).'

Said Śītalā, 'Listen to My words, Oh King! Think intently. I am that very same person.'

The King said, 'In my dream I saw a female ascetic. How am I now to recognize You in this astrologer's garb? If you will give this luckless one the shade of Your feet, if you are gracious (*jadi āche dayā*), do please put on the guise of the ascetic.'

Hearing the King speak thus, the Mother, who is the refuge of the bereft, began to smile. 'Hear, Oh Queen. Take your son. Your King recognized. [. . .']

At this, the Queen took her babe, as Daivakī took Gadādhar on her lap; [. . . as Yaśoda was called. . . . So beheld the Queen . . . receiving her son. . . .]

Leaf XV. Side a. [. . . Her garment soiled, her hair ripened to the color of conch-shells, her form but skin and bones. . . .] Thus the old woman blessed the King: 'May you increase in wealth and progeny, Oh King. May your years be long. [This pauper woman . . . in your Bardhamān] I will dwell in Bardhamān ultimately (*nidāne*). From today there will be no fear of my disease. You will be the King and I the subject,' thus said Śītalā.

Said the King: 'Be the ruler of this land. Revive the subjects (*bāchāgane*, perhaps "children") and let me die. If You wish me to be the King of the land—my subjects have all died. Of what shall I be King?'

Śītalā said: 'King, I will revive your country of Bardhamān. It will not be otherwise, if you have the golden pot (*hemghaṭ*) that is in Vijayānagar brought here and worship me in it.'

Said the King: 'Why need I go to Vijayānagar? I will make a golden pot right here. I have priceless jewels in my store. How much wealth is needed for a golden pot? What single golden pot do You speak of Mother? I can give You a hundred golden pots.'

Śītalā said: 'King, first let Me explain! I am not satisfied (*santuṣta*) by a golden pot from here. I will tell you about the golden pot kept in Vijayānagar. In that golden pot Brahmā, Viṣṇu, and Śiva, having become pitiable (*haiyā sakaruṇ*), have worshiped me. Indra, King of the Gods, Yama, the Terrible, and Varuṇa of the Waters have given My worship in that pot,

Leaf XV. Side b. and in it shall Bīrsiṃha worship me.'

Having said, 'As you command,' the King declared his determination (*nidān*).

Sings Kavi Jagannāth—now Bardhamān revives.

FOURTEEN. *Payār*

King Bīrsiṃha wept, clutching her feet, 'How will the country live? Please revive it.'

Śītalā said, 'Wait a while. I will pay a visit to Indra's world and return. Of Indra I will ask the showers of immortality, and revive everyone's life.'

Said the King: 'What lengths You go to deceive me. Where will I wander, searching for You? Until I get back the country of Bardhamān, I will not let go these lotus feet that I now clasp.'

Said Śītalā, 'King it shall be thus: Ultimately your land of Bardhamān will revive.'

The King said, 'You know what You know, Śītalāi. If You do not revive Bardhamān, I will not give You worship.'

Hearing this, the Goddess went to Indra's world and, seeing her, the son of Kaśyapa (Indra) was very joyous. [. . .] Touching the Goddess's feet, he did obeisance.

Said Śītalā, 'Indra [. . . Give me the showers of immortality . . . in Bardhamān, Bīrsiṃha by name. . . . Ultimately . . . I will revive. . . .]

[Beyond this the page is badly damaged and Leaf XVI is lost.]

The *Śītalā Maṅgal* of Mānikrām Gāṅgulī

Translated by Aditi Nath Sarkar & Ralph W. Nicholas

Introduction

The text of Mānikrām's *Śītalā Maṅgal* here translated is taken from *Dvādaś Maṅgal*, edited by Pañcānan Maṇḍal and published in the Series *Sāhityaprakāśikā* (vol. 5) by Viśvabhāratī (Śāntiniketan, 1966), pp. 285–294. It is printed from manuscript no. 1622 in the Palli-śrī Library at Śāntiniketan.

There has been some controversy over Mānikrām's dates. Bijitkumār and Sunandā Datta, in their Introduction to Mānikrām's better-known *Dharma Maṅgal* (Calcutta University, 1966, pp. xvii–xix), date that work to the eighteenth century, pointing to some modern features of the language as well as to their decoding of the chronogram as reading 1703 *śakabda* (= 1781 AD). Other authorities have read the chronogram as 1489 *śak* (= 1567 AD) and even as early as 1389 *śak* (= 1467 AD) (see Āśutoṣ Bhaṭṭācārya, *Bāṅgla Maṅgalkāvyer Itihās*, 5th ed., Calcutta: A. Mukherji & Co., 1970, pp. 699–702 for a full discussion).

There is no chronogram in Mānikrām's *Śītalā Maṅgal*. However, the language of the text is not archaic. Moreover, the composer lived in what is now the Arambagh subdivision of Hooghly District (then known as Jahanabad), surrounded by the locales of several other *Śītalā Maṅgal* poets, strongly suggesting that he too participated in the eighteenth century efflorescence of her cult. Thus, we accept the Dattas' eighteenth century date for Mānikrām and would place him somewhere in the middle of that century.

Like other *maṅgal kāvyas*, the *Śītalā Maṅgal* is made up of separate *pālās*, discrete 'dramas' concerning the Goddess, performed on successive nights. Each night's performance begins with a *bandanā*, a hymn praising the deity. In the case of *Śītalā Maṅgal*, this is generally followed by an episode in which, her worship denied, she marshals her army of diseases. On the basis of this pattern, the Viśvabhāratī manuscript seems to consist of one whole drama, the Munipur *pālā*, as well as a fragment of a Gokul *pālā* (see Section V and Appendix A), and, perhaps, a fragment of a third *pālā* conflated with the others. The dimensions of a complete drama can be seen by reading Section I–III, IV less the repetitions and replacing vv. 57–71 by vv. 228–242, V–IX. Evidence in the *bandanā* (Section I, vv. 3–4) suggests that the Gokul *pālā* was performed before the Munipur *pālā*. The entire poem, apart from the *bandanā*, is composed in units of 16 to 18 verses, with multiples of two or three times this number indicating the relative importance of the episode. Omitting repetitions, there are 221 verses in this text.

We have spoken of this myth as being 'performed,' which it is today in villages and towns of West Bengal. A fuller discussion of the nature of these performances may be found in 'Śītalā and the Art of Printing' pp. 192–211. Briefly, contemporary performances are done by a company of singers, either as a kind of oratorio (without costumes but with different singers taking different parts), or operatically (with costumes and acting). References in the text to the 'performance' or 'stage' (*āsar*), the 'protagonist' (*nāyak*), 'rhythm' and 'meter' (*mān, tāl*), and 'song' (*gīt*) all suggest that the contemporary style of performance was in vogue in the eighteenth century. If this was so, then, the manuscripts probably served as librettos for singers, who may have pulled together pieces by various hands in order to make up a single performance or to prolong their performance over several nights with *pālās* from different sources. Thus, in the manuscript tradition of the *Śītalā Maṅgal*, the composite text may have been the ordinary type.

The *Śītalā Maṅgal* of Mānikrām Gāṅgulī

Note: The *bandanā*, or praise song, of Śītalā, which is here presented as the first section of Mānikrām's *Śītalā Maṅgal*, appears at the end of the printed text. This may be due to the fact that this *bandanā* was intended to precede a *pālā*, or drama, that has since been lost from the manuscript leaves. Since the *bandanā* is always sung or recited before the drama on any night of *Śītalā Maṅgal* performance, we have here included it first. The *bandanā* is in *tripadī* verse; the remainder of the text is in *payār*, except for Sītā's lament (Section VIII), which is in *ekpadī*.

I

Obeisance to Sitala

Tripadī

1. My heart intent on no other, I seek to praise Śītalā Devī, She who causes disease and grief, and She who afflicts with Fever (*santāp-kāriṇī*).

   Seated on your mount, the Ass, whose gait is like that of the Greatest among Elephants, in your hands shine a vessel (*kalas*) and a broom (*mārjanī*).
2. The sixty-four poxes constantly attend You, sportive in their glee. You were born in the womb of the lotus. Whoever displays pride (*ahaṃkara*) finds no salvation (*nistār*). The Mother Herself becomes adverse to him.
3. The Gods (*devatā*), the *kinnara* (superhuman beings), men (*nara*), the Primordial Being of Creation (*ādibhūta carācare*) all, You can send flying at a glance.

   In the hope of protecting Gokula, Govinda worshiped (*seva*) You with particular knowledge (*jñāna*) and devotion (*bhakti*) in that Goṣṭha (i.e., Vṛndāvana) of Wisdom (*jñānagoṣṭhe*).
4. Sītā and Rāma did your worship and Lava-Kuśa received [back] life; in the City of the Gods (*surapure*) Indra worshiped you. Hara (Śiva) himself worshiped you, as did the Higher than High (*parātpar*). Who [indeed] knows all Your boundless glory?
5. [You] upon whose feet tinkle belled anklets, whose waist is embellished by a girdle, whose auspicious head is adorned with a winnowing fan (*sūrpa*)—Descend in my presentation (*āsar*),

remove the obstacles to the music, and protect Your own protagonist (*āpan nāyake*).

6. The neglect of You is the cause of going to perdition of the unwise who do not understand.

    Show Your intrinsic grace (*dayā*) and allow me the shadow of Your two feet; let my mind dwell on those red feet.

7. You are the Mother of the World (*jagat-jananī*). What do I know of Your glory? Hear him who attends you (*abadhāne kara abagati*).

    Dvija Śrī Mānikrām of Belḍihā village, then, prostrates himself at your feet.

II

Śrī Śrī Rāma. Obeisance to Śītalā

Payār

8. One day Śītalā, happy in Her mind, called Jvarāsur to Her and said:
9. 'Come, we will go to Munipur (Abode of the Sages) to receive worship. We will give the *Biṣ-muṅgā* (Poison-mouthed) pox to Lava-Kuśa.'
10. Said Jvarāsur: 'Mother, let me submit to you that Sītā is Lakṣmī, Śrī Rāma is Nārāyaṇa himself.
11. That heartless (*pāṣaṇḍī*) Kaikeyī has given her enough grief, she has wandered in forests these fourteen years.
12. And then Rāvaṇa abducted Sītā, and the grief-stricken Rāma, aided by Hanumān, bridged the sea.
13. Sītā was rescued [only] after the sea was crossed and Rāvaṇa slain.
14. After their return home there were fateful pronouncements, and he again banished Sītā to the forest.
15. The Lord knew not that Sītā was five months gone with child. Mother Jānakī stayed in the house of Vālmīki.
16. Lava was born in Vālmīki's house, and Sītā tended him with great affection.
17. [One day] Sītā addressed Vālmīki with gentle speech: 'Father, look after Lava while I go to fetch water.'
18. 'Go, child,' said the *muni*, sitting down to meditation. Forgetfully, Sītādevī got up [and left] with Lava.

19. [Then] the *muni*, not seeing Lava, exhaled and gave life to Kuśa.
20. In this fashion, the two brothers Lava-Kuśa came to be; they dwelt happily in the *muni's* house.
21. So much has the daughter of Janaka suffered. Oh, Mother! Do not grieve her again.'
22. Śītalā said: 'Child! It just cannot be otherwise. How else will my worship become well-known?'
23. At this, Jvarāsur melted with pleasure, 'Today I will behold the lotus-feet of Sītā.'
24. The Goddess called the poxes in terrible glee: 'Come, we will go to Munipur for the sake of [my] worship.'
25. At her command all the poxes got ready. Dvija Śrī Mānik recites the Śītalāmaṅgal.

III

Payār

26. The *Cāmudal* (Skin Eruptions) went, with the sixty-four diseases; the *Rakta-muṅgā* (Bloody-mawed) pox got ready gaily.
27. The exceedingly terrible *Beṅgcyā* (*baiñcā*, Jujube) pox, that jeopardizes life and has Death as an ally, prepared.
28. *Tilyākalyā* (Sesamum-cake), the *Kā̃ṭhalya* (Jack-fruit) of terrible strength, and the *Musuryā* (Smallpox, lit., pox resembling *masur* pulse) and *Dhukuṛyā* (? pox associated with a coarse sack) eruptions (*cāmudal*) got ready.
29. The *Agni-muṅgā* (Fiery-mawed) pox, most terrible, lined up; in its burning, life goes away, taken to the house of Death.
30. The *Biṣmuṅgā* (Poison-mouthed) poxes of various kinds got ready, as did the *Atika* (Bundle) pox, with the *Ḍumuryā* (Fig) for company.
31. *Garula* (*garal*, poison) and *Tẽtulyā* (Tamarind)—these principal poxes prepared themselves, and the rambunctious *Batryā* (?) and *Ṣiphuryā* (?).
32. The *Alkusyā* (Cowage) pox got ready in great glee; and the *Ṭiuryā* and the *Chapryā* (? Blotchy) readied themselves along with the *Biśālyā* (Huge).
33. The accoutred *Milāmilā* (Measles) went with the *Mataryā* (resembling *maṭar* pulse), which, once it seizes hold, does not let go while life remains.
34. The *Suci-muṅgā* (Needle-mouthed) pox got ready swiftly; and

Paṭalyā (*paṭal*, a small cucumber-shaped vegetable) and *Pāniphalyā* (Water-chestnut), the intractable ones.

35. The *Luā-garā* (Iron-clad) pox accoutred itself in great style, [the one] that appears after a person dies, on the stiff corpse.
36. Many a *Dhān-śisā* (Rice-whisker) pox rushed forth, [as did] the *Mādāryā* (*Mādār*-fruit) and the *Nīl-badan* (Blue visaged).
37. *Galagaṇḍa* (Goiter) got ready with a sinister passion, and all of the *Khos* (Scabies) prepared, together with the *Bisphoṭak* (Poisonous boils).
38. In this way the various species of pox readied themselves; they came to the Goddess's feet and saluted.
39. Said Śītalā, 'I have a great desire to hear what power (*pratāp*) each one of you has, so tell me.'
40. Signature [probably intends a repetition of v. 25].

IV

Payār

41. Hearing this, the *Cāmudal* (Skin eruptions) spoke, with their hands folded together: 'He whose body we seize, his blood we turn into water.
42. Even though time remains in his pre-ordained span of years (*paramāyu*), yet we can take his life. Even Dhanvantari (the heavenly physician) himself cannot preserve him.'
43. *Garalyā* (Poisonous) pox said: 'My qualities (*guṇa*) are plentiful. He who is stuck with me, his fate has indeed turned [for the worse].
44. I hide inside and do not show myself outside. Even if a person's ordained span of years is not over, I take him to the abode of Death.'
45. *Dhukuṛyā* [see v. 28] pox said: In ten days I ruin the lineage of him whom I seize.'
46. The *Milmilyā* (Measles) went, accoutred, with the *Maṭaryā* (*Maṭar* pulse-like), which, once it seizes hold, does not let go while life remains [repeats v. 33].
47. The *Sucimuṅgā* pox got ready swiftly; and *Paṭalyā* and *Pāniphalyā*, the intractable ones [repeats v. 34].
48. *Galagaṇḍa* got ready with sinister passion, and all of the *Khos* prepared, together with the *Bisphoṭak* [repeats v. 37].
49. In this way the various species of pox readied themselves they came to the Goddess's feet and saluted [repeats v. 38].

50. Said Śītalā, 'I have a great desire to hear what power each one of you has, so tell me. [repeats v. 39].
51. Hearing this, the *Cāmudal* spoke, with their hands folded together: 'He whose body we seize, his blood we turn into water' [repeats v. 41].
52. Even though time remains in his pre-ordained span of years, yet we can take his life. Even Dhanvantari himself cannot preserve him' [repeats v. 42].
53. Said *Biṣ-muṅgā* (Poison-mouthed), 'One by one, I crush the entire lineage of him to whose house I go.'
54. *Garalyā* pox said: 'My qualities are plentiful. He who is stuck with me, his fate has indeed turned [for the worse] [repeats v. 43].
55. I hide inside and do not show myself outside. Even if a person's ordained span of years is not over, I take him to the abode of Death' [repeats v. 44].
56. *Dhukuṛyā* pox said: 'In ten days I ruin the lineage of him whom I seize [repeats v. 45].
57. While one is being cremated, another breathes his last (*ek jane agni dei ār jan śvase*); such is my might, by your blessing.'
58. Said *Ālkusyā* (Cowage), 'Mother, hear my speech! Him whom I seize, I ruin.
59. Before his ordained time, I take him to Yama's house. I do not allow the cremation-ground fire to be extinguished for ten days [at a time].'
60. *Tīlyākulyā* (Sesamum cake) said: 'In your presence, Mother, I say—my particular strength is on Saturdays and Tuesdays [these are generally regarded as unpropitious and unlucky days].
61. I appear and then submerge myself [in a person's body]. I take his ordained span of years and hoist it up a tree.'
62. *Kā̃ṭhyālā* (Jack-fruit) pox said: 'I would like to submit that Nārāyaṇa knows how strong I am.
63. Before the rest of the body, I plug the throat. Vidhātā is unable to preserve [such a person; for him] survival becomes impossible.
64. Said *Khosu* (Scabies): 'The person I seize I fill with spontaneous pleasure. He sheds his clothes and prances about and, lighting a fire, toasts himself.
65. He scratches to his heart's content without knowing the cause. But he rolls on the earth when I commence the burning.
66. If I favor man and woman at once, they run mad at every turn of their daily lives.

67. [The] man caresses the woman's creamy-soft (*nunisyā*) body with his hand and in boundless pleasure they rise heavenwards.
68. [But] when life is about to depart because of the burning, then the mind weeps aloud.'
69. Thus each spoke of his own particular strength. Śītalā said: 'Well, then, all is ready for my service.
70. Come children, go sprightly to Gokul. Today I will receive flowers and water from Kṛṣṇa.'
71. Saying this, the Goddess set off. Dvija Śrī Mānik sings the Śītalāmaṅgal.

V

Payār

72. The Mother arrived at the bank of the Yamunā. Jvarāsur and the poxes remained out of sight.
73. Using her transformative power (*māyā karyā*), the Mother became a very old woman. A torn quilt (*kā̃thā*) she wore; her skin was flaked like chalk.
74. Her basket of poxes in the crook of her arm, she sat in the middle of the road. Teasingly, the children of Vraja addressed her with much laughter.
75. 'Whence do you come old crone, where is your home? Tell us why you have come to Gokul town?
76. What's in your hamper? Give it to us to eat.' Said the old crone, 'Children, all I have are pulses,
77. obtained by begging. . . .'

[Here the text breaks off. When it resumes the setting is quite different.]

VI

Payār

78. Jvarāsur, in great good humor, went in front, mounted on a bear, a quiver of sharp arrows in hand.
79. The poxes went in sacks by cart; the journey of six *kroś* (about twelve miles) seemed never-ending.
80. Using her transformative power, Śītalā became an old crone, a colorful basket in the crook of her arm and a red staff in hand.

81. The Mother went along behind, happy inside, like Dāmodar (Kṛṣṇa) going to trick Bali.
82. Bhagavān (here Viṣṇu) became a span in form (i.e., a dwarf), and King Bali made him the gift of three steps of earth.
83. One step went to heaven, the second to earth, and finally the third step came to rest on Bali's head.
84. Similarly went the Mother, rapid of motion, and arrived at Munipur (the Abode of the Sages) without delay.
85. Śītalā then called out to Jvarāsur, 'Pitch a tent and put down the sacks of poxes.'
86. While Jvarāsur did as commanded, Śītalā herself remained unseen.
87. Lava-Kuśa played with the boys of the sages. They laughed, danced, and sang, lost in happiness.
88. Candracūṛ, Cintāmaṇi, Caturbhuj, Hari, [and all the other boys of Munipur] came to the old woman in a tumult.
89. Lava-Kuśa said: 'Old woman, whence have you come? Where did you get such a colorful basket?
90. What are in all these sacks? For what purpose? Explain! Tell us your name, old woman, introduce yourself.'
91. Said Śītalā: 'My home is in Surpur (City of Immortals). I peddle, wandering from country to country.
92. In all creation my name is Śrīmati Maṅgalā. Look my dears! These are my sacks of pulses.'
93. Hearing this, the children gleefully [said], 'Today we'll eat the old hag's pulses!'
94. Some said, 'Why would the old woman just give them [to us]?' Others said, 'We'll find out only if we ask.'
95. Still others said, 'If not, we'll rob her and eat them.' Some said, 'Or else we'll pay the price.'
96. Some said endearingly, 'You are very fortunate, old woman! The merit (*puṇya*) for feeding pulses is limitless.'
97. The old woman said, 'I will not give away anything free.' Lava-Kuśa began tugging violently at the sacks.
98. Inwardly angry, the Mother jested: 'Why did you come here to die?
99. You sons of Śrī Rāma are so arrogant! You will be ruined and die, shattered by pox!
100. King Parīkṣita had been arrogant, and for that reason received as his just desert a Brahman's curse.

101. "You will be bitten by a snake within the week!" The King became immobilized on hearing this.
102. The King listened to [recitation of] *Śrīmadbhāgavata* for seven days, but the Brahman's words were not annulled.
103. King Duryodhana, who lived in the city of Hastinā, arrogantly spoke rude words to Kṛṣṇa.
104. "All your life has been spent driving cattle. You who were nourished on the rice of cattle-keepers, how can you be so lordly (*ṭhākurāl*)?"
105. For this arrogance he died with his entire lineage. Yudhiṣṭhira became king in Hastinānagar.
106. Where did Māndhātā go because of his pride? And the *daityas* (demons) Śumbha and Niśumbha died because of pride.
107. Listen, O Lava-Kuśa, to these merciless words—I will here and now crush your pride.'
108. Said Lava-Kuśa: 'Old hag, you've said a mouthful. [But] we are Śrī Rāma's sons and do not fear.
109. Right now we'll take your life with one slap and eat up all the pulses that there are.'
110. Having heard these words, beside herself with joy, Śītalā went far away into the great forest.
111. Lava-Kuśa ate the plundered pulses; wondrous sweet they were, like the nectar of the lotus.
112. All the sons of the sages who had come with them took some and ate them.
113. Thereupon, the Mother called Jvarāsur and said: 'Go and possess all their bodies.
114. One by one I will dispatch all the poxes. This day will I be worshiped in every household in Munipur.'
115. Hearing this, Jvarāsur took his leave happily. Dvija Śrī Mānik sings the Śītalāmaṅgal.

VII

Payār

116. When he received the Goddess's command, Jvarāsur became enflamed. He began by seizing Lava-Kuśa.
117. And all of the sage's sons who had come with them—one by one he possessed the bodies of all of them.

118. They fainted and fell to earth. Some said, 'Ah, what has happened? A calamity! My life is lost!'
119. Some asked themselves, 'Why did you eat the old woman's pulses? How can you go home; your feet won't move?'
120. Some lamented, as they sat clutching their heads. Some said, 'It looks as if the old woman has cursed us.'
121. In a chorus they wept aloud; and, sitting at home, Jānakī heard them.
122. Each sage's wife heard the voice of her own and hurried at once to the place, extremely distressed.
123. Each lifted up her son and clasped him to her breast. Mother Jānakī grieved, stricken with distress.
124. Then she took Lava-Kuśa and went home. Vālmīki asked, 'Child, what is the cause [of your grief]?'
125. Jānakī said: 'Oh, father, I am so unfortunate! I do not know what has happened to Lava-Kuśa.
126. 'I have neither father nor mother and I dwell banished in the forest. [Yet] with your consolation I had forgotten all my sorrows.'
127. Said Vālmīki: 'Dear child, you are Lakṣmīśvarī and Śrī Rāma is Viṣṇu himself, this I know.
128. Cursed by her husband, Ahalyā turned to stone. By the touch of the dust [of his] feet she found release.
129. Who knows of [all] the glory of the supremely compassionate Rāma, because of whose quality boulders float on the bottomless ocean.
130. Because of whose quality the forest ape becomes captivated; reciting whose name Śiva has become victorious over death (Mṛtyuñjaya).
131. I am evil-souled (*durātmā*) and sinful-minded (*pāpmati*). Out of his own quality, Rāma, son of Daśaratha, has shown me mercy.
132. I could not recite "Rāma, Rāma" aloud; I became an ascetic reciting "Death, Death (marā marā)."
133. What man in the world is as fortunate as I? You, his wife, are Lakṣmī in my house.
134. When you address me as "Father," and I hear it, I am fulfilled.
135. I bless Lava-Kuśa with all my thoughts. Do not be concerned, all harm and distress will go away.'
136. Having said this, the sage went away to his meditation. Over here, Śītalā called the poxes to Her and said:

137. '*Biṣ-muṅgā*, dear child, go and seize Lava-Kuśa! Before possessing the rest of their bodies, choke up their throats.
138. Go, *Agni-muṅgā*, to Agastya's residence! If [he] does not worship, ruin him.
139. *Ālkusyā*, go to Vaśiṣṭha's house! If he does not worship, slay him with his whole lineage.
140. Go, *Beṅgcyā* pox, into Gautama's house! If [he] is arrogant, you will slay him with his lineage.'
141. Having thus set the poxes to work, the Mother vanished and remained in secrecy.
142. Thereafter, during the first two days, Jvara possessed sovereignty. On the third day, pox appeared.
143. He whom *Dhukuṛyā* pox went and seized, his life began to leave him because of the burning.
144. The blood of persons seized by *Ālkusyā* and *Agni-muṅgā* turned to water during the first watch of the night.
145. He whom the *Kā̃ṭhālayā* (Jack-fruit) pox came and seized—his flesh cracked [like the skin of a jack-fruit], his blood flowed, and his arms [seemed to] drop off.
146. He who had *Cāmudal* pox had his throat plugged, and eating was impossible for him.
147. In house after house in Munipur there arose lamentation. Now, friends, hear a little more about Lava-Kuśa.
148. *Biṣ-muṅgā* is an irresistible pox, and therefore Lava-Kuśa's lives were in jeopardy.
149. One moment they were senseless, and would regain consciousness in the next. Then did their lotus-like faces become dull.
150. The eyes of Sītā wept incessantly. Dvija Śrī Mānik sings the Śītalāmaṅgal.

VIII

Ekpadī

151. Holding Lava-Kuśa on her lap, in a flood of tears [she said]:
152. 'I have neither mother nor father. I am the terrible unfortunate Sītā.
153. In Rāvaṇa's city of Laṅkā there was a threatening Rākṣasī.
154. She used to beat me with a cane. Fallen to the ground, I would weep.

155. Yet I did not die then. What was my life saved to witness?
156. To behold you crying out for your luckless mother—it rends [my] breast.
157. Oh, my jewels! Oh, my treasure! How can I go on living?
158. Who else do I have? In whose company will I stand?
159. How can life be made to leave this unfortunate one?
160. Can life endure this? Why did I not die?'
161. Said Lava-Kuśa: 'Listen! Why should we shed tears?
162. Fate (*Vidhātā*) has inscribed on our foreheads that we will die young.
163. Fruitless are your illusory attachments of affection (*māyā moha*); bid us farewell in this adversity.
164. If you cannot bring us back to life, take us on your lap for one [last] time.
165. Our life-breath (*parāṇ*) feels restless. No words move on our lips.'
166. Hearing her sons' words, [Sītā] fell to the earth.
167. The wives of the sages rushed forth and, raising her up, sprinkled her face with water.
168. Dvija Śrī Mānik sings, contemplating Śītalā.

IX

Payār

169. Thus wept Mother Jānakī; in the meantime the sage Nārada was getting ready.
170. Seated in an affected pose on his rice-husker (*ḍhẽki*), he went playing a *vīṇā* and singing ecstatically of the many qualities of Govinda.
171. The rice-husker spoke up, 'I can't move! My pedal wobbles. The pestle is out of order, its iron band has come loose.'
172. Hearing this speech, the divine sage said, 'I'll repair all your trappings as soon as we get back from this trip.'
173. Thereupon, swiftly the sage arrived in Munipur.
174. He praised the fear-dispelling feet of Jānakī and asked the cause [of her distress].
175. Jānakī said, 'Oh, sage, a calamity has occurred! Please bless Lava-Kuśa, they are about to perish.'

176. Said Narada: 'Mother, allow me to submit that you are Lakṣmī and Śrī Rāma is Nārāyaṇa himself.
177. Your sons Lava-Kuśa are mighty. Do not be distressed, nothing ill will happen.
178. The Lord's servitor, the heroic Son of the Wind (Pavananandan i.e., Hanumān) would come forthwith if you just remembered him.
179. The physician (Vaidya) Dhanvantari is famed all over the world; send Hanumān and fetch him here.'
180. Upon hearing this, Mother Sītā, pleased in her mind, remembered Hanumān.
181. That hero was gleefully spending his time in a banana orchard (*kadali kānan*), his lips silently reciting 'Jay Rāma, Śrī Jānakī.'
182. The very moment the summons of his guru's wife reached his ears, the great hero arrived there.
183. Prostrating himself on the ground, the hero saluted [her] feet. The Mother blessed him with reassuring speech.
184. 'Girdling the ocean, you slew Rāvaṇa. You gave Lakṣmaṇa his life when he [was struck by] the *śaktiśela* (a mythological missile).
185. Risking your life, you have rescued this unfortunate woman. Now give life to Lava-Kuśa.
186. Go and summon the physician known as Dhanvantari, you who are the highest treasure of my Lord's life.'
187. Having heard this, Hanumān departed and appeared before Dhanvantari.
188. Thereupon, seeing Hanumān, Dhanvantari, inwardly happy, palms pressed together, did obeisance.
189. [He said], 'Today I have seen you and I am fulfilled. Tell me in all candor for what reason you have come.'
190. Upon hearing this speech, the God among Apes said: 'Mother Jānakī sent me; come to Munipur.
191. *Biṣ-muṅgā* pox has afflicted Lava-Kuśa, and so I have come. Now I have told you the particular [reason].'
192. Said Dhanvantari: 'I cannot go with you. Śītalā, if she hears, will be extremely angry.
193. Pox is a terrible disease. He who is seized by it—know, Oh Hero!—Fate is indeed against him.
194. Lava-Kuśa will not live. Now they must die!' Hearing this,

Hanumān became like the All-consuming Fire (Hutāśana) in anger.

195. How dare you speak such cruel words while Mother Jānakī is beside herself with grief for her sons!
196. I am Hanumān the Hero, I have no fear. I have ravaged the golden Laṅkā with fire.
197. Effortlessly have I tied mountains with single short hairs 'pon my fur! I will dunk you in sea-water for half-hour or so!
198. So just come along quietly, if you know what's good for you, or you'll see a nice variety of blows!'
199. On hearing this, Dhanvantari trembled and shook [and said], 'I bow down to you, Great Hero. Oh, save me!'
200. Hanumān went in front, with Dhanvantari behind, and swiftly arrived in Munipur.
201. Then Śītalā spoke as a voice from the sky: 'Be careful, boy! Don't slight me!'
202. See that my worship is published in Munipur, or I'll bring disaster on your house.
203. At once *Dhukuṛyā* eruptions will attack, and I'll take your family to perdition.'
204. Then Dhanvantari said with humility, 'I will publish your worship, as you command.'
205. Having said this, he went quickly and arrived where Jānakī was.
206. Prostrating himself, he saluted her feet. Weeping all the while, Sītā entreated [his help].
207. Said Dhanvantari, 'Mother, do not weep any more. Your Lava-Kuśa will receive life.'
208. Hearing the name of Dhanvantari, the sages all came. Some said, 'Save my boy.'
209. Some said, 'Give my son the gift of breath.' Still others said, 'Son, may your well-being increase.'
210. Dhanvantari said: 'Masters, to your hearing I submit this: let all in Munipur worship Śītalā.
211. The medical treatment I will conduct with all suitable effort; all will be cured. Do not worry.'
212. Hearing this, the sages became happy and commenced the service of Śītalā.

213. Establishing the pot, they did the invocation and single-mindedly worshiped the fear-dispelling feet.
214. Thus praised the sages, with hands cupped together: 'Thou art Bhadrakālī, destroyer of worldly fear (*bhavabhaya-vināśini*).
215. Thou art Māheśvarī (? spouse of Śiva, or Supreme Goddess), Maṅgalā (The Beneficent), Śītalā (the Cool One), Mahāmāya (She of Great Transformative Power). Jayantī (The Triumphant) Maṅgalā (Auspiciousness) art thou; thou art Sarvajayā (She Who Conquers All).
216. Thou art Paramkāriṇī (She Who is the Ultimate Actor), Patitapāvanī (She Who Rescues the Fallen), Ādyāśakti (The Primal Force), Aṣṭabhujā (The Eight-Armed), and Anantarūpiṇī (She of Endless Forms).
217. Be favorable, Mother, at Munipur. We will worship you forever from this day.'
218. Thus the sages sang praise with joined palms. The Mother, her mind satisfied, was well-pleased.
219. Dhanvantari tinctured them (*chob dila*, perhaps 'innoculated them') and the pox pustules rose. Bringing *nim* (margosa) branches, he spoke *mantras* over them.[100]
220. On the fifteenth day the pox pustules ripened, and when they had seen this, the sages were happy at heart.
221. All intent on the service of Śītalā, on the twenty-first day they gave [the patients] the bath-of-recovery (*arogyasnāna*).
222. Dhanvantari took his leave and went home. Great was the joy that arose in Munipur.
223. So ends the song of the Munipur *pālā*, says Dvija Śrī Mānik, thinking of Śītalā.

Thus: end of *pālā*, date 20th Caitra (about the 3rd of April, ten days before the Bengali New Year).

Appendix A

These verses are presented by the editor as Appendix B. On the basis of the rather slim evidence contained in v. 227—a reference to Govinda—we suspect that this may be the end of the Gokul Pālā, which is begun in the text but breaks off at v. 77. If this is so, then it might be followed by the material in Appendix B, which would constitute part of the following night's performance.

Payār

224. [first half of verse missing] . . . in this form, purely, did they worship ceaselessly.
225. Applying water and flowers to everyone's body, all were cured through the mercy of the Goddess.
226. Here ends this *pālā* sung by Dvija Śrī Mānik, meditating upon Śītalā.
227. Friends, make the sound of 'Hari' loudly. All creation is a husk; the feet of Govinda are the kernel.

Appendix B

These verses are presented by the editor as Appendix A. They evidently form part of the introduction to the Munipur Pālā, which appears to have been quite similar to the introduction to the Gokul Pālā, except for the reference to Śītalā's receiving worship from Sītā (v. 241) rather than Kṛṣṇa (v. 70).

Payār

228. While one is being cremated another breathes his last, such is my might by your blessing [repeats v. 57].
229. Said *Biṣ-muṅgā*, 'One by one I crush the entire lineage of him to whose house I go' [repeats v. 53].
230. *Agni-muṅgā* said, 'He whom I go and seize—his life goes out with the burning' [cf. v. 29].
231. *Beṅgcyā* pox said, 'Within one night I turn the blood of him whom I seize to water' (cf. vv. 27, 41).
232. Said *Ālkusyā*: 'Mother, hear my speech! Him whom I seize, I ruin [repeats v. 58].
233. 'Before his ordained time, I take him to Yama's house. I do not allow the cremation-ground to be extinguished for ten days [at a time]' [repeats v. 59].
234. *Tilyākulā* said: 'In your presence, Mother, I say—my particular strength is on Saturdays and Tuesdays [repeats v. 60].
235. I appear and then submerge myself [in a person's body]. I take his ordained span of years and hoist it up a tree' [repeats v. 61].
236. *Kaā̃ṭhālyā* pox said: 'I would like to submit that Nārāyaṇa knows how strong I am [repeats v. 62].
237. 'Before the rest of the body, I plug the throat. Vidhātā is unable to preserve [such a person; for him] survival becomes impossible' [repeats v. 63].

238. Said *Khos*: 'The person whom I seize at my whim, sheds clothes and prances about and, lighting a fire, toasts himself [repeats v. 64 with variation in word order].
239. He scratches to his heart's content without knowing the cause. But he rolls on the earth when I commence burning' [repeats v. 65, vv. 66–68 omitted].
240. Thus each spoke of his own particular strength. Śītalā said: 'Well, then, all is ready for my service [repeats v. 69].
241. Come, children. Come speedily to Munipur. Today I will receive water and flowers from Sītā' [almost identical to v. 70 except for references to Munipur and Sītā instead of Gokul and Kṛṣṇa].
242. Saying this, the Mother went with swift motion. Dvija Śrī Mānik sings the Śītalāmaṅgal.

Obeisance to Śrī Śrī Durgā. Obeisance to Gopal.

7. *The Goddess Śītalā and Epidemic Smallpox in Bengal*

White-bodied one, mounted on an ass, in your two
hands a broom and a full pot,
To mitigate fever, you asperse, from the full pot,
with the broom, the water of immortality.
Naked, with a winnowing fan on the head, your body
adorned with gold and many gems, three-eyed,
You are the quencher of the fierce heat of pustules;
Śītalā, I worship you.

(Nirmalānanda 1967: 196)

Thus is the worshiper directed to contemplate the Hindu Goddess of Smallpox. A disease that so often disfigured or blinded its victims, when it did not kill them, is serious enough to be granted its own deity in a pantheon of specialist gods and goddesses. But Śītalā is unlike the other Indian godlings of affliction, which are mostly localized and called by a great variety of names. Śītalā is known by a single name throughout the Indo-Aryan speaking region of India and Nepal (and by a small number of other names in south India). And she is usually the recipient of large-scale community worship by the villages in which she dwells.[1]

In rural southwestern Bengal, during the spring, her worship is carried out with as much splendor and celebration as each village can manage. 'Śītalā,' say the farmers and fishermen who predominate in that locality, 'is the Mother of our village. She takes away the fear of smallpox.' Most of these people have been vaccinated more than once, and the area has been free from smallpox for more than a decade. Moreover, many people think that smallpox is—or was—an infectious disease transmitted by an ineffable seed from an active case to a previously uninfected person. But such knowledge and experience seem to have no influence on their reverence for Śītalā.

Westerners have often supposed that the relationship between the goddess and the disease is direct, if mystical, so that the eradication of smallpox will bring with it the disappearance of Śītalā worship, if not of the goddess herself. Among the early travelers to India, to whom smallpox was a matter of intimate personal experience, there seemed little doubt that the source of the anxiety from which the goddess was generated lay in the terrifying visage of the victim, studded with fulminating pustules, disfigured almost beyond recognition, and, in the late stages of the infection, redolent of decaying flesh. If the horror of the sight could not be translated by reasonless Hindu superstition directly into a weird goddess, then 'tradition' was invoked as well. James Moore, in his *History of the Small Pox*, reflected on a drawing of this goddess: 'In a country, where every thought, word, and deed, are mere repetitions of those of their progenitors, a composition, like this, bears the stamp of great antiquity.' It seemed to Moore, as it did to many others in nineteenth century Europe, that nothing in Oriental societies ever changed. He found a clear demonstration of this in the history of syphilis (the other pox, a disease too terrible for him to name), which was introduced into the East by the Portuguese, where it 'spread widely, and produced inexpressible misery' but gave rise to no symbolic rites: 'No image adorned with appropriate types has been erected in any Chinese or Hindoo temple: for invention has long abandoned these his primitive abodes' (Moore 1815: 34–35).

Although the Occidental assumption that India has no history has also now been long abandoned, it has continued to exercise a curious influence on the writing of the history of smallpox. J.Z. Holwell, the British East India Company physician who is best remembered for having survived imprisonment in the Black Hole of Calcutta, has been a particularly influential disseminator of the idea that smallpox was a part of the unchanging Indian landscape. In 1767 he addressed an 'Account of the Manner of Inoculating for the Small Pox in the East Indies' to the College of Physicians in London. The portions of this paper that are based on Holwell's own observations are quite valuable, but it also includes the following paragraph:

> . . . [A]t the period in which the *Aughtorrah Bhade* [*Atharva Veda*] scriptures of the Gentoos were promulgated, (according to the Brahmins three thousand three hundred and fifty six years ago;) this disease must then have been of some standing, as those scriptures institute a form of divine worship, with *Poojahs* or offerings, to a female divinity, stiled by the common people *Gootee ka Tagooran* [probably *guṭikā ṭhākurāṇī*] (the goddess of spots [smallpox, Skt. *guṭikā*]), whose aid and patronage are invoked during the continuance of the small pox season, also in the measles, and every cutaneous eruption that is in the smallest degree epidemical. Due weight being given to this circumstance, the long duration of the disease in Indostan will manifestly appear; and we may add . . . that not only the Arabians, but the Egyptians also, by their early commerce with India through the Red Sea and Gulf of Mocha, most certainly derived originally the small pox (and probably the measles likewise) from that country, where those diseases have reigned from the earliest known times. (p. 146)

While Sanskritists (Orth 1900: 393; Jolly 1901: 93) reported their inability to locate such worship in the *Atharva Veda* or any other ancient text, the history of disease went its own way, perhaps excessively ready to believe that a horrifying malady like smallpox originated in the hot, moist putrefaction of the tropics. It is difficult to say how many times Holwell's account has been repeated, but one of the most influential authors to do so was the cautious August Hirsch (1883: 125), who concluded that 'although the origin of smallpox remains an unsolved problem . . . the *native foci of smallpox* may be looked for in *India* and in the countries of *Central Africa*' (p. 127).

Donald Henderson, chief medical officer of the World Health Organization (WHO) Smallpox Eradication Campaign, reiterated an expanded version of the story in 1976, adding to it the reasonable epidemiological speculation

> that in ancient times only the more densely populated areas of India and China were able to sustain the continued transmission of smallpox. If it was occasionally introduced in less populated central and western Asia, Europe and Africa, it might have persisted for a time in such a region as the Nile delta, but eventually the chain of transmission would have been broken. The slow pace of travel in pre-Christian times and the infrequency of long journeys could have served to confine smallpox largely to Asia during that period. (pp. 26–27)

And Holwell's speculation reappeared, with an added fillip, in the recently popular *Plagues and Peoples* (McNeill 1976):

> As for India, the existence of temples for worship of a deity of smallpox shows that the disease (or something closely akin thereto) was of considerable significance in Hindu India from time immemorial—however long that may be historically. Unfortunately, absence of records permits no account whatever of Indian encounters with infectious disease before 1200. (p. 144)

Indian medical texts, composed at various times over the period in which smallpox became known in the region, indirectly relate a great deal of the history of the disease. The history of smallpox in India and the history of the Hindu Goddess of Smallpox are, of course, quite different things. However, the interpretation by Hindus—both common people and intellectuals—of their experience of the disease and of divinities makes a connection between them. There are many interesting things to be learned from each of these histories, but what is least well understood—and, thus, most interesting of all—is their relationship. Pursuit of that relationship had led me into factual territory usually worked by anthropologists who claim they are not concerned with people's interpretations of natural phenomena, but rather with some order that is intrinsic in the phenomena (including the human participants) themselves.

A search for material causes behind the 'mystification' of native religion is associated with methods of social and cultural analysis that assume that what a people 'knows' is mostly false consciousness, but that their culture generally protects them from their ignorance by preadapting the relationship between their biological needs and their natural environment. This position—adopted by some cultural ecologists and 'cultural materialists'—shows less respect for demonstrably pertinent facts than it appears to do: at most, it accords only subordinate importance to the natives' explanations of their own practices. There are aspects of ecology, epidemiology, and disease history discussed here that do not form part of the collective consciousness of Bengal. However, they are not, in my view, digits of an unseen hand that constructs a culture regardless of human understanding. The religious interpretation people in rural Bengal place upon infectious disease does not exclude a naturalistic comprehension. They would almost surely not produce all of the facts of biological history considered here, but their reverence for Śītalā does not require them to reject such facts.

Smallpox

Two viruses of the genus *Orthopoxvirus* cause what is commonly known as smallpox among human beings. One of these, the variola minor poxvirus, causes a relatively mild form of the disease, sometimes called alastrim, that has a low case fatality rate. It seems to have been rare in India and will not be of concern here. Variola major smallpox has a case fatality rate of 20 to 40 percent, sometimes reaching 50 percent when exacerbated by malnutrition or secondary infections. This is the virus that has impinged most heavily on the lives and consciousness of people in India. There are related poxviruses that infect other animals, and, as is well known, it was Edward Jenner's observation that a limited cowpox infection conferred immunity from smallpox that led to the development of vaccination (Rhodes and van Rooyen 1958: 165–66; Dixon 1962: 1–7).

The virus enters the body through the upper respiratory tract and multiplies in the mucosa, passing into regional lymph nodes, from which it invades the blood and localizes in the internal organs where it undergoes further multiplication. At the end of the incubation period, which lasts from six to twenty-two days, averaging about twelve, there appears to be a massive release of viruses into the circulatory system. This phase is probably responsible for a typical smallpox prodrome that is well described in Indian texts: a sudden, sharp rise in temperature, severe headache and pains in the chest, back and limbs, vomiting, prostration, and, in particularly severe cases, a rash. From the third to the fifth day after the onset of the prodromal illness, the characteristic smallpox begin to appear on the body. The virus localizes in the skin, particularly the peripheral areas, the face, and the lower limbs, hands, and feet, although there may be some macules over all parts of the body. The lesions turn into papules that fill with fluid, becoming vesicles prone to secondary infections, for which reason they are commonly called pustules whether or not they contain pus. Temperature often falls to near normal with the appearance of the focal eruption and may remain there throughout the nine days or so it takes (if there is no secondary infection) for the pustules to be reabsorbed by the body. Victims who survive the pre-eruptive phase of the disease often recover unless the tissue destroyed by the eruption simply cannot be replaced rapidly enough. Rapid replacement of damaged tissue is dependent on the nutritional status of the host; the synergism of malnutrition and infection is responsible for the high fatality rates of smallpox epidemics in India (Rhodes and van Rooyen 1958: 166–69; Deutschmann 1961: 3; Dixon 1962: 5–43).[2]

Although there is some evidence of naturally occurring smallpox in monkeys and apes (Hahon 1961), recent epidemiological experience suggests that it is a 'two-factor complex: virus and host' (Deutschmann 1961: 1), with neither an intermediate reservoir of infection in a nonhuman population nor any essential animal vector. Viruses are shed by smallpox victims from the epithelium beginning from the onset of the focal rash and continuing until the pustules are completely healed. Anything with which the patient has come into contact—bedding, clothing, utensils, even the dust of the sickroom—is likely to become contaminated, and the virus may remain alive and infective for up to a year outside the body (Rhodes and van Rooyen 1958: 171–72). A person who has recovered from an infection is thereafter immune to the disease. There are no known cases of passive carriers of smallpox virus, although persons with mild and nondebilitating cases have passed it on to others who suffered severe infections.

These facts have bearing on the natural history and epidemiology of smallpox. Roughly speaking, once the smallpox virus became established in a human host, someone had to be infected with it almost all the time for the virus to survive. There might be periods of up to a year during which the virus subsisted in the dried crust of epithelium shed by a sufferer, but, if the virus could not propagate itself afresh in a previously uninfected person, it would die out. This characteristic is responsible for the guarded confidence now expressed by the WHO that smallpox has been eradicated. Historically, when smallpox has first invaded relatively small, isolated populations with no previous experience of the disease, almost everyone has come down with an infection, leaving the surviving population virtually 100 percent immune. The disease then died out in that population, to be reintroduced from outside when a significant nonimmune group had developed among persons born after the previous epidemic. Without an endemic home in a human population sufficiently large and in sufficiently close contact to guarantee fairly continuous propagation, smallpox would have wiped itself out (Hare 1967: 119–20). Thus, the search for the ancestral home of this disease can reasonably be restricted to a few centers of high population density among the old world civilizations.

Early history of smallpox in India

For about the last 2,000 years a disease called *masūrikā* has been recognized in the Indian medical compilations. The name is derived from *masūra*, the hard, lenticular orange pulses that are a common part of diets throughout South Asia today; the derivation is based on the similarity of the eruptions of the disease to the color, shape, and consistency of the pulse. Although it does not appear among the diseases mentioned in the *Atharva Veda*, *masūrikā* is mentioned in the early medical compilations of Caraka and Suśruta, which appear to have taken shape before the Christian era and to have been put in final form by the fourth century AD. Because *masūrikā* is certainly the term used to designate smallpox in later texts, these early appearances suggest that smallpox is an ancient disease in India. However, as elaborate as Caraka and Suśruta are on many other ailments, they say extremely little about *masūrikā*. Caraka does not include it in the enumeration of diseases, but takes it up briefly, together with measles, in the section on treatment, where it is said to be an eruption of the entire body to be treated like erysipelas and leprosy (Jolly 1901: 93). Suśruta (1915) is slightly more elaborate, offering this description:

> *Masūrikā*—The copper-colored pustules attended with pain, fever, and burning, appearing all over the body, on the face, and inside the cavity of the mouth, are called *Masūrikā*. (13.36; Bhishagratna 1911; 2:90)

This is a good description of smallpox except for one detail: it is taken from Suśruta's discourses on 'minor diseases' (*kṣudra-roga*), which consist mostly of cutaneous exanthemata, including acne.

As is usual, the observations of Caraka and Suśruta are repeated in later medical compilations. The first small but significant addition to the description of *masūrikā* was made by the physician Vāgbhaṭa. In his *Aṣṭāṅgahṛdaya-saṃhitā* (2.5. 111) is the following new verse: 'He on whose body the *masūrikā*, appearing like coral globules, break out then swiftly vanish, dies quickly' (Jolly 1901: 93; Hilgenberg and Kirfel 1941: 205). This, the first suggestion in Indian medicine that *masūrikā* may be a fatal disease, is not definitely dated, but the evidence points toward the seventh century, and perhaps to the early part (Hilgenberg and Kirfel 1941: xv; Filliozat 1964: 14; Meulenbeld 1974: 424). In other words, Vāgbhaṭa was probably a contemporary of the Christian physician Ahrún of Alexandria, who wrote the first treatise in the Mediterranean world definitively identifying smallpox and measles (Greenhill 1847: 164).

The *Nidāna* of Mādhava-kara, composed early in the eighth century, included an extensive and knowledgeable chapter (54) on *masūrikā*, treating measles and chickenpox together with smallpox, all of which seem to have been quite familiar to him (Mādhava-kara 1920: pp. 355–60; Meulenbeld 1974: 19–20). Thus, it appears on the evidence offered by the early medical authorities, that in India smallpox became widespread enough to be quite familiar, and dangerous enough to demand careful attention in the course of the seventh century—the same century in which it was established in the countries around the Mediterranean (Greenhill 1847: 101–105). The antiquity of smallpox as it was known until its recent eradication, at least as far as India is concerned, is not as great or as obscure as has often been thought. But this was well understood over a century ago by the sage physician of Dacca, Dr Thomas Alexander Wise, who wrote of the early Indian descriptions of *masūrikā* (1867):

> It may have changed its character, like some other diseases, from unknown causes, but it is more probable that the peculiar and dangerous epidemic, small-pox, is a new form of disease. According to this opinion, it is at a much later period that the small-pox is described by Hindu writers in its present formidable form; probably not long before Rhazes described it [ca. AD 910], some time after which it appeared in Europe. (2: 108–109)

In addition to making clinical distinctions among numerous types of pustular eruptions, Mādhava also supplied humoral and dietary explanations for the various forms of smallpox, measles, and chickenpox. If the underlying theory is accepted, Mādhava's treatment of the poxes was exclusively biological, and his commentators in the twelfth and thirteenth centuries followed his lead in this respect, not raising the name of any deity or demon in connection with these diseases. However, someone unknown—possibly one of the commentators—probably about the late fifteenth or early sixteenth century added an appendix (*pariśiṣṭa*) on 'The Pathology of Śītalā' to his text (Mādhava-kara 1920: 494–95). The appendix provides an account of pox eruptions complementary to that given in the text, but based on the theory that they are caused by the Goddess Śītalā. There is a hint of this new theory of pox in the twelfth century commentary of Ḍalhaṇa at Suśruta 2.13, which identified *śītalikā* as the 'popular designation' of *masūrikā* (Suśruta 1915: 25). Since smallpox is characterized by fever, the typical treatment that was developed in India emphasized continuous cooling of the patient throughout the course of the disease. Jolly (1901: 94) thinks the use of *śītalikā*, a feminine form meaning 'cool one,' is derived from the therapy prescribed.

The *Bhāva-prakāśa*, an early sixteenth century medical text compiled by Bhāva Miśra (1958: 375–82), greatly elaborated the discussion of smallpox. He repeated everything Mādhava had said about the malady and added a detailed section on the therapy appropriate to different types of pustules. He included the appendix on the pathology of Śītalā within his text and added to it both recommendations for the medical treatment of *śītalā* and instructions for the worship of the Goddess: 'A Brahman, possessed of faith, should recite the hymn of Śītalā Devī in the presence of *śītalikā*; then *śītalās* abate' (p. 380). This hymn speaks repeatedly of the 'terrible fear' or 'dreadful calamity of pustules' (*visphoṭakabhayaṃ mahat/ghoraṃ*), language which is absent from the earlier discussions of smallpox. Diseases, it seems, are for physicians, but calamities are for priests.

By the sixteenth century in India, there were two fully fledged interpretations of smallpox: one based on the biology of humors and diet of Ayurveda and deriving appropriate therapeutic procedures from it, the other based on the conception that the disease is a divine affliction and stipulating that the worship of Śītalā is indispensable to treatment. The one element that proved most significant to European observers in the eighteenth century—the procedure for inoculating the smallpox, or variolation—is, however, not present in Bhāva Miśra's discussion, nor is it found in any of the earlier texts.

Variolation

Intentional infection of a nonimmune person with smallpox under conditions conceived to produce a mild case was widely practiced in many parts of the world before the introduction of the Jenner vaccine in 1798, and for a considerable time thereafter.[3] This practice depends on the ability to distinguish among smallpox, chickenpox, measles, and scarlet fever, because an inoculation with measles, for example, would not produce immunity from smallpox. Thus, it is unlikely that variolation was used prophylactically in the Western world before the tenth century. Although it was contested by some authorities, the theory that smallpox was caused by a 'fermentation of the blood' rather than by a factor extrinsic to the body prevailed among European physicians into the late seventeenth century (Rolleston 1937: 17). Notwithstanding the learned theory, however, European peasants practiced variolation at least as early as the seventeenth century; physicians began to adopt it during the eighteenth (Langer 1976). Accounts of variolation techniques used in Turkey became the basis for a wide range of experiments with methods, including means of attenuating the virus, in England and on the Continent (McVail 1893: 408–416). Variolation continued as a prophylaxis in competition with vaccination in the nineteenth century, but it lost ground because of two important disadvantages: although the average variolated case was milder than the average case contracted naturally, there was no means of guaranteeing this result, so there were occasional instances of death and disfigurement, and variolated cases were fully contagious, thus contributing to the spread of the disease.

Variolation, also known as 'inoculation of the smallpox,' was called in Bengali *ṭikā* (derived from the Sanskrit *vaṭikā*, a small lump or globule), the term later used to refer to vaccination. It was based on the idea that smallpox was produced from a seed (*bīja*) mixed with the blood of a person, implying a theory of infection not contained in the Ayurvedic humoral explanation of the disease. In other words, Śītalā did not stand in the way of advancing clinical knowledge of smallpox. Since the subject engaged such keen interest in England, several observers who encountered variolation in Bengal recorded descriptions of it. In 1731 one Robert Coult in Bengal wrote in a letter to Dr Oliver Coult in England (Dharampal 1971):

> Their method of performing this operation is by taking a little of the pus (when the smallpox are come to maturity and are of a good kind) and dipping these in the point of a pretty large sharp needle. Therewith make several punctures in the hollow under the deltoid muscle or sometimes in the forehead, after which they cover the part with a little paste made of boiled rice.
>
> ...
>
> The feaver insues later or sooner, according to the age and strength of the person inoculated, but commonly the third or fourth days. They keep the patient under the coolest regimen they can think of before the feaver comes on and frequently use cold bathing. (pp. 141–42)

Dr Edward Ives (1773: 54), a British naval surgeon, observed a procedure very similar to that described by Coult when he visited Bengal in 1755. The Dutch naval commander Stavorinus (1798) visited the Dutch factory at Chinsurah in Bengal in 1770. He wrote: 'Inoculation is known among the Bengalis, who practice it by powdering some smallpox particles, which they make the patients swallow in some liquid. There are very few who use it for insertion' (pp. 325–28). This remark, evidently based on hearsay evidence, was sharply challenged by Cossingy (1799, 2: 110), who cited observations of the insertion of the virus in an incision on the left wrist as the procedure of inoculation used at the Portuguese settlement in Bandel, Hooghly.

Dr Francis Buchanan (1808) witnessed inoculation early in the nineteenth century in Dinajpur District (pp. 12–14). Matter freshly extracted from pustules on the body of a smallpox victim was introduced into small needle punctures made in the skin of uninfected people, usually children between three and ten years of age. Buchanan said that the inoculators were local cultivators, both Hindu and Muslim, who were not otherwise esteemed as physicians. In the 1840s the smallpox inoculators in Dacca were garland-makers and barbers; medical specialists of the highranking Vaidya caste did not perform this operation (Wise 1867, 1: lxxxviii; Risley 1891, 2:61–62). The Rev. William Ward (1970 [1822], 1:96) of Serampore, early in the nineteenth century, noted that Daivajñas, low-ranking astrologer Brahmans were inoculators. In the latter half of the nineteenth century, Risley (1891) wrote that it was an occupation of barbers (Nāpit), who 'possess a textbook, Vasanta-tikā (Smallpox-inoculation), but few study it' (2:128).

In the light of these observations, the experiences reported in Holwell in 1767, presumably from Calcutta, take on additional significance. He says:

> Inoculation is performed in Indostan by a particular tribe of Brahmins, who are delegated annually for this service from the different Colleges of Bindoobund [Brindaban], Eleabas [Allahabad], Banaras, &c. over all the distant provinces; dividing themselves into small parties, of three or four each, they plan their travelling circuits in such wise as to arrive at the places of their respective destination some weeks before the usual return of the disease; they arrive commonly in the Bengall provinces early in February, although they some years do not inoculate before March, deferring it until they consider the state of the season, and acquire information on the state of distemper. (pp. 146–47)

Whatever kind of Brahmans these may have been—and inoculation, like other occupations that require bodily contact with heterogeneous persons, is not an estimable job for a Brahman—they were certainly specialists. The interpretation is further borne out by the elaborateness of their procedures. They made the insertion anywhere on the body but preferred the outside of the arm. The spot chosen was rubbed vigorously with a dry cloth for eight to ten minutes, then fifteen or sixteen minute incisions were made in a small circle using a steel tool about four and a half inches long—'the instrument is precisely the same as the Barbers of Indostan use to cut the nails, and depurate the ears of the customers.' A small wad of cotton 'charged with the variolous matter' and moistened with two or three drops of Ganges water was placed on top of the wound and allowed to remain in contact with it for several hours. 'The cotton, which he preserves in a double callico rag, is saturated with matter from the inoculated pustules of the preceding year, for they never inoculate with fresh matter, nor with matter from the disease caught in the natural way, however distinct and mild the species' (pp. 150–53). Throughout the operation, the inoculator continuously recited the worship of the Smallpox Goddess, Guṭikā Ṭhākurāṇī. Thus, although procedures for smallpox inoculation were known and used in mid-eighteenth century Bengal, the specialists were itinerants from up-country, who had superior procedures, including means of attenuating the virus, and who called the goddess not by the Sanskrit Śītalā, used in the medical texts, but by a vernacular name.[4] By the beginning of the nineteenth century the technique was established among a variety of Bengali inoculators. It is difficult to prove anything on the strength of Holwell's remarks, but they suggest that smallpox may have been better known in northern India than in Bengal in the early eighteenth century.

The history of Śītalā

The Smallpox Goddess emerged in the medical texts about the beginning of the sixteenth century and, although the earliest reference does not contain a description of the Goddess that would allow us to identify her decisively with her later familiar form, there are several twelfth century icons that are unambiguous. An image from a temple at Modhera in Gujarat shows her mounted on an ass, naked, a winnowing fan on her head. There is a similar figure on the outer wall of a twelfth century temple at Sejakpur in Saurashtra.[5] Another from Osia in Rajasthan, carved into a temple constructed in 1178, depicts the same conception (Majumdar 1965, Pl. LII; India, Archaeological Survey: 109). Several images of Parṇaśabarī, a Mahayana Buddhist goddess of diseases, unearthed from a tenth to twelfth century site in eastern Bengal, clearly depict Śītalā: she rides an ass, carries a broom in her right hand and a winnowing fan in her left (Bhattacharya 1958: 196–97, 232–33, Figs. 140, 173, 174; Sahai 1975: 239–42). It is over a thousand miles from Gujarat and Rajasthan to Bangladesh, and it is highly improbable that such an iconographic innovation would appear simultaneously in widely separated regions. The absence of similar images in the intervening areas is, no doubt, due in part to Muslim iconoclasm, but, most likely, there are some specimens that I have not yet located.[6]

The historical connection between Śītalā and the ancient pilgrimage place of Banaras is a recurrent theme in the Sanskrit writings about the Goddess, but evidence concerning the antiquity of this connection is extremely scarce, if only because most of the temples in the city have been destroyed and rebuilt several times over (Sukul 1970: 717). A recent observer includes a temple of Śītalā Devī among the city's most ancient temples (Eck 1978: 177). Meena Kaushik (1979) reports that Śītalā-mātā

> is worshipped by all castes in Varanasi. She has a large temple dedicated to her at Shitalā Ghāṭ . . . This temple has one entrance which opens towards the North and the deity faces the East. The main idol of Shitala-mata occupies the central place in the temple, and is made of silver. (pp. 17–18)

Early in this century Havell (1905) saw the temple of Śītalā Ghāṭ:

> It is a small box-like structure, without any attempt at architectural embellishment, but it is, nevertheless, much frequented by worshippers anxious to avert the evil influence of the goddess. She is represented by an old piece of stone-carving from which almost every detail has been obliterated, placed on a repouseé shrine of modern workmanship.[7] (pp. 113–14)

Sherring's detailed account of Banaras in the mid-nineteenth century does not mention Śītalā Ghāṭ. He discusses four temples devoted to this Goddess, but all of them appear to be small shrines included in the compounds of Śiva temples (Sherring 1968: 65, 85, 100, 130).

It is tempting to find in this progression of temples evidence of the recent rise of a cult of Śītalā in Banaras. However, the oldest Sanskrit literary evidence concerning the Goddess connects her to this city at a much earlier date. In the midst of Bhāva Miśra's sixteenth century discourse on the variety of smallpox known as śītalā, he quotes a *Śītalāṣṭakastotra* (Eight-part Hymn of Śītalā) said to be taken from the *Kāśī-khaṇḍa*, or section on Banaras, of the *Skanda Purāṇa*. Although the published editions of the *Kāśī-khaṇḍa* do not include this hymn, versions of it are often repeated in modern *smārta* compilations and it has appeared as a separate publication.[8] I quote here a section from it:

I celebrate the goddess Śītalā—mounted on a donkey and having as her garments the quarters of the world [i.e., naked]—whom, having approached, one may turn back the great fear of pustules.

Whoever, afflicted by fever, should say, 'O Śītalā! Śītalā!', his dreadful fear of pustules immediately vanishes.

A man who, having resolved in his mind in the midst of ablutions, should deeply revere you, in his family the dreadful fear of pustules does not arise.

O Śītalā, for a man scorched by fever, become foul smelling, and whose vision is destroyed, you they regard as the living medicine.

I bow down to Śītalā Devī, mounted on a donkey, having for garments the regions of the world, accompanied by her broom and pot, and having her head, decorated with a winnowing basket. (Bhāva Miśra 1958, 2:380; cf. *Śabdakalpadrumaḥ* 1931–34, *s.v. masūrikā*)

The close correspondence between the description of the Goddess in this passage and the twelfth century icons clearly indicates a common source.

During the sixteenth century, at about the same time that Bhāva Miśra was creating a place for Śītalā in the medical literature, the great Bengali *smārta* Raghunandana Bhaṭṭācārya was creating a place for her in the Hindu religious year (Kane 1930–62; 5:428). 'Śītalā's eighth' (Śītalāṣṭamī) is the eighth lunar day of the dark fortnight of Phālguna; it may fall between the middle of February and the end of March. The significance of this season will become apparent presently; the significance of the dark lunar fortnight at any time of the year is generally death and inauspiciousness. Other late Sanskrit works on ritual, *tantras*, and digests of observances, also recognized Śītalā, although I know of no work of the sixteenth century or earlier that makes her out to be anything other than a minor deity.

It is difficult to overestimate the importance of the period beginning in the late fifteenth century and extending through the sixteenth in the formation of the Bengali literature and the closely intertwined regional religious culture of Bengal. A great many Bengali compositions—most of them metrical narratives dealing with deities and their worship by human beings—predate this period, but, in numbers, variety, and quality of literary products, the sixteenth century is outstanding. There are Bengali translations of Sanskrit texts about most of the major divinities, as well as compositions relating local traditions about the deities of the Sanskrit pantheon. And there are numerous works concerning deities little known outside of Bengal, often presiding over dangers and threats to life commonly encountered by rural people.

Caṇḍī, the Bengali version of the goddess of the *Devīmāhātmya*, is the subject of what is widely regarded as the greatest work of this class, a long poem known as the *Kavikaṅkaṇa-Caṇḍī* composed in the middle of the sixteenth century by Mukunda Cakravartī (Sen 1975: 2). Among local divinities, Manasā, the Goddess of Snakes, is by far the best represented, being the subject of innumerable texts written throughout Bengal from the fifteenth through the eighteenth centuries (Bhaṭṭācārya 1970: 306–402). Today, in Hindu villages, Caṇḍī, Manasā, and Śītalā are the village goddesses (*grāma-devatā*) par excellence. Therefore it is quite strange to find not a single word about Śītalā in the extensive Bengali literature of the sixteenth century, when she appears to have been well known to prominent Bengali authors writing in Sanskrit at the time. Whatever the cause for her belated acceptance into village pantheons, she cannot be interpreted as having ascended from the Bengali earth into an ever more exalted heaven.

The earliest extant Bengali poem about Śītalā dates from about 1690, coincidentally, the year Calcutta was founded, and was composed in Saptagram, which is not far north of Calcutta.[9] About 1750 a sudden outpouring of compositions began: at least six can be dated to the period between 1750 and 1770, and I have heard indirectly about others that may be dated to 1738 or 1764. Moreover, these texts were all written in a comparatively small locality in southwestern lower Bengal (see pp. 107–109). The longest and most popular of the Śītalā poems, the one that has been printed and reprinted in cheap editions, nowadays forming the basis for most performances of the narrative of the Goddess, and which contains the most elaborate and colorful detail about types of poxes and related eruptions, was composed by Nityānanda Cakravartī (1931). Nityānanda, who evidently knew his smallpox and did not simply rework some patent list of pustules, was court poet of Rājā Rājanārāyan (ruled 1756–1770) of Kāśījoṛā, a small kingdom adjacent to the area of my fieldwork in eastern Midnapur. Nityānanda's composition makes use of many of the usual conventions of poems of this class, but it appears that he had no literary example in writing about Śītalā and that he followed principally local tradition, which included the Sanskrit iconography but went far beyond that in its creation of a narrative career for the Goddess among human beings. In summary, it appears that Śītalā, the Goddess of Smallpox, who had been a minor deity, emerged as a major object of worship in south-western Bengal during the eighteenth century.

Western Bengal in the eighteenth century

The eighteenth century was a time of serious troubles in Bengal. The Mughal empire was in decline, laying the ground for the British acquisition of power. Between 1742 and 1751 the Maratha cavalry repeatedly plundered south-western Bengal, carrying away whatever they could loot and laying waste to the rest. It is difficult to judge the extent of population displacement resulting from Maratha depredation, but a contemporary Bengali observer saw it as very great (Dimock and Gupta 1965: 26–36). It is usual for land to fall out of cultivation during such a period and for food scarcity, if not famine, to prevail. After their victory at Plassey in 1757, the British gained control over the districts of Burdwan and Midnapur, in western Bengal, as well as Chittagong in the east. The British pressed the zamindārs in their concessions for payment of revenues, and, as usual, when the zamindārs were under financial duress, they pressed the cultivators. A severe drought in 1769 led to a disastrous famine in Bengal and Bihar in 1770, in which ten million people are estimated to have perished (Sinha 1967: 88). Stavorinus, a Dutch naval commander, who happened to be in Chinsura in 1770, wrote movingly of the tragedy he witnessed (1798) and also said:

> This famine arose in part from the bad rice harvest of the preceding year; but it must be attributed principally to the monopoly the English had over the last harvest of this commodity, which they kept at such a high price that most of the unfortunate inhabitants—who earned only a sou or a sou-and-a-half a day to sustain their family—found themselves powerless to buy the tenth part of what they needed to live.
>
> To this scourge was added smallpox, which spread among persons of all ages and of which they died in great numbers . . . Mortality could not have

> but augmented, especially after my departure from Chinsura; Director F. was one of the victims carried off by the smallpox, I learned after leaving Batavia. (p. 125–28)

The Dutch director was not the most eminent victim of the smallpox epidemic that followed the famine of 1770; the Nawab Nazim of Bengal, Saif-ud-daula, also died of the disease in that year (Marshman 1850: 80).

Information about famines prior to 1770 is sketchy, but the Calcutta Consultation Book for 9 July 1711, noted that the British Company waived monthly rents and distributed 500 maunds (about 20 tons) of rice among the poor: 'there having been a Famine in the Country for this severall months, so that severall thousands have famished for want of rice . . .' (Wilson 1895, 2:15–16). There were famines again in 1783–84 and 1787 (Greenough 1977: 408).

Smallpox was apparently endemic in Bengal in the eighteenth century and it had an epidemic cycle based on the rate of replacement of the unimmunized population. Holwell observed in 1767:

> The general state of this distemper [smallpox] in the provinces of Bengall (to which these observations are limited) is such that for five and sometimes six years together, it passes in a manner unnoticed, from the few that are attacked with it; for the complexion of it in these years is generally so benign as to cause very little alarm; and notwithstanding the multitudes that are every year inoculated in the usual season, it adds no malignity to the disease taken in the natural way, nor spreads the infection, as is commonly imagined in Europe. Every seventh year, with scarcely any exception, the small pox rages epidemically in these provinces, during the months of March, April and May; and sometimes until the annual returning rains, about the middle of June, put a stop to its fury. On these periodical returns (to four of which I have been witness [1744, and presumably 1751, 1758, and 1765]) the disease proves universally of the most malignant confluent kind from which few either of the natives or Europeans escaped, that took the distemper in the natural way, commonly dying on the first, second, or third day of the eruption . . . (p. 144)

Holwell observed smallpox epidemics in Bengal at the same time that the principal Bengali narratives concerning Śītalā were being composed. It is difficult to say when the population threshold for smallpox endemicity was crossed in lower Bengal, but it seems likely that it was before 1690, when the first known poem about the Goddess was written. The disease was recognized in Indian medicine for about a thousand years before that, and it must have had an endemic home somewhere in the region during the period from the twelfth to the sixteenth century, when it acquired a deity of its own and a prominent place in medical texts. The efflorescence of compositions about Śītalā, containing anguished statements about horrifying pustular diseases, written in the middle of the eighteenth century in a restricted locality along the lower Hooghly River and immediately westward from it, suggests a qualitatively different kind of encounter with smallpox. The testimony is synchronous with turmoil in the Mughal empire, and the area from which it originated corresponds roughly with the territory of the Maratha raids. A large number of displaced people spreading infection more rapidly than usual, interruption of a regular annual schedule of variolations, disruption of quarantine arrangements for freshly variolated children, and malnutrition, owing to land fallen out of cultivation and distressed rent-extraction, exacerbating the death rate, all may have played a part in transforming smallpox from a disease into a calamity. However, there is no way of showing how any or all of these elements might have presented themselves to a person in eighteenth century Bengal, so I shall leave this picture in impressionistic form and turn abruptly to the twentieth century. It is always easier to search where the light is brighter.

The endemic-epidemic cycle

The twentieth century statistics on reported smallpox mortality represented in Figure 1 give a crude quantitative dimension to the endemic-epidemic cycle. The statistics are, of course, rough: they are reports of mortality rather than of infection, mostly provided by village watchmen who were rarely literate, not to say lacking in clinical diagnostic skills; and vaccination was widespread, reducing the mortality rate. Nevertheless, it is safe to say that the peaks on the graphs show epidemics of smallpox. The districts selected for detailed examination are all, of course, rural and agricultural: Dacca is densely inhabited, lying in the well-watered delta in the east; Mymensingh is also in the east, but has only moderate population density, and the best agriculture of the four sample districts; Murshidabad is an old delta district in western Bengal, with moderate population density and average agricultural productivity; Midnapur is active delta on the eastern half, but raised gradually toward Chota Nagpur in the west, so that population is dense and agriculture good in the east, but both decline toward the west.

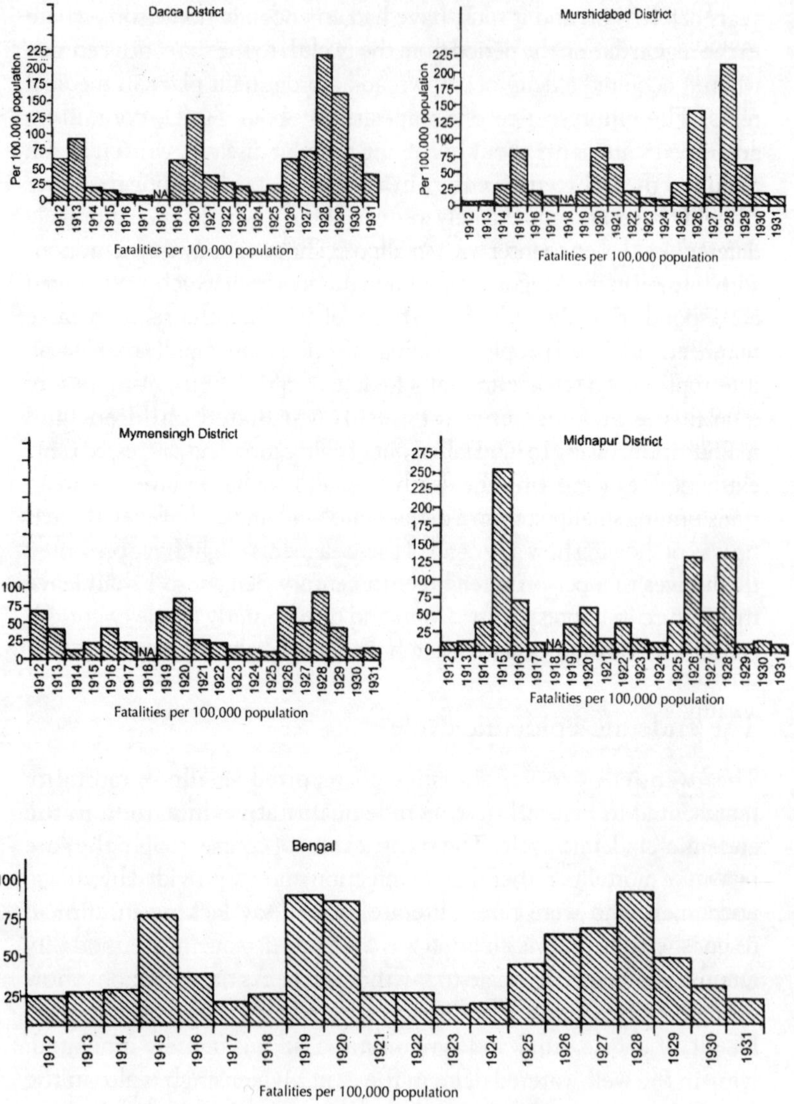

Figure 1. Annual smallpox mortality in Bengal and selected districts, 1912–1931
Sources: Bengal, Sanitary Commissioner (1912–1913); India, Sanitary Commissioner (1918).

Over the twenty-year period between 1912 and 1931, Bengal as a whole had three smallpox epidemics, in 1915, 1919–1920, and 1928. The 1915 epidemic was predominantly in western Bengal, 1920 in the east and north, and all parts shared in the 1928 epidemic. Only Dacca demonstrated a regular endemic-epidemic cycle: the epidemic of 1913 was followed by four or five years of low death rates, a gradual buildup in 1919 toward a major epidemic in 1920, a regular progression downward for four years, then upward for three to the terrible epidemic of 1928, which did not cease until 1929. In each of the other sample districts, additional variables intrude into the demographic process of accumulating nonimmune youngsters in the population. Four variables are largely responsible for the erratic pattern of epidemics in Mymensingh, Murshidabad, and Midnapur: (1) the movement of people between centers of infection, principally in urban areas, and the countryside, (2) vaccination, (3) rainfall, and (4) food supply. They were probably of different relative importance in each district.

1). Pilgrimage places, particularly Puri in Orissa, were foci of infection for the Bengal countryside before the twentieth century. In addition to these centers, in the 1912–1931 period there was increased movement of people between villages and Calcutta, district headquarters, and divisional towns such as Dacca. Such movement spread smallpox more rapidly throughout the region than occurred during the eighteenth or nineteenth century.

2). Vaccination was differently regarded by different groups of people in various parts of Bengal during this period. Among Hindus, some government vaccinators usurped the roles of the old inoculators, becoming priests of Śītalā. However, there were die-hard communities and localities that refused to have anything to do with what appeared to be interference in the domain of Śītalā. Resistance to vaccination among uneducated Muslims was frequently quite strong. Thus, it was difficult to obtain a uniform pattern of vaccination in an epidemic locality.

3, 4). Rainfall and food supply are closely linked to one another, and each is independently connected to smallpox epidemiology. Malnutrition increases the chance of infection and the chance of mortality due to infection; the food shortages that produce malnutrition usually follow droughts. Holwell noted that smallpox raged epidemically in the hot, dry months just before the onset of the monsoon in mid-June, and that it declined with the rainy season. Subsequent epidemiological research has shown that the transmissibility of the smallpox virus declines with increased atmospheric humidity (Rogers 1926; Russell and Sundararajan 1929). In addition to reducing the size of the harvest, thus bringing about malnutrition and its infectious sequelae, a drought also increases the transmission of smallpox viruses and the risk of infection.

The unexpected increase in smallpox mortality in Bengal in 1919 is explained in part by the fact that 1918 was a year of below-average rainfall and a correspondingly low rice harvest. This relationship is presumably an old one, pre-existing vaccination and metropolitan foci of infection in Bengal, and it is culturally acknowledged in a way. Famine, disease, and rapacious tax-collectors are seen as connected to one another—and, at a certain level, as naturalistically connected. That is, the links between low rainfall and low rice harvest, low rice harvest and increase in the proportion extracted as revenue, increase in revenue and dimunition in nutrition, reduced diet and increased disease are all clearly made by ordinary people in rural Bengal. But what they add up to is more than the sum of the parts, often dramatically characterized as the cataclysmic end of the present cosmic epoch (*yugāntara* or even *manvantara*), when chaos and universal destruction reign. Behind such widespread distress lies the general sinfulness of human beings, who neglect their gods and their dharma. Agriculture, meteorology, disease, and nutrition have been studied in a recognizably scientific way for a long time in India. But the sciences have not provided a root answer to the 'why' of human suffering. It is to provide a meaningful—that is to say, fundamental and adequate—answer to the 'why' of smallpox that Śītalā comes to be fitted into the already crowded Bengali pantheon.

The structural advent of Śītalā

The places of Śītalā in village pantheons and in the religious year seem so obvious and so integral as to create the illusion of eternity. Yet the historical evidence is that these systems were opened up to incorporate her, then closed around the innovation without revealing a trace of the original disturbance. The historical track of such a change is difficult to follow, but the structure of the calendrical and ritual systems into which the goddess was received make it possible to discern something about the process.

'In twelve months, thirteen festivals,' the Bengalis say with rare and uncharacteristic restraint. There are, in fact, about a hundred important rites held around a typical year in a Bengali village. However, all of these rites belong to a limited number of contrasting sets, of which the most important ones—the ones that give the structure to the whole year—may be called the 'rites of autumn' and the 'rites of spring.' The central autumnal rite is Durgā Pūjā, fixed on the lunar calendar, and, before the organization of modern 'committee *pūjās*,' carried out by Hindu kings and their petty successors under the Mughals and British, the zamindārs and related rural magnates. The Durgā Pūjā was traditionally given by a single *yajamāna* for the benefit of his family, household, and subjects, all arranged in hierarchical order on the model of the ancient Indian royal sacrifice. The social universe of Durgā Pūjā is a conceptual kingdom, however devoid of sovereignty it may nowadays appear.

The principal rite of spring is the Gājan, a 'popular' (*laukika*) ritual for which authority is not found in Sanskrit texts. This ritual is directed to Śiva, conceived to be the husband of Durgā and the fertilizer of the earth. Its dates are fixed on the solar calendar and it is carried out by ordinary villagers with comparatively little participation by high caste people. However, not every village possesses a Śiva temple, and only a few are equipped to perform the Gājan. Although it is done in villages and by villagers, it is not thought to be for the benefit of villages but rather for the whole universe.

Villages also possess deities of their own, conceived to be peculiar to the persons and localities delimited by particular village boundaries. These deities, sometimes inchoate stones that manifested themselves in the earth of the village, sometimes old sculptured images, or pottery or brass figurines, are housed at the feet of especially significant trees or in small temples, where they are often given regular service and worship year-round. Goddesses are more numerous than gods among village deities, and Caṇḍī and Manasā hold places of importance in many villages. However, in the deltaic portions of lower West Bengal today, Śītalā is the most usual village deity. She often appears alongside Manasā, but where I have found the two together, it is Śītalā's worship that sets the schedule; Manāsā is not ignored, but she is worshiped on the occasions of Śītalā worship and as an adjunct to her. The conception that it is a particular village and not any other unit that receives the benefit of her worship is in some instances enacted by processions circumambulating the village, planting flags where paths cross the village borders, or otherwise bounding the village before her pūjā is begun. In other words, the social niche where Śītalā found her place is predominantly the village. In eastern Midnapur District, individual village Śītalās are most commonly called 'Mother of such-and-such village' (*amuk grāmer mā*), the name Śītalā being reserved for occasions of worship. In some instances it would appear that she usurped the place of an earlier village mother, often a rough stone Caṇḍī, and subordinated a more highly marked goddess, such as Manasā, in taking her present position.

Finding the appropriate place for her elaborate annual worship (see Nicholas 1978) was a different kind of problem, and one that is solved in somewhat idiosyncratic ways by various villages even now. The sixteenth century Bengali authority on the *śāstras*, Raghunandana, assigned the eighth lunar day of the dark fortnight of Phālguna (February-March) to her worship.[10] This is not the kind of decision an erudite Brahman would reach arbitrarily, and it most likely reflected what was then known as 'learned practice' (*śiṣṭācāra*). Apart from the appropriateness of the dark lunar fortnight to the worship of a Goddess who controls death and destruction (Das 1977: 97–99), how did the month of Phālguna come to be chosen for the worship of Śītalā? Since the transmissibility of the smallpox virus is retarded by atmospheric moisture, the data displayed in Figure 2 are what might be expected: average monthly mortality rates from smallpox were at their highest during the hot, dry months from February through May, then declined abruptly in June with the onset of the monsoon rains. The seasonal pattern of smallpox outbreaks is now a fact deeply lodged in Bengali culture. While the earlier Sanskrit name for smallpox—*masūrikā*—has not been forgotten, it has been replaced in common parlance by the term *basanta*, which was earlier simply the name of the spring season. If a term is sought to distinguish smallpox from springtime, it is usually *basanta-roga*, 'spring disease.'[11]

It is not only in the language that the seasonal pattern of smallpox is given clear and explicit recognition. Spring is also the season when the elaborate annual worship of Śītalā is carried out by each village. Raghunandana's date, for practical purposes today, marks the beginning of the period of Śītalā worship in south-western Bengal.[12] And worship continues, in different villages at different times, over the next four months, until the rains begin. The occasions of worship are spread out for a variety of reasons, but the most important ones have to do with the necessity of staging a complete, more or less fully dramatized,

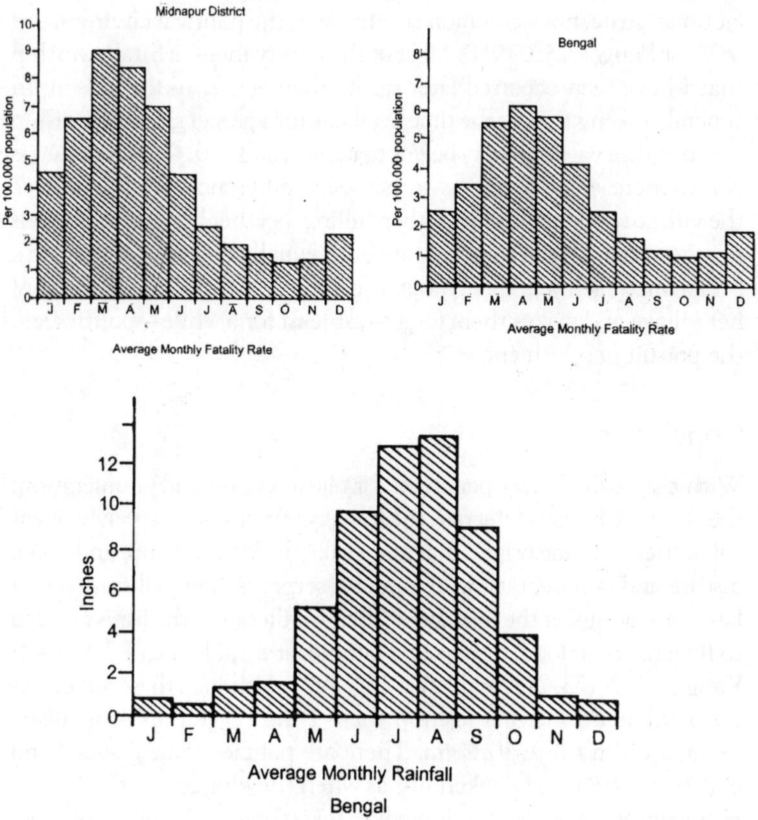

Figure 2. Monthly smallpox mortality rate in relation to rainfall, Bengal and Midnapur Districts, 1912–1931.
Sources: Bengal, Sanitary Commissioner (1912–1931), Department of Agriculture (1912–1931); India, Sanitary Commissioner (1918).

enactment of Nityānanda Cakravartī's version of the Śītalā myth (see pp. 206–209). The singers and musicians who present these performances are specialists who come from other villages and work fairly steadily throughout the smallpox season. They book their engagements in advance, agreeing to perform for one to ten nights, according to the desire of the village and its ability to pay. Payments are made out of contributions subscribed by village families, and willingness to contribute is usually directly linked to the moral well-being of the village at the approach of spring. Moral well-being means freedom from factional strife, not a common condition in the political environment of West Bengal since 1950. Most of the observances of Śītalā worship that I have seen occurred later rather than earlier in the season. In general, it seems that, as the time available for a proper splendid worship diminishes, a vague anxiety begins to mount, and with that anxiousness comes increased willingness to put aside differences for the sake of the village's goddess. Like a mother pulling together her quarreling sons so as to remind them that they are both equally offspring of her body, Śītalā once each year quietly but forcefully draws together the sons of her village and makes them forget—at least for a while—politics and the pursuit of selfish ends.

Conclusion

With a schoolteacher's penchant for classification and enumeration, the classic of Indian statecraft, the *Kauṭiliya Arthaśāstra* lists eight 'great calamities of divine origin' that may strike the kingdom: fire and flood, disease and famine, rats, wild animals, serpents, and evil spirits. In a later passage, under the heading of 'divine afflictions,' the list is reduced to five: fire and flood, disease and famine, and epidemic (4.3.1; 8.4.1; Kangle 1969: 133, 211, and 1972: 262, 397). Although these afflictions are attributed to divine agency, there is no suggestion of fatalistic resignation in the *Arthaśāstra*. There are policies to be pursued and effective actions to be taken just as when the kingdom is threatened by human enemies. Ayurvedic medical texts composed at different times over the career of smallpox in India express a closely related attitude toward that disease, even while they move toward the recognition of the goddess behind it.

Although a disease resembling smallpox—and called by the same name (*masūrikā*) later used for what is undoubtedly smallpox—is mentioned in one of the oldest Indian medical texts, it was not described as serious or as sometimes fatal before the seventh century. By the first half of the eight century, however, medical knowledge of the disease was well established. The etiology of smallpox in these texts is based on a biological theory about diet, heat, and bodily humors used to explain most other ailments. Then, in about the twelfth century, Śītalā, the Goddess of Smallpox, was introduced as a second form of explanation for the disease. The Goddess did not displace the naturalistic medical picture of the disease; a progressively more refined rational therapy was developed at the same time as her worship. But, while the treatment of a person suffering from a disease was the work of a physician, an epidemic was a divine affliction of the whole kingdom against which doctors were helpless.

The mid-eighteenth century, when Śītalā suddenly became so important in south-western Bengal, was a time of turmoil that came perhaps as close to anarchy as most people might ever have known it. What remained of Hindu kingdoms in the region had mostly been converted into agencies of the Mughal revenue-collecting apparatus. As Mughal authority evaporated and, in the ceded districts, the British sought a way of supplanting it, the Maratha cavalry claimed everything it could carry away. It is likely that people displaced from their homes during this period, spread the smallpox virus more rapidly than usual and that widespread malnutrition increased the death rate. The famine of 1770 showed too clearly the fatal interaction of drought, malnutrition, and smallpox: failure of the monsoon in 1769 led to a severe food shortage in 1770; the ensuing smallpox epidemic carried away some millions of the weakened population.

This experience, over two centuries in the past, is registered today in the pre-eminent cult of the villages in the afflicted region. Domestic worship of Śītalā is not prohibited, and it is occasionally performed by a family in which a child is suffering from measles or chickenpox. But the most usual ritual carried out by the village as a collectivity for the benefit of all its residents and not others is the worship of Śītalā. Among fellow villagers, shared awareness of a common fate might persist even when the kingdom had fallen into disunity, and—on the evidence from contemporary village rites—might serve to reunite them when parties and interests from outside the village had led them into disunity. Some of the most significant 'natural facts' about smallpox—its seasonality, the periodicity of epidemics, the method of transmission, and the obtaining of immunity—have been acknowledged in Bengali culture during the epoch of Śītalā's great importance. But Bengalis have subordinated biology to sociology and transformed calamity into community.

8. *Śītalā and the Art of Printing: The Transmission and Propagation of the Myth of the Goddess of Smallpox in Rural West Bengal*[1]

In contemporary rural Bengal, myths[2] and other important social and religious information are communicated in three principal ways: orally, in manuscripts, and in printed books. Anthropological and folklore studies place great value upon the oral tradition—the handing down of narratives orally from generation to generation. Myths and tales learned by an old man years ago at the knee of his aged grandmother, by an adept of some cult, or by an initiate into a secret society are frequently recorded by anthropologists and folklorists for fear that they will soon disappear entirely. Certainly, there is a distinct romantic satisfaction to find oneself the first to have recorded a particular myth or tale; how much more so if one is the last.

Oral transmission and direct learning are the most ancient means by which the continuity of human cultures has been maintained; they are also, in many respects, the least efficient and the most likely to give way to improved methods, of preservation and transmission. Although the oral tradition in India, clearly embodied in the *guru*-disciple relationship, has occupied a place of importance alongside the literary tradition, anthropologists have done relatively little in this field. Major emphasis in the study of Indian mythology has been philological, with the manuscript as the basic source. However, in contemporary rural West Bengal, neither the manuscript nor the oral tradition is as important a means of transmitting myths as is the inexpensive printed book.

The distinction between the 'transmission' and the 'propagation' of a myth that I make here is particularly important in a society such as that of Bengal in which specialization is the rule. I use the term 'transmission' to refer to the processes by which myths are communicated from one generation to the next—to their cultural preservation. In rural Bengal, the transmission of myths is primarily the task of specialists who are necessarily concerned with the completeness, detail, and accuracy of the narratives that they control. Virtually everyone in the society knows the general outlines of the most common myths, but the specialists require full knowledge. By 'propagation' I mean the processes by which myths are communicated to and reinforced in the minds of most members of the society.[3] In rural Bengal, those who propagate the myth are also specialists; thus, propagation is primarily communication from specialists to the nonspecialist public. There is some overlap between these processes, even where specialization is marked. In a less differentiated society than that of rural Bengal, there might be nearly complete identity between the two processes, with transmission taking place almost exclusively in the context of propagation.

Like most culturally significant tasks in Indian society, reading and writing themselves were specialist functions until comparatively recent times. The British conception of education and the demands of the modern job and marriage markets resulted in the fact that nearly half the men and about an eighth of the women in the rural area that I shall be discussing are 'literate.' Among them only a portion can read a religious text. Moreover, among the owners of religious texts, it is likely that a majority do not read them and have never read them; these books (and, in a few cases, manuscripts) lie in bundles before family shrines, where they are worshiped along with the family deities. However, among the specialists in the transmission and propagation of myths, I have seen a few well-worn books that have performed their functions many times over.

In this paper, I shall be concerned with the transmission and propagation of myth in a cluster of eight villages, collectively know as Kelomal, located in the Tamluk Subdivision of Midnapur District, West Bengal. There are, of course, many parts of rural India in which rates of effective literacy are even lower and where printed books are even less commonly available than in this area. Nonetheless, I believe certain generalizations concerning the effects of media upon the transmission and propagation of myths are valid.

Śītalā

A goddess who is thought to control smallpox, and often, a variety of other contagious diseases, is found in almost every part of India. She goes by a wide variety of names in the South;[4] but she is generally called Śītalā, or something derived from it, in the North. Most deities who are as widely worshiped as the smallpox goddess(es) make an early appearance in Indian religious literature and, if their names are not to be found in the Vedic corpus, undergo a personality syncretism with some Purāṇic deity. However, as best as I can determine, Śītalā—with whom I am principally concerned here—appears only twice in brief passages in Sanskrit works of late composition: the *Picchilā Tantra*, a work of such obscurity that it does not even merit mention in Kane's *History of Dharmaśāstra*, and the *Skanda Purāṇa*, a late, largely derivative work (Bhattacharya 1952: 56; Banerjea 1956: 24–25; Mukhopādhyāya 1965: 453–55).[5]

In northern and central India, Śītalā appears primarily in the oral tradition;[6] only in Bengal, so far as I have been able to discover, is there a substantial vernacular literature devoted to her. This literature belongs to a distinctively Bengali class called *maṅgal-kāvya*, which is primarily narrative interspersed with lyrical passages. Edward Dimock (1963: 6) characterizes it as 'village poetry' and says

> The legends which the *maṅgal* poems contain are old; though few of the poems themselves seem to be earlier than the fifteenth century, it is certain that they were passed down orally over many centuries before being put by a particular writer into the form in which we have them today. The dating of a particular version of the poem does not necessarily reflect the dating of the legend itself. (p. 197).

Most of the poems of the *maṅgal* class, which go by a variety of Bengali names, are myths that eulogize particular gods and goddesses and relate their careers, particularly their dealings with mortal men and the establishment of their worship on earth. Some of them concern deities well-known all over South Asia and in ancient Sanskrit literature—Lakṣmī and Sarasvatī, for example. Some deal with gods and goddesses, such as Jagannāth and Caṇḍī, known all over India but of primarily regional importance. The most interesting of these, however, are the *maṅgals* of purely Bengali divinities: Manasā, the goddess of snakes; Dakṣin Rāy, the tiger god; Ṣaṣṭhī, who is responsible for the welfare of children; and Dharmā, the white god. The *Śītalā-maṅgal* belongs to this latter category. Although Śītalā is known throughout the Indo-European speaking portions of South Asia by a name closely resembling that in Bengali and is generally associated with smallpox and other contagious diseases, the myth of the *Śītalā-maṅgal* seems to be peculiarly Bengali and the personality attributed to her in it is apparently not established elsewhere.

Some of the *maṅgal* poems have proved exceptionally valuable to students of social history (e.g., Inden 1967, Dimock and Inden 1969) because they contain such clear representations of their authors' conceptions of the social order. Others have received the attention of historians of religion, because of the insight they provide into ancient and obscure religious belief and practice; or of philologists, because of the archaism of their language. Some of the *maṅgal-kāvyas* have attracted scholars of literature because of the artistic merit of their poetry. The various versions of the *Śītalā-maṅgal*, however, have not received much attention from any scholars: they contain little information of historical importance, are mostly of relatively recent composition, are highly imitative of earlier *maṅgals* in style and content, and, generally, little can be said for them as literature.

The defects of the *Śītalā-maṅgal*, from the perspectives of scholars in other disciplines, create awkward problems for an anthropologist. It would have been most useful to have had a collaborator in the field of Bengali language and literature with competence in the literary manifestation of the goddess. Nevertheless, I have undertaken the study of both the village Śītalā and the Śītalā of the *maṅgal-kāvya*, since the people among whom I worked consider her in both forms.

Śītalā-Maṅgal

Dimock, quoted earlier, mentions that the myths that appear in *maṅgal* poetry forms were doubtless transmitted orally prior to their having been written down. The four manuscript versions of the *Śītalā-maṅgal* about which I know something are clearly derived from different, although connected, oral traditions.[7] The earliest written version of the Śītalā myth appears to be that of one Daivakīnandan (who calls himself Kavi Vallabha) who lived in Burdwan District and wrote during the early part of the seventeenth century (Bhattacharya 1952: 62; D.C. Sen 1954: 321). The two 'dramas' (*pālā*) in his poem are quite different stories from those known to me. The second version is a minor work among a long series of *maṅgal* poems composed by Kṛṣṇaram Dās who lived in a village just to the north of Calcutta; it dates from about 1690.[8] The other two versions, those of Māṅikrām Gāṅgulī and Nityānanda Cakravartī, are of late eighteenth century composition (S. Sen 1960: 140–144). Māṇikrām was a poet of the Rarh country; Nityānanda lived in the deltaic eastern portion of Midnapur district. It is this latter area and Nityānanda's version of the myth that concern me most.

Nityānanda was a courtier of the Rājā of Kāśījoṛā Parganā, named Rājnārāyaṇ, whose age, Āśutoṣ Bhaṭṭācārya (1952: 66–67) tells us, 'cannot be known'.[9] However, as a Bengali zamindār, Rājā Rājnārāyaṇ's name could not fail to appear in connection with a land dispute, in the course of one of which one Kāśīnāth Bābu, Security of his estates, tells us that he inherited his father's zamindārī estate in 1756–57 and died without a legitimate heir in 1770–71 (Sengupta and Bose 1962: 24–26). Thus, the text is clearly dated.

Raghunāthbāṛi, the capital of Kāśījoṛā Parganā, lies about seven miles northwest of a group of villages called Kelomal in which I did fieldwork in 1968–69 and about six miles west of villages in which I worked in 1960–61. One of these latter villages, which I have called Govindapur, was a part of Kāśījoṛā Parganā; it was in Govindapur that I first saw and heard a performance of the *Śītalā-maṅgal*. Like four public performances of the myth that I witnessed in 1969, the 1960 performances were by men of the locality who are specialists of some repute: they are hired by villages and neighborhoods all over the deltaic portion of south-western Bengal to perform for them. They travel to villages in Howrah and Hooghly Districts and in the deltaic portions of their home district, Midnapur. In addition, they are often hired by organizations sponsoring neighborhood pūjās for Śītalā in Calcutta. Śītalā seems to be less important in the villages lying to the west of the delta margin, in western Midnapur and Bankura Districts. Thus, I think that there is a relatively clear territory over which there may be broad similarities in the myth and cult of Śītalā; I may have accidentally selected something near the religious center of the territory as the site of my field research.[10]

The goddess

Śītalā's *dhyāna-mantra*, taken from the *Pacchilā Tantra*, describes her as being of white complexion, sitting on an ass, holding a broom resting on a full pitcher of water from which she sprinkles life-giving water by means of the broom, naked, with a winnowing fan on her head, ornamented with gold and jewels, three-eyed and mitigating the terrible suffering of skin eruptions. A similar description is contained in her *stotram*, taken from her *Skanda Purāṇa* (Mukhopādhyay 1965: 553–55; Bhattacharyya 1952: 56). It is in this form, (although not naked, but dressed as a married woman), seated side-saddle fashion on her *vāhana*, the ass, that she is most commonly represented by the potters who make images for neighborhood pūjās in Calcutta. Such images are established at convenient outdoor locations during the hot, dry weather of May and June, immediately preceding the monsoon. The goddess is worshiped both by a Brāhmaṇ priest and in a public performance; then she is either immersed in some body of water, or her spirit is released from the image by the immersion *mantra*, the lifeless image being allowed to stand where it is, giving a kind of second-class *darśan* to passers-by.

Representations of Śītalā found in the villages of Kelomal have little evident connection with the anthropomorphic figures of Calcutta or with the goddess described in the *dhyāna-mantra* or *stotram*. In Kelomal and the surrounding area, the image of the goddess may be made of stone, metal, or pottery. There are some figurines of brass, mostly modern, that are fully anthropomorphic but that lack any obvious characteristics that might distinguish them from a variety of other goddesses; this is true of the baked pottery representations also, although these seem to be usually older than the brass images.

Stone is not native to the Bengal delta and stone working is not an art for which this area is famous. Stone images of Śītalā are usually crudely shaped. One that I know of amounts to no more than a rough sphere with a slightly raised nose and slightly depressed areas corresponding to eyes. A locally renowned goddess, from the nearby village of Mahisālī, has a brass face with cowry shells for eyes, and a nose and tongue made of sheet silver; her entire face is studded with silver pustules.[11] The stone form in which she originally appeared is concealed behind a silver breast-plate. She has detachable silver hands and legs.

Most of these figures are heavily coated with vermilion (*sindūr*), giving them a crimson complexion quite unlike the white one described in her *mantras*; however, in the case of vegetarian Śītalās, the image is sometimes allowed to remain the color of the material from which it is manufactured. She is invariably dressed as a married woman in red cloth or a red-bordered sari.

Vegetarianism is only one of the characteristics in which the Śītalās of different villages vary one from another; each goddess of standing has a reputation for distinct personality characteristics, likes and dislikes. There are separate, although similar, myths concerning the origin of many images; most of these are as frequently called 'Mother of such-and-such village' as they are called Śītalā. Thus, while Śītalā remains the goddess of smallpox, she is also the *grām*-Caṇḍī for most villages in or near Kelomal. Not all villages, however, have a permanent image of Śītalā; and not all villages that have permanent images have public temples to house them or agricultural land set aside to support them. Where villages do not have images of the goddess, the common village Śītalā pūjā is done *ghaṭ sthāpana*, that is, by invoking the deity into a specially prepared earthen pot, which is immersed at the end of the ceremony.

Śītalā is never worshiped alone. At minimum she is accompanied by her companion, Jvarāsur,[12] the Fever Demon, and by her serving woman Raktābatī, who receive worship secondary to that which Śītalā receives. Where there is a village temple for the goddess, it often also houses other deities, such as Manasā, the goddess of snakes, who cannot be ignored when worship is given to Śītalā, although the worship of other gods and goddesses is clearly secondary to that given the village mother. There is, however, one deity whose worship is essential when a village Śītalā pūjā is held: she is Olābibi,[13] the Muslim goddess of cholera. There are, for practical purposes, no Muslims in any of the eight Kelomal villages. Pūjā is given to Olābibi by a Muslim priest from a neighboring community on behalf of the village that is holding the ceremony. While not so much time or money is devoted to the worship of Olābibi as is given to Śītalā, her pūjā is clearly of some importance.

Olābibi is represented aniconically by an outdoor shrine.[14] In the Kelomal villages, this is usually built of brick plastered with cement and consists of a set of three steps, altogether about two feet high and three feet across, topped by three mounds side by side. Some villages do not have such a permanent shrine but construct one out of mud a few days before the pūjā. In other villages, the cement holding the bricks together has decayed and these are put back together with fresh mud in advance of the ceremony. In nearby villages, some of the Olābibi shrines have four pillars situated on a high mound or under a small arched roof. None of the local Olābibis has a particular reputation or distinct personality; there is, however, one in a village near Raghunāthbāṛi, the capital of Kāśījoṛā Parganā, who is held in great repute, and her shrine is maintained year-round by the Paṭidār (or Paṭuyā) caste, in whose neighborhood it is located. I shall return to a consideration of Olābibi in connection with her myths.

The myth

The reason that only the version of the *Śītalā-maṅgal* written by Nityānanda Cakravartī will be considered here has already been stated. And I shall deal only with the edition published by Tārācā̃d Dās and Sons of Calcutta, which is the edition used by performers of this myth whom I know. This edition first appeared in 1931; however, on the back of the title page, we are informed that 'this book was originally published it 1285 *sāl* (1878–79) by Binodbihārī Śīl in the Māṇik Library. Now we hold exclusive rights.' It seems, then, that Nityānanda's work was printed a little more than a century after he wrote it, an interesting fact in view of the complete absence of 'modern' content in the work, the ferment that was taking place in Bengali intellectual life in Calcutta at the time of its publication, and the significant advance that Western education had made in Bengal by that time. Moreover, the edition of Tārācā̃d Dās and Sons has gone through at least twelve printings; while I do not know the size of those printings, it is clear that many thousands of copies are in circulation and have been in the last ninety years. I mention these facts in order to indicate that while it is a rustic narrative with which I am concerned, it is one that has been of interest to some millions of people over the last two centuries! I give here only a brief summary of the myth of Śītalā as written by Nityānanda.

Nityānanda's *Śītalā-maṅgal* begins with the birth of the goddess and progresses through a series of episodes called *pālās*. The word *pālā* most commonly means 'turn' (as when village families take monthly turns in offering food at the common village Viṣṇu temple), but in this case it means a kind of drama. Performers of the myth assert that they can divide the entire story into ten separate *pālās* to be performed on ten successive nights. They are rarely called upon to do this; most villages cannot afford to hire them for more than two nights and most lay primary emphasis upon one night, on which the performance is carried on until it is nearly dawn. The audience watching such a performance is thought to be keeping a vigil (*jāgaraṇ*) for the goddess; the devotion thus displayed is regarded as generally meritorious. The entire *maṅgal* poem is subtitled

Śītalār jāgaraṇ pālā, 'The Drama of the Vigil of Śītala.' The largest *pālā* in the myth is the *Birāṭ pālā*, in which Sitala humbles the great King of Birāṭ and makes him her worshiper.[15] There are many subordinate *pālās* within the *Birāṭ pālā* so that it can be expanded and contracted in performance and the subordinate *pālās* may be performed on separate nights.

Śītalā was born from the cooled remains of the fire in which the heavenly King Nahuṣa offered a sacrifice in order to obtain a son. She appeared as a beautiful young woman with a winnowing fan on her head. Brahmā, the Creator, asked who she was, and she said that she did not know. Therefore, he named her Śītalā, 'The Cool One,' because she had been born from the cool ashes of the sacrificial fire.[16] He directed her to go to the land of mortal men, where she would be worshiped as a goddess. He provided her with various kinds of lentils (which later become the means by which she gives pox to those who humiliate or reject her on earth). She requested two boons from Brahmā before she began her earthly adventure: that her worship first be performed in heaven, so that mortals would know how to do it, and that she be given a companion. Brahmā sent her to *Śiva* to present these requests. Śiva created the mighty Fever Demon, Jvarāsur, from the perspiration on his forehead. The Fever Demon so terrified the gods and goddesses that they asked Viṣṇu to destroy him. Viṣṇu sent his discus, which cut the monster in three parts and killed him; Śiva restored him to life but left him with three heads, six arms, six legs, etc.

Śītalā, dressed as an old Brāhmaṇ woman, and with the terrific Fever Demon disguised as a child, went to the court of the mighty Indra. There she had to afflict all the gods and goddesses with smallpox and fever before they performed her pūjā. Śiva told those who had insulted Śītalā of the tragic error they had made; they immediately worshiped Śītalā and became her devotees, whereupon all were cured of their various maladies.

Accompanied by the Fever Demon, the goddess began her adventures on earth, principally in the kingdom of Birāṭ. She first appeared before the king, a devout Śaivite, in a horrible dream containing explicit portents of the destruction to come if he did not worship her. This dream, however, did not break his single-minded devotion to Śiva. There follows, in the narrative, a long interlude in which Śītalā marshalled her resources, in the form of poxes and other communicable diseases of far greater variety than the Western taxonomist of pathologies can muster. Here also appear Śītalā's vehicle, the ass, and her serving woman Raktābatī ('She who possesses the blood,' one of the names of smallpox).

Śītalā's first confrontation in the kingdom of Birāṭ was with a boatman named Nimā, who insisted that she pay the fare for a ferry ride from her stock of lentils. She sent him home with some of her 'peas of eternal life'; his sons found these exceptionally delectable, but six days after they had eaten them, they were seized with smallpox and died. Nimā was on the point of taking his own life when Śītalā, still in disguise, revealed herself to him and said that she could restore his sons to life. She turned their corpses to stone. Nimā and his wife took the stone bodies home and, eventually, when the Birāṭ Rājā worshipped Śītalā, they were restored to life.

Next, Śītalā spread the devastation of her diseases throughout the entire kingdom, selling lentils in the markets. She killed the king's own sons, the last three of whom he made strenuous efforts to hide from her, and nine lakhs of his subjects. The king's principal wife, Sudeṣṇā, and his youngest son's wife remained devotees of Śītalā throughout this period of trial. Eventually, the king offered worship to the goddess and Śītalā pūjā was done, with blood sacrifices, in every house in the kingdom. The goddess then restored her victims to life.

In the next 'drama' a sādhu and physician from the Birāṭ kingdom, Debdas Datta, at Śītalā's command and under her protection, undertook a long journey to bring the goddess's golden pot to the Birāṭ court. He visited a number of lands, both known (Vṛndāvana, Banaras, and Gayā) and imaginary Māyādeś and Pākisā. Finally, there is a short *pālā* called *Gokul pālā* in which the inhabitants of Gokul are humbled by the goddess, who saved Kṛṣṇa and Balarām themselves from smallpox.

This is an outline of the Śītalā myth as presented in the most commonly used printed text. In performance, some sections are expanded and embroidered upon, others are de-emphasized, and some are omitted entirely. Each group of specialist performers attempts to create a distinctive performance of the myth. Local references and the names of local persons are inserted in amusing contexts. And Vaiṣṇava *kīrtans* that are appropriate in mood to various parts of the story are sung as a kind of interlude at many points, according to the length of performance desired. The basic line of the story and the specific actions related, however, are highly consistent from one performance to the next. By contrast with this consistency, I examine two versions of the Olābibi myth.

The Olābibi myth

The first version of the *Olābibi Gan* (song of Olābibi) that I relate was performed by a group under the leadership of Śrī Kuñja Bihāri Nandi, Utkal *śrenī* Brāhmaṇ of Āmgechyā village.

Nārāyaṇ decided that he should have worshipers among Muslims as he did among Hindus and decided that the best way to manage this was to be born a Muslim. The Bādshāh's daughter lived a secluded life, as became a Muslim woman of high birth. She saw only her mother and a few courtiers, the sixteen serving women who constantly attended her, and her religious teacher who came regularly to read 'kitāb and *Korān*' to her. One day the teacher told her that she had heard all of the Muslim scriptures and that it would benefit her more to have a bath (*ghosal*) in a river. She asked her mother's permission to leave the palace for a bath. This was an alarming prospect but the mother consented with the provision that the entire path from the houses to the banks of the Yamunā be enclosed in cloth and that the sixteen serving women go with her.

The arrangements were made and the girls were playing in the water when a lotus came floating past. The lotus was Nārāyaṇ himself, transformed by his *māyā*, or power of illusion. The princess sniffed the lotus and, unknown to anyone, the seed of Nārāyaṇ entered her body as the perfume of the flower. Later they returned to the palace and, as the days went by, it became increasingly clear to the princess that she was pregnant. First the serving women learned of this; then her mother found her crying and discovered her secret. Her mother questioned her closely but could find no connection with a man through which the girl might have become pregnant. The serving women urged the queen to arrange the girl's marriage as quickly as possible. The queen said that she had long been requesting the Bādshāh to give her in marriage but he thought that there was no groom suitable for his daughter.

The queen went to the Bādshāh and told him of their misfortune. He was shocked. She asked him again to arrange for the girl's marriage and criticized him for not having done it long ago. The Bādshāh summoned his chief minister (*ujir*) to discuss the problem. He proposed to the minister that he have the girl killed outright but the minister warned him of the great sin of killing women, Brāhmaṇs, and cows. The minister went to the princess and again questioned her closely. She told him the story of the lotus and also suggested that there might have been a man watching from a distance as she bathed. The minister discounted these possibilities and returned to the Bādshāh without any explanation of the mysterious pregnancy. The Bādshāh had become concerned about his reputation in his kingdom and asked the minister what he could do. The minister suggested that the princess be confined to prison with sentries and with thirty-two serving women to be with her constantly. 'When the child is born, we can examine his face and determine which man it resembles; the father shall be punished with death,' the minister concluded.

The scene is shifted to the prison. Nārāyaṇ spoke to the princess from within her womb. He requested that she give him a tiny piece of cloth with a small hole in it so that he might not be born naked. The princess was understandably astounded to hear a voice coming from her belly and told him of her unhappiness. He said, 'Well, I know everything, but for the time being I need a small piece of cloth.' She tore a piece from the end of her sari. Immediately, the labor pains began; the child was born but disappeared before the mother could even see it. (The performers here interposed the information that 'this is *māyā* [the illusory power of a deity], this is the *māyā* of a god, this is the *māyā* of Nārāyaṇ.') Only a flower lay on the ground at the place of delivery.

The serving women immediately reported to the king the birth and strange disappearance of the princess's child. The furious king summoned his minister, upbraided him for having proposed the unsuccessful plan, and ordered him to take the princess into a jungle filled with wild animals where she would be killed. The minister did as he was ordered and abandoned the princess in the jungle without food or shelter. She began to lament: '*Hāi* Āllāh. I was raised in the seclusion of the *zenānā*. Now I am alone in the jungle surrounded by wild animals. Yet, I believe that I am free from sin.' Immediately, Olābibi appeared and addressed her as 'Dear mother.' [Here, again, is the deity's *māyā*, the male god Nārāyaṇ appearing as the female Olābibi.] Olābibi described herself as the princess's child and told her that she could suffer no harm, even in so dangerous a place, because she was under the protection of Olābibi.

When the minister had left with the princess, Olābibi had struck down his son with cholera. Olābibi reappeared in the Bādhshāh's court and told the minister that she could restore his sons's life if he would worship her with an offering of *śiraṇi.*[17] He quickly did this and the son was restored to life. The minister took to the Bādshāh some of the *prasād* of his offering to Olābibi. The Bādshāh enquired about the source of this *śirani* and the minister related the story of his meeting with Olābibi and his son's restoration to life. The Bādshāh was contemptuous and said, 'Olābibi is a goddess of the Bengalis and the beggars.' The minister, however, said that he would continue to worship her.

Next, Olābibi presented herself to the Bādshāh; she asked him to worship her. He told her that he did not recognize her and demanded proof that she was the powerful goddess she claimed to be. 'There is a *jagaddal pāthar* [immovably heavy stone that weights down the universe] in our pilgrimage place at Mecca. That stone is suspended with no support. I would like you to show that stone to me here,' the Bādshāh challenged her. Olābibi said that she would bring it to him and then instantly produced the stone. The Bādshāh acknowledged Olābibi's divine status, then asked her who she was and how she came there. She described herself as the child of his unmarried daughter. The Bādshāh then realized the significance of the earlier events and worshipped Olābibi. 'From that time,' the performers concluded, 'the pūjā of Olābibi became prevalent in the *Kaliyuga*.'

I relate a second version of the Olābibi myth principally in order to show the great variety among the several versions. This one was performed by a group from Ilkā village in Mahishadal Thānā under the direction of Śrī Śakti Pada Miśra, a Byāsakta *śrenī* Brāhmaṇ. Kṛṣṇa was standing beneath his heavenly *kadamba* tree when a *Rākṣasī* (anthropophagous demoness) appeared before him. She instantly resolved herself into four sisters, through her *māyā*. They were Olā ('She who comes down,' i.e., the discharge of the bowels in cholera), Uṭhā ('She who comes up,' i.e., the vomiting in cholera; *Olāuṭhā* together means cholera), Hasan (a smile), and Campak (the flower of a magnolia-like tree). Kṛṣṇa asked the four sisters what work they would do. Olā said. 'I will cause diarrhea and, together, Olāuṭhā will cause death.' Uṭha said, 'I will kill with a glance.' Hasan said, 'I will kill with a smile.' And Campak said, 'When I smile together with Hasan, all will be killed.'

Kṛṣṇa agreed that Olā and Uṭhā could go into the world of mortal men but he required Hasan and Campak to remain behind. He told

Olā and Uṭhā that they might go wherever the name of Hari (Viṣṇu) was not heard, but that they could not go where *Hari Nām Kīrtan* was sung. He charged them to remember his command 'in the name of Allah' (*āllār dohāi*) and said that this was Allah's wish but that no one would know of it except them.

Throughout the *Satyayuga*, the *Tretāyuga*, and the *Dvāparayuga*, when men were religious, Olā and Uṭhā could find no opportunities to use their destructive power. But in the present age (*Kaliyuga*), when:

> the institutions of caste do not remain
> and people don't respect their *gurus*;
> proper social distinctions do not remain.
> Then it will cease to rain,
> jackals will climb trees, tigers will give birth to goats,
> girls of the Oilpresser caste will become princesses
> and leather-workers will become kings;
> Hunters will become ministers
> and Caṇḍalas will carry the umbrellas of Brāhmaṇs.

In this age, Olā and Uṭhā found employment. They went first to the Bādshāh and asked him to offer them worship. He refused to acknowledge their divinity. Then they went out into his kingdom; they found two cowherd boys playing in a field and offered them sweets containing the poison of cholera. The boys died immediately.

When the boys did not return home with the cattle, the parents began to follow the cattle tracks and found their two dead sons in the field. Olā and Uṭhā appeared before the sorrowful parents and said that if the parents could obtain worship for them, they would restore their sons to life. The parents asked, 'Who are you?' 'We are Olābibi,' the sisters said. 'We can bring your sons back to life if the Bādshāh gives us pūjā.' The parents went quickly to the Bādshāh and told him their story. The Bādshāh agreed that if Olābibi could restore the boys to life, then he would give her (or them) pūjā. The parents related this to Olābibi, who sprinkled a little water on the bodies of the boys, re-animating them. Then the Bādshāh, the parents, and all of the Bādshāh's subjects offered worship to Olābibi.

The remarkable differences between these two versions of the creation and deeds of Olābibi are paralleled by considerable discrepancies in the identification of the mythical figures represented by the three (or four) mounds that stand atop the Olābibi shrines. People simply did not agree about the identities of these mounds; numerous conceptions were presented as authoritative. These discrepant versions of the Olābibi myth were recorded by hand in school notebooks; this, no doubt, is what remains of the Bengali manuscript (*pũthi*) tradition in an age of cheap printing and widespread literacy. I shall return to the problem of discrepancy and coherence in mythology after considering the performances of these myths.

The propagation of the myth

I have postponed explaining what is meant by the 'performance of a myth' until this point because performance is a complex event and it is the myth rather than its presentation that primarily concerns me. Moreover, I am omitting entirely any consideration of the Brāhmaṇical ritual that is performed along with the myth. The performance of pūjā to Śītalā by a Brāhmaṇ priest on behalf of the village is theoretically just as important as the performance of the myth. It is the performance of the myth, however, that excites public attention and that provides the principal stimulus for the organizing of the ceremony. The organization of a factionalized village to hold such a ritual, despite its obvious importance for the community,. is a difficult problem and a fascinating example of an occasion in which high normative coherence embraces embattled camps and unites them in a common effort. All of these considerations will have to be left aside now, however, and I turn instead to the organization of the performing group which is hired by the village to present the myth to them.

What I have called 'the performing group' is known as *śayāl gān dal*. *Śayāl* means something like 'traveling about for pleasure,' *gān* means 'song,' and *dal* means 'party' or 'group,' so that the entire expression means approximately 'a party of traveling singers'; it has a happy or positive connotation. What I have called the 'performance' is known in the local idiom as *śayāl gān*, and is a pleasurably anticipated occasion for all villagers, but especially for youngsters and women.

A *śayāl gān* may go on for up to ten days. However, I have seen none longer than two days; most last only one, at least most did in 1969, after two or three years of especially bad crops. The expense involved in presenting *śayāl gān* goes up rapidly when the performers stay for several days: not only do their fees rise proportionately, but they must be housed and fed at village expense. Although a contract is made with the entire *dal*, through its leader, for the performance desired, the cost is usually from Rs 3 to Rs 5 per member for an afternoon and evening's performance, plus a meal, breakfast, and *biṛis* to smoke. The *dals* that I saw ranged from ten to twenty-five members, so the total expenditure for this part of the ritual is very large from the perspective of a poverty-stricken Bengali villager.

Most of the members of the *dals* that I saw were Māhiṣyas, members of the numerically dominant agricultural caste of the locality; and so were most of the members of their audiences. Although she is equally 'Mother' of all villagers, Śītalā is most closely associated with the Māhiṣyas, and what are called 'village affairs' are primarily Māhiṣya-organized and controlled, even in villages where other high-ranking castes are economically and politically dominant. A few members of some *dals* were caste Vaiṣṇavas, and the leaders of two of the four *dals* were Brāhmaṇs, one of the Byāsakta *śrenī*, which does the household pūjās of the Māhiṣyas, and the other of Utkal *śrenī*, a group, said to originate in Orissa, that provides priests for some collective Māhiṣya ceremonies and cooks for major feasts where members of several different castes are to be fed. There were no members of high-ranking Brāhmaṇ or Kāyastha castes in any of these groups.

Śayāl gān, which, for practical purposes, means 'Śītalā's song,' and *Olābibir gān* ('Olabibi's song') are, as their names imply, sung. A performance has the quality of an opera, complete with arias, duets, trios, choruses (none of these, unfortunately, harmonized), and recitative. There are also, as I mentioned before, interludes of Vaiṣṇava *kīrtans*, selected to match the mood in the story at the points in which they are introduced. The minimum musical accompaniment for any of these *gāns* is the *khol* and *karatāl*. The *khol* is a distinctively Bengali form of *mṛdaṅga* with a pottery base, small and light enough to be suspended around the player's neck by a strap and danced with in delightful stylized steps. The *khol* is basically an accompaniment for Vaiṣṇava *kīrtan*, although it is played in almost any kind of religious music (and never with secular music). The *karatāl* is a pair of small brass cymbals that also invariably accompany Vaiṣṇava devotional singing and are used in other religious music, as well as in some secular music. Most of the *dals* also have a harmonium, about which the less said the better, from my point of view. Some use bamboo flutes as additional accompaniment and one group, which did a *yātrā*-style performance of the myth, even used a cornet (which members of the group referred to as a 'brass flute').

Almost all *śayāl gān* performances are done in ordinary dress, with the lead singer—usually the man taking the part of Śītalā—distinguished by a black yak-tail fly-whisk (*cāmar*) which he carries constantly. The fly-whisk is used to honor Olābibi during the afternoon offering of pūjā to her, and to honor Śītalā during the *ārati*, or display of lights before her image, in the early evening. The fly-whisk is thought to acquire some special power from these uses as well, perhaps, as from its being carried by someone representing Śītalā herself. Thus, in groups that have Brāhmaṇ members, the Brāhmaṇ is also often the lead singer and may be the only one to handle the fly-whisk. However, in other *dals* the fly-whisk is constantly handled by Māhiṣyas and is even used by them to give blessings (by laying it on the back of the neck) to members of the audience.

One of the *dals* that I saw—the one that gave by far the most persuasive performance of the *Śītalā-maṅgal*—used costumes and elaborate props, just as is done in the Bengali *yātrā*. Members of the 'orchestra' and 'chorus' did not wear costumes, but all of the principal players—Śītalā, Jvarāsur, the ass, Nimā the boatman and his wife, the Birāṭ Rājā and his chief queen Sudeṣṇā, and Debdās Datta, the *sādhu* and physician, as well as a number of minor characters, were costumed. Some of the actors played several roles and the Fever Demon doubled as an instrumentalist.

In ordinary *śayāl gān* performances there is usually a degree of dramatization that goes naturally with the fact that each singer enacts the role of only one character in each episode. Dramatization went much further than usual in the costumed performance, however, so that the major events in Nityānanda's *Śītalā-maṅgal* were communicated to the audience in an exceptionally persuasive manner. When the performance concluded, at about 2 a.m., many people, including almost all of the young married women with children in their arms, rushed forward to take dust from the feet of Śītalā. The goddess in this case happened to be a young Māhiṣya man who had taken over the role from a Brāhmaṇ, originally selected to play the part. This young Māhiṣya may have had the experience of having the dust reverentially taken from his feet on only a few previous occasions—perhaps by his younger sisters or by the young children of his elder sisters when they visited his house. When it happened after his performance of Śītalā, he was evidently nonplussed at first; but he soon began to move among the audience, accepting reverence and allowing the dust to be taken from his feet, giving blessings (by the laying on of his fly-whisk), and accepting small coins as *dakṣiṇā* (the fee of a Brāhmaṇ). This event was, in my estimation, the clearest indication of the effectiveness of this oral and dramatic method of propagating the myth of Śītalā that I saw. But the other forms of *śayāl gān*, although less dramatically effective, are nonetheless persuasive reminders of what everyone already knows.

The transmission of the myth

The propagation of the myths of Śītalā and Olābibi is done entirely through the oral and dramatic medium. Three media, however, are employed in transmitting the myths: Oral transmission, handwritten manuscripts, and printed material. Oral transmission takes place in the context of the *guru*-disciple relationship and in the somewhat more permissive version of this relationship that exists within the *śayāl gān dal* between the leader (*mālik*) of the group and its members. The leader has the role of artistic director for his company; he determines which portions of the myths are to be sung, which recited or enacted in dialogue, and which ommitted entirely.

Since each company attempts to make its performance distinctive and especially attractive, so that they will be employed more frequently, there is a good deal of variation in the presentation of those sections of the myth that are sung and great differences among *dals* in the language used in the songs.

Except for the fact that a manuscript may outlive a particular *guru*, in Bengal the transmission of myths by handwritten manuscripts is almost as private as the *guru*-disciple relationship itself. Manuscripts are generally transmitted either through the teacher-pupil lineage or through the family. Thus, discrepant versions of a myth, such as the *Olābibi gān*, may persist side by side over sustained periods of time, whether they are eighteenth century manuscripts, carefully written on country-made paper, or twentieth century ones, hastily written with blotting fountain pens in school notebooks.

A manuscript may have been used to teach hundreds of performers or may have lain untouched at a family shrine, receiving only ritual attention; in either case it exists apart from its author and so, while basically a private thing, it transmits its contents in an impersonal way. A greater degree of 'dissociation' has occurred than would be the case in oral transmission.

Edward Sapir (1949: 566) speaks of varying degrees of 'dissociation' between a symbol and 'its original context.' All of the words of any language, of course, are symbols in that they stand in a purely arbitrary relationship to the things, events, and relations to which they refer. Thus, it is sensible to say that the word, as a symbol, is dissociated from its referent in that the two bear no necessary or inherent relation to one another. There is an additional sense of 'dissociation' between spoken and written words. The primary context of utilization of linguistic symbols is in speech, that is, in direct communication between speaker and hearer; the ideal form of verbal communication is conversation, in which the responses of one person indicate to the other whether or not he is communicating what he intends. When words are written with the intention of communicating (as opposed to being written for mnemonic purposes), the dissociation is not only between symbol and referent and between the primary and secondary contexts of utilization, but also between the 'encoder' and the 'decoder' of the message. The reader is ordinarily deprived of the capacity to check the intention of the writer, although such a check is an inherent part of conversational use of language.

The Indian manuscript tradition is partially free from the communication problem inherent in writing. Insofar as the contents of a manuscript are taught by a preceptor to his disciples and, in recopying, are made more intelligible to succeeding generations of readers, the manuscript may be thought of as having a mnemonic function. Since manuscripts contain sacred knowledge, they are intended for specialist use and inevitably have esoteric aspects. In India, sacred knowledge is thought of as being powerful in itself; it should be made available only in limited degree to women and Śūdras; the most esoteric aspects should be restricted to those who have been initiated by a particular *guru*.

Printing and publishing completes the dissociation between writer and reader. The marketing of printed books is absolutely contradictory to the idea of private knowledge, sacred or profane. The technology of printing implies the existence of a large enough literate population to constitute a 'mass' market (although the definition of 'mass' is obviously quite variable). The market, with the requirement that goods be displayed and attractively priced, and the anonymous relationship that exists between buyer and seller, means that esoterism cannot be preserved.[18] And the 'mass' characteristic of the product means that it must be standardized.

Standardization is not a common characteristic of Bengali manuscripts, however devoutly it may have been sought by writers and copyists. While the number of manuscripts of myths in Bengal can never have been very large, relative to the number of printed books that now exist, the lack of concord between any two of them supposedly relating the same material is so customary that scholars take it for granted. As I mentioned much earlier, the four versions of the *Śītalā-maṅgal* that are known to Bengali literary scholars have little in common with one another than the goddess herself.[19] These were, of course, written by different men, at different times, and in different parts of Bengal. So long as they existed solely in manuscript and oral form only local tradition caused one to predominate over another.

Dimock and Ramanujan (1964) have examined a number of different texts of the *Manasā Maṅgal* and found that while they were written in quite different places at different times, they share a large common core. This is particularly true of the very popular episodes concerning the humbling of Cā̃d Sadāgar, the merchant prince, the killing of his youngest son Lakṣmindar, by one of Manasā's snakes, and his restoration to life through the devotion of his wife, Behulā. In other words, there was a degree of standardization in the Manasā myths current in Bengal prior to their publication.

The printing of Nityānanda's *Śītalā-maṅgal* changed the balance among the various Śītalās, even though several publishers issued ostensibly different popular editions. It seems possible that printing the myth in its various versions would have the potential of diversifying as well as standardizing it. I have examined in a cursory way three cheap editions of the *Manasā Maṅgal* that were available in Bengali book stalls in 1968 and 1969; they appear to bear the same relationship to the originals as do *Reader's Digest* condensed books. While the author's language seems to be largely preserved, divergent *pālās* have been eliminated so that the congruity among the various versions is increased. Thus, the effect of printing and publishing for a relatively large public has been the standardizing of Bengali mythology and, probably, the creating of a possible 'orthodoxy' that may prevent further mythological development. Numerous copies of inexpensive *maṅgal* books, like museum reproductions of fossil animals, will remain to remind us of the past age of autonomy and creativity in the religion of rural Bengal.

End Notes

Chapter 2
Vaiṣṇavism and Islām in Rural Bengal

1. I am indebted to a number of people for suggestions on the earlier version of this paper. I am most grateful, however, to Tarasish Mukhopadhyay both for his collaboration in the field research and for his contributions to this paper. The Foreign Area Fellowship Program made possible the fieldwork on which this paper is based and the Asian Studies Center at Michigan State University enabled me to write it.

Chapter 3
Understanding a Hindu Temple in Bengal

1. Fieldwork was done in eight villages, known collectively as Kelomal, in Tamluk Subdivision during 1968–9 with support from a Fulbright-Hays Senior Research Fellowship. For many of my own 'understandings' of Bengali Hinduism I am grateful to Dr Tarashis Mukhopadhyay who has been my colleague and close friend throughout my work in Bengal. I am indebted to Ronald Inden for many of the ideas contained in this essay, and particularly for insight into the structure of Hindu kingship.
2. Accounts of the career of Chaitanya, based on sources composed by his followers in the years after his death, are readily available (e.g., De 1961; Kennedy 1925).
3. The notion of a 'dominant orientation' should not be understood as

excluding the worship of non-Vaishnava deities, including goddesses who have a terrifying aspect. The goddess Sitala, who is considered mistress of smallpox and other diseases, is particularly an object of worship by Mahishyas (see pp. 105ff).

4. Continuity and identity between the old *tulasī* pedestal and the new Hari temple is often marked by the inclusion of some part of the pedestal, such as the figure of Garuda, in the temple. Consecration of the temple seems to have the effect of deconsecrating the pedestal, which may thereafter be ignored.
5. Before *caturbhuja* he said '*caturvyūha* Narayana,' referring to the four embodied manifestations of Vishnu as Krishna, Balarama, Pradyumna, and Aniruddha (or alternatively, the manifestations of Purushottama as Vasudeva, Samkarshana, Pradyumna, and Aniruddha), thus offering the possibility of yet another exegesis of the temple. However, he said no more about this subject.
6. I think his learned reference here is to a certain Rukmangada in the Naradiya Purana. He was a king of Kalinga (present day Orissa and northern Andhra Pradesh) who decreed that anyone in his kingdom under eighty years of age who ate food on Vishnu's day (*ekādaśī*, the eleventh day of each lunar fortnight) would be liable to corporal punishment, fine or banishment (Kane 1930–62, v, 5: 892); see also Brihannaradiya-Purana in *Hazra* 1958: 309–45). My informant proceeded to specify that the temple should receive worship on the eleventh or twelfth day of the lunar fortnight, and not, as the common people did, on full-moon night.
7. The proposition that, in Bengali Hindu culture, no sharp distinction is drawn between the 'natural' substance of a person's body and his 'moral' code for conduct is developed more extensively in chapters 1 and 2 of Inden and Nicholas 1977.

Chapter 4
The Village Mother in Bengal

1. I am grateful to Raymond Fogelson and Ronald Inden for a critical reading of this manuscript, and to fellow panelists and discussants at the session of the 1975 American Anthropological Association meeting that dealt with mother worship for contributions to its final form.
2. In the nineteenth century this caste was most often designated Kaibartta; it included both cultivators and fishermen. Around the turn of the century the cultivators ceased giving daughters in marriage to fishermen and began referring to themselves as Mahishya, a name indicative of Shudra origins superior to those of the Kaibarttas. There are now two

distinct castes, and the fishermen call themselves Rajbangshi, 'Of Royal Clan.'

3. Although it has its roots in the Mughal period, the zamindari (*zamindār* ='land-holder') system is a product of British revenue administration. To simplify somewhat, a zamindar was responsible for the collection of taxes from a group of villages and for the annual payment of a fixed sum to the government. Such persons were usually high caste Hindus and filled a 'royal' role in local society.
4. Pargiter made a complete English translation of the *Mārkaṇḍeya Purāṇa*. There are several translations of the 'Caṇḍī' portion of this Purāṇa; the copiously annotated one by Agrawala (*Devī Māhātmyam*), which includes the full Sanskrit text, is useful. Although the myth is read aloud as part of the worship of the goddess, the procedures of worship are contained in manuals (*paddhati*) derived from three other Puranas, the *Devī*, *Kālikā*, and *Vṛhan-nandīkeśvara*. It is also customary in certain households to include a reading of a sixteenth-century Bengali myth of the goddess, the *Kavikaṅkana-Caṇḍī* composed by Mukundaram.
5. A discussion of Shitala mythology and translations of two versions of her myth are available in Chapter 6. 'The Fever Demon.' See also Bang (1973).
6. I have presented a brief discussion of Olābibi and her mythology in Chapter 8.
7. This is an eighteenth-century text composed by Nityānanda Cakravartī, who lived only a few miles from Kelomal. His version, much more detailed than any of the others, was printed in Calcutta in 1878 and is still in print (*Bṛhat Śītalā Maṅgal*).
8. This is a brief summary of a complex symbol. For a fuller discussion see Inden and Nicholas, *Kinship in Bengali Culture*.
9. Although I have not yet been able to document this contention fully, Sarkar and I have shown that the printing of Shitala's myth first took place during a great malaria epidemic in the nineteenth century. (Chapter 6).
10. For north India see Freed and Freed, 'Two Mother Goddess Ceremonies'; for Nepal see Nepali, *The Newars*; for central India see Babb, *The Divine Hierarchy*; for Rajasthan see Carstairs, 'Patterns of Religious Observance'; for Punjab see Singh, 'Religion in Daleke'; for Malwa see Mathur, 'The Meaning of Hinduism'; for Gujarat see Naik, 'Religion of the Anavils'; for Nagpur District, Maharashtra, see Junghare, 'Songs of Shitala.' For a village in Poona District, however, Orenstein discusses the worship of a smallpox goddess called 'Marai' (1969: 199). This name is similar to that of Mariamma, the most common name of the smallpox goddess

in Tamil country, according to Whitehead, *Village Gods of South India*, pp. 31, 32. He found a Sitalamma in Telugu country, but she was identified there as a water goddess (p. 23).

11. Translated from Cakravarti, *Śītalā Maṅgal*, pp. 13, 14.

Chapter 5
Caṇḍī

1. For the dating and provenance of the *Mārkaṇḍeya Purāṇa* and the *Caṇḍī* see Pargiter (1904: viii–xx), Agrawala (1963: iv–xi), and O'Flaherty (1975: 17–18).
2. I have followed the usual Bengali practice (observed elsewhere in India as well) of numbering the chapters 1–13 rather than 81–93. However, I have not been able to follow another custom, which is to count the verses of the text so as to make them number 700. The *Bhāgavad-gītā*, probably the most widely read of works used in solitary religious observances, contains 700 Sanskrit couplets. In an effort to place the *Caṇḍī* on a footing with the *Gītā*, it is commonly enumerated so as to include 700 'verses,' and is then designated the *Durgā-saptaśatī*, '700 [Verses] of Durgā.' However, many of the 'verses' identified in these versions are nothing more than such unversified statements as *ṛṣir uvāca*, 'the sage said.' Even counting all such unmetrical inclusions, a total of 700 'verses' is not achieved, and a number of couplets must be divided to produce the desired total. Authorities differ on where these breaks should be made, so I have followed the scholarly if less pious enumeration of Agrawala (1963), which produces only 577 verses.
3. The Sanskrit version in Bengali characters and 700 verses (Mukhopādhyāya Bhaktibhūṣaṇa 1375) is closest to that generally used in Bengal. Two Bengali monks of the Ramakrishna order have published the Sanskrit text as used in Bengal, but in Nāgarī characters, together with English translations (Jagadīśvarānanda 1955; Tattwananda 1962); the English of Jagadīśvarānanda is the best of any I have seen. Pargiter (1904) did a complete translation of the *Mārkaṇḍeya Purāṇa*, including the *Devī-māhātmya* (pp. 465–522). The modern scholarly edition of Agrawala (1963), whose enumeration of verses I have followed, contains a learned introduction and lengthy annotations. A recent French translation by the Sanskritist Jean Varenne (1975) is noteworthy not only for scholarship and elegance of language but also for its inclusion of a complete Romanized Sanskrit text with *sandhis* broken, which is invaluable to anyone who, like me, is an amateur in Sanskrit studies. Two scholarly English-language anthologies of Hindu myths contain translations of episodes from the *Caṇḍī*: that of Dimmitt and van

Buitenen (1978: 232–240) includes 1.45–53, 61–78; 2.1–68; 3.20–41; 7.1–23, and 12.29–37; O'Flaherty (1975: 248–249) has 3.20–41. Versions of the *Caṇḍī* narrative are repeated in many of the later Purāṇas, and these are sometimes cited by Bengalis as aids in the exegesis of the Mārkaṇḍeya version, but none of the others is used in worship. The sixteenth-century Bengali *Kavikaṅkana Caṇḍī* is used in the Ghoṣ Bāṛi Durgā Pūjā in Kelomal.

Chapter 6

The Fever Demon and the Census Commissioner: Śītalā Mythology in Eighteenth and Nineteenth Century Bengal

We wish to thank Paul Greenough, David, Curley, Paul Finkleman, and Raymond Fogelson for their painstaking reading and criticism of an earlier version of this paper.

1. Hunter 1897: 28–29.
2. We cannot deal with the characteristics of this type of poetry here. Good discussions are available in Dimock 1963: 197–200, and Clark 1967: 9–17.
3. The manuscript is no. 'c' 5675 in the Library of the Asiatic Society of Bengal. See Satyanārāyaṇ Bhaṭṭācārya 1958: iv–vi. Despite its early date, it consists of three *pālās* ('dramas') that resemble those in the eighteenth century works: (1) *Jagāti Madan Dās Pālā* (2) *Kāzi Pālā*, and (3) *Hṛsikeś Sādhur Upakhyān*. Krṣṇarām lived in village Nimita near Saptagrām, about eight miles north of modern Calcutta.
4. Harideva's *Śītalā Maṅgal* is known from four manuscripts in the Library at Shantiniketan. See Mandal 1960: 175–272; Mandal 1963: 406–07.
5. This text is known to us from a manuscript of twelve leaves, collected from a village near Tamluk, and now in the possession of Ralph Nicholas. See the translation pp. 132–148.
6. This text is known from a manuscript in the Library at Shantiniketan published in Mandal 1966: 283–294. See the translation pp. 148–165.
7. These are in two different manuscripts in the Library at Shantiniketan published in Mandal 1966: 254–270.
8. A possible sixth mid-eighteenth century composer of a *Śitalā Maṅgal* is a poet known only as Śaṅkar and represented by three fragmentary manuscripts in the Shantiniketan Library. See Mandal 1958: 365–66, 371–72; and Mandal 1963: 381. In one fragment a merchant is said to worship Śītalā with plentiful offerings; the other concerns one Raghu Datta, also a merchant and a worshipper of Maheśvara.
9. We have encountered references to an article by Vyomokeś Mustāphi,

in the *Sāhitya Pariṣad Patrika*, vol. 5, pp. 32–70, that may be based on a manuscript but we have been unable to locate a copy of this article. Mandal (1952), mentions the existence of eight pages of a manuscript of Nityānanda's text in the Library at Shantiniketan.

10. This is found in the India Office Library, Vernacular Tracts Bengali no. 1775.
11. We cannot rule out the possibility that Nityānanda's *Śītalā Maṅgal* had been translated into Oriya but the evidence is clear that it was written in Bengali. However, the close similarity between the language of the Trailokyanath Datta edition and that of the edition that is now published by Tārācād Dās and Sons, which makes no claim to being a translation, strongly suggests that it was Trailokyanath who was perpetrating the fraud.
12. This is found in the India Office Library, Vernacular Tracts Bengali no. 1339. We do not know the date of its composition. However, the composition of Śītalā poetry had not yet quite come to an end in the 1870s. In 1922–23 one Nīlkānta Bandopādhyāy, who was born in Bikrampur in 1867, published a long poem entitled *Śītalā Sambhava (Kāvya)* (Calcutta: Baradākānta Cakravartī). He explains in his introduction that literature of quality concerning Śītalā, a *jāgrata devatā*, was not available, so he composed this, relying on some literary sources, upon performances he had heard of *Śītalār Bhāsān Gān*, and on his own imagination. His version of the *Virāṭa Pālā* suggests that he had heard performances of Nityānanda's version of the *Maṅgal*.
13. H. Beverley, *Report of the Census of Bengal 1872* (Calcutta: Bengal Secretariat Press, 1872), p. 86. Hereafter *Report 1872*.
14. *Report 1872*, p. 81.
15. For a comprehensive and lucid account, see Klein 1972: 132–160.
16. *Memorandum on the Census of British India of 1871–1872: Presented to Both Houses of Parliament* (London: Eyre & Spottiswoode, 1875), p. 9. Hereafter *Memorandum 1871–72*.
17. *Report 1872*, Appendix B, 'Selections from the Reports of District Officers.'
18. E.g., Hooghly, 1045 persons per square mile, 24 Parganas-Calcutta, 951, Saran, 778 Patna, 742. Seventeen districts in Bengal had over 500 persons per square mile, whereas only 7 English counties did; 8 of these were larger than the West Riding of Yorkshire, the largest English county.
19. *Report 1872*, Part II, p. 83.
20. *Report 1872*, Part II, p. 93.
21. *Memorandum 1871–72*, p. 9.
22. *Report 1872*, Appendix B.

23. *Report 1872*, Appendix B.
24. Regarding the absence of any exact knowledge about the causes of the epidemic, it is sufficient to note here the confession of one physician writing from Midnapur: 'The disease is due to the action of a poison which we call malaria for want of a better name.' If this should remind us of the effort to explain the effect of opium by an appeal to the 'dormitive principle' in the poppy, the situation is frankly acknowledged: 'Notwithstanding . . . the many and indeed probable causes that have from time to time been discussed . . . it is certainly very clear that all these conditions have existed for many years without producing any other effect on the public health except those periodic outbreaks of fever with which every European resident in Bengal is familiar.' W.W. Hunter, A *Statistical Account of Bengal*, vol. 3 (London, Trübner & Co. 1876), p. 242. Hereafter *Hunter 3*.
25. *Report 1872*, p. 86, paragraph 204.
26. *Report 1872*, pp. 145–146, paragraph 396–97.
27. *Memorandum 1871–72*, p. 9.
28. *Report 1872*, p. 82, paragraph 192.
29. *Report 1872*, p. 84, paragraph 196.
30. *Report 1872*, 'General Department,' pp. 2–3, paragraph 4. It is not possible to tell how much of the population decrease (which must in any event be viewed as approximate given the basis of Buchanan's estimates) was due to disease-related deaths and a decline in fertility. Many families fled the area for the more salubrious and agriculturally more productive districts of eastern Bengal. At the back of all of these population changes, however, is a declining ecosystem.
31. *Report 1872*, p. 83.
32. *Report 1872*, p. 94, paragraph 223.
33. *Report 1872*, pp. 93–95. A fuller account of Bayley's studies is found in *Asiatick Researches*, vol. 12.
34. *Report 1782*, pp. 93–94. It should be noted that there are some discrepancies between this source and *Memorandum 1871–72*, p. 9, where Bayley's study is also reported. However, to quote the *Report 1872* at greater length: 'No great reliance perhaps can be placed upon estimates based upon the number of houses in this country, the term being rarely understood by any two people in the same sense. Mr. Bayley himself says:—'It is scarcely necessary to observe that many dwellings, especially those of the more opulent classes of inhabitants, include several distinct buildings, huts or out-offices within an enclosure, and frequently contain distinct families of several brothers or other near relatives. A dwelling of this description, whatever may be the number of buildings contained in it, is intentionally considered and rated as one building . . .' Mr. Metcalfe, the present Magistrate, however, informs me that this was

precisely the definition of house adopted for the present census; and if this is so, we have this result, that while the number of houses has largely increased, the average per house has fallen . . . In order to test the accuracy of the present figures, I have endeavoured to compare the returns of the 98 villages of which Mr. Bayley procured a detailed census. In 54 villages, which I think I have succeeded in identifying, I find that there are at present 16,121 houses, against 16,200 in 1814; but the inhabitants only number 76,510 against 92,725. The average number of persons to a house therefore is 4.7 instead of 5.7.' Some of this difference is doubtless due to the fact that it was not possible in 1872 to determine what Bayley may have taken the boundaries of the village to be. Also, the returns were obtained by Bayley through 'the agency of respectable native proprietors of estates, and . . . by the aid and influence of European gentlemen residing in the interior.' Nevertheless, we doubt that such factors could account for the total differences in the population figures for these villages.

35. *Report 1872*, 'General Department,' pp. 2–3.
36. *Sanitary Report on Bengal, 1868* (Calcutta, 1869), p. 184.
37. See the translation of Jagannāth's text in the appendix, p. 147.
38. See, for example, J.A. Boudillon, *Report on the Census of Bengal, 1881*, 3 vols. (Calcutta: Bengal Secretariat Press, 1883), vol. 1, Chapter 5, 'Statistics of Increase and Decrease,' pp. 39–71, especially paragraph 147. Hereafter *Bengal 1881*.
39. W.W. Hunter, *A Statistical Account of Bengal*, vol. 2: Districts of Nadiya and Jessore (London: Trübner & Co., 1873), pp. 212 ff. Hereafter *Hunter* 2. Hunter's account, which was published between the first two censuses, is remarkable for its detailed description of the epidemic in the several districts. It was based on data 'collected for the most part in the years 1870–72' and thus offers a different perspective on the period of the first census.
40. *Hunter* 2. p. 139, and *Bengal 1881*, vol. I, pp. 58–59, paragraph 147.
41. *Bengal 1881*, vol. I, pp. 58 ff., para. 147 ff. for contemporary accounts of the fever epidemic in the several districts, see: for Hooghly, *Hunter 3*, pp. 418–427; for Midnapur, *ibid.*, pp. 229–244; for Burdwan, *ibid.*, pp. 177–192. Though abated east of the Hooghly River, fever can hardly be said to have disappeared. From July 1880 to December 1881, Nadia, for example, was 'terribly ravaged by malarious fever carrying off over 125,000 people during that time.
42. *Report on the Census of British India, Taken on the 17th February 1881* (London: Eyre and Spottiswoode for Her Majesty's Stationery Office, 1883), vol. 1, Chapter 6, pp. 153–54. Contrast, for example, the rates of increase in other divisions during the same period, where fever had not been a factor: Chota Nagpur, +34.3%; Patna, +14.8%; Dacca, +14.6%.

43. *Bengal 1881*, vol. 1, p. 57.
44. *The Sanitary Commissioner's Report for 1873*, part 2, p. 61, quoted in *Bengal 1881*, vol. 1, pp. 59–60, paragraph 149.
45. *Bengal 1881*, vol. 1, p. 54, paragraph 136.
46. *Bengal 1881*, vol. I, p. 54, paragraph 136.
47. *Bengal 1881*, pp. 53–54, paragraph 135.
48. *Bengal 1881*, pp. 53–54, paragraph 135.
49. F.W. Strong, *Eastern Bengal District Gazetteers: Dinajpur* (Allahabad: The Pioneer Press, 1912), pp. 46–47. Hereafter *Dinajpur 1912*.
50. *Dinajpur 1912*, pp. 46–47.
51. These figures are given in Radhakamal Mukherjee, 1938: 80.
52. *Bengal 1881*, vol. 1, p. 54, paragraph 136.
53. J.A. Vas, *Eastern Bengal and Assam District Gazetters: Rangpur* (Allahabad: The Pioneer Press, 1911), p. 51.
54. *Dinajpur 1912.*, p. 44.
55. *Hunter 7*, p. 147.
56. L.S.S. O'Malley, *Bengal District Gazetteers: Murshidabad* (Calcutta: Bengal Secretariat Book Depot, 1914), pp. 89–93.
57. J.C.K. Peterson, *Bengal District Gazetteers: Burdwan* (Calcutta: Bengal Secretariat Book Depot, 1910), pp. 80–81.
58. Nityānanda in Panskura and Jagannāth in Tamluk.
59. See pp. 206–209.
60. *Hunter 3*, p. 220.
61. *Hunter 3*, p. 222.
62. *Hunter 3*, pp. 222–23.
63. L.S.S. O'Malley, *Bengal District Gazetteers: Midnapore* (Calcutta: The Bengal Secretariat Book Depot, 1911), pp. 90–92. Hereafter *Midnapore 1911*.
64. For an unusual contemporary account of the Maratha raids, quite unlike anything in the *Maṅgal-kāvya* literature, see Dimock and Gupta 1965.
65. For a convenient summary of events in this period, see Sinha 1967.
66. Sinha 1967: 88.
67. Details on the rivers and ecosystems of the Bengal delta are available in: Spate and Learmonth 1967; S.P. Chatterjee 1948; and Nicholas 1962.
68. For the political history see Basu 1940, and *Midnapore, 1911*. For changes in the course of the Kansai see S.P. Chatterjee, maps 4 and 5.
69. See Āśutoṣ Bhaṭṭācārya 1970: 799, on the *ādi kavi* distinction.
70. See pp. 108–109 above.
71. For another consideration of the standardization of a Bengali myth through printing and the respective positions of oral, manuscript, and printed myths see pp. 192–211.
72. See note 12 above.
73. The only partial exception is that of Dvija Harideva, where Jvarā

is one of her two lords-lieutenant, the other being called Basantarāy.

74. Dvija Nityānanda Cakravartī (fl. 1756–1770), *Bṛhat Śītalā Maṅgal bā Śītalār Jāgaraṇ Pālā*, 12th printing (Calcutta: Tārācād Dās and Sons, c. 1968) ('Text A'), pp. ii–iii.
75. Dvija Nityananda Cakravarti, *Śītalār Jāgaraṇ Pālā arthāt Matsyadeśe Śītalā Devīr Māhātmya Varṇana*, 1st ed. (Calcutta: Trailokyanāth Datta, 1878) ('Text B'), p. 10.
76. Text B, p. 4.
77. *Hunter 3*, p. 239.
78. *Hunter 3*, pp. 421–22.
79. Hippocrates, I, pp. 83–85, 135. See Jones 1909: esp. pp. 23–81.
80. Boyd 1949 I: 11–12. See this work for a review of the development of medical knowledge concerning malaria.
81. Boyd 1949 I: 12.
82. Boyd 1949 I: 12–13.
83. Boyd 1949 I: 419–27.
84. Weber 1968: 245.
85. For a further treatment of *āndolan* see Nicholas 1973.
86. Inden 1967.
87. Dimock and Inden 1969.
88. A *cā̃dmālā*, or 'garland of moons,' is a kind of ornament commonly used in Bengal to decorate the image of a deity during worship. The ordinary variety is made by members of the Mālākār, or Garland-maker, caste from pith (*solā*) and tinsel.
89. The word used is *ādeś*, which may also mean 'indication,' or even 'direction,' as does the word *upadeś*. Used in a familiar context, however, the hierarchical connotation is mitigated.
90. The ms. is damaged at the point where, according to the signature line, this section should begin. However, the *puspikā* at the end of this section is numbered 'three,' so we think that the whole section consists of two parts, the first enumerating diseases thought to be caused by humoral disorders, the second consisting primarily of diseases with eruptive symptoms.
91. *Pān*, or 'betel' as it is often glossed in English, is a preparation of areca nut, spices, and scent, rolled in a betel leaf. The offering of *pān* is a formal and courteous gesture.
92. Yama's speech suggests that the present drama was performed in conjunction with (or at least that the audience was familiar with) a *Svarga* or *Yampur Pālā* in which Śītalā ravaged Heaven or the City of Yama (Death) in order to obtain worship.
93. While Śītalā speaks of her 'grace' referring to its explicit form as pox, the Jāgāti, with his limited perception, is able to understand the term only in its apparent and beneficent sense.

94. This seems to be a reference to a *Svarga Pālā* (see note 5).
95. This may be from *keblāni*, 'a dull-witted woman,' or something like 'the village madwoman,' who is a familiar figure in Bengali villages, often feared as a kind of witch. Muhammad Sahīdullah, *Purba Pākistāni Āñcalik Bhāṣār Abhidhān*, vol. 2 (Dacca: Bāṃlā Akāḍemi, 1965) has *kāolāno*, 'to wander aimlessly,' and *kāulāno*, 'to beg plaintively.' However, it is also possible that this word should be read as *kalāiwālinī*, 'female pulse seller.'
96. The first three of these are of the Solar dynasty of heroes of the *Rāmāyaṇa* and the other three of the Lunar dynasty of the *Mahābhārata*.
97. Kṛttivās, in the fourteenth century, in his classic Bengali *Rāmāyaṇa* (*Ayodhyākāṇḍa*: 12, Baṅgiya Sāhitya Pariṣat edition) used this very image and phrasing in a similar situation.
98. The notation *dhuyā* after this sentence suggests that it was meant to be sung as a refrain.
99. The ms. is written over at this point and we cannot make out the next word.
100. This intriguing hint of an indigenous medical procedure for the treatment of pox is unfortunately neither clear nor detailed. However, it is suggestive of procedures reported by Dr James Wise as practiced by the Mālākār, or Garland-maker caste, of Dacca District in the early nineteenth century. Wise's description is quoted at length by H.H. Risley in *The Tribes and Castes of Bengal. Ethnographic Glossary*, vol. 2. (Calcutta: Bengal Secretariat Press, 1891), pp. 61–62.

    'One of the chief occupations of this caste is innoculating for small-pox and treating individuals attacked by any eruptive fever. Hindus believe that Śītalā, the goddess of small-pox, is one of seven sisters, who are designated Motiya, Matariyā, Pakauriya Masūrikā, Chamariya, Khudwā, and Pansā. The first four are varieties of small-pox, the names referring to the form, size, and colour of the pustules; the fifth is *Variola maligna*; the sixth is measles; and the seventh is water-pox. Every Mālākār keeps images of one or more of these goddesses, and on the first of Chait (March 15th) a festival is held, and the Mālākārs superintend the details. It is popularly called 'Mālībāgh,' from the garden where the service is performed, and thither Hindus and Muhammadans repair with offerings of clotted milk, cocoanuts, and plantains in the hope of propitiating the dreaded sisters.

    'When small-pox rages, the Mālākārs are busiest. As soon the nature of the disease is determined, the Kabīrāj retires and a Mālākār is summoned. His first act is to forbid the introduction of meat, fish, and all food requiring oil or spices for its preparation. He then ties a lock of hair, a cowrie-shell, a piece of turmeric, and an article of gold on the right wrist of the patient. The sick person is then laid on the 'Mājh-pattā,' the young and unexpanded leaf of the plantain tree, and milk is prescribed as the sole article of food. He is fanned with a branch of the sacred *nīm*, and any one entering the chamber is sprinkled with water. Should the fever become aggravated and delirium ensue, or if a child cries much and sleeps little, the Mālī performs the Mātā pūjā. This consists in bathing the image of the goddess causing the disease and giving a draught of the water to drink. To relieve the irritation of the skin, pease-meal, turmeric, flour, or shell-sawdust is sprinkled over the body.

'If the eruptions be copious, a piece of new cloth in the figure of eight is wrapped round the chest and shoulders. On the night between the seventh and eighth days of the eruption the Mālī has much to do. He places a waterpot in the sick room, and puts on it alwā rice, a cocoanut, sugar, plantains, a yellow rag, flowers, and a few *nīm* leaves. Having mumbled several *mantras*, he recites the *kissa*, or tale, of the particular goddess, which often occupies six hours.

'When the pustules are mature, the Mālī dips a thorn of the karaundā (*Carissa*) in til oil, and punctures each one. The body is then anointed with oil, and cooling fruits given. When the scabs (dewli) have peeled off, another ceremonial, called 'Godām,' is gone through. All the offerings on the waterpot are rolled in a cloth and fastened round the waist of the patient. These offerings are the perquisite of the Mālī, who also receives a fee.

'These minute, and to our ideas absurd, proceedings are practised by the Hindus and Muhammadans, including the bigoted Farazi, whenever smallpox or other eruptive fever attacks their families. Government vaccinators earn a considerable sum yearly by executing the Śītalā worship, and when a child is vaccinated a portion of the service is performed.'

Dr Francis Buchanan, during his tour of Dinajpur District in 1808, also observed the practice of innoculating children against smallpox (India Office Library, Mss. Eur. D 71, *Buchanan Hamilton Collection*, 'Account of the District or Zila of Dinajpur, 'Book II. People, pp. 12–14). He reported that the smallpox season generally began between February 10 and March 12. During that time innoculators, both Muslim and Hindu, would open pustules on the bodies of smallpox victims, extract the matter on cotton wool, and rub it over needle punctures on the skin of uninfected people, usually children between three and ten years of age. Children under three were separated from those to be innoculated and given sugar water over which 'some incantations to Sitola have been performed by a Brahmon.' A child to be innoculated was bathed, 'and afterwards is not allowed to eat fish, meat is nearly out of the question; but it seems to be allowed whatever else it chooses, except cakes or bread;

and sugar plantains, water-melons, cucumbers and cold boiled rice are recommended as the most proper diet.' The child was bathed two or three times a day and, if he became feverish, he was given water over which a *mantra* was said by the innoculator. Buchanan said that the innoculators were cultivators not otherwise esteemed as medical practitioners, and that they knew nothing of the vaccine innoculation.

Chapter 7
The Goddess Śītalā and Epidemic Smallpox in Bengal

1. Although I did not know it at the time, the research embodied in this paper was begun in 1960 when I first saw a performance of Nityānanda's *Śītalā Maṅgal* (1931) in a Midnapur village. In consequence of such a long period of work on the subject, I have accumulated more debts than usual, and I would like to acknowledge the major ones. Research was supported by a Foreign Area Training Fellowship, a Fulbright-Hays Research Fellowship, the Asian Studies Center at Michigan State University, and, at the University of Chicago, by the Committee on Southern Asian Studies, the Lichtstern Research Fund of the Department of Anthropology, and the U.S.P.H.S. Biomedical Research Support Grant to the Division of the Social Sciences at the University of Chicago. Many scholars have contributed to this research in ways so various that I cannot mention them here: I am especially indebted to K.C. Bahl, Dr. and Mrs F.B. Bang, A.L. Basham, P.R. Brass, V. Das, E.C. Dimock, F. Fenner, R. D. Fogelson, E. Gadon, P. Gaffney, P.R. Greenough, R.B. Inden, J. Jepson, J.K. Kallgren, C. Leslie, M. Marriott, T. Mukhopadhyay, M.R. Nicholas, I.H. Rosenberg, A.N. Sarkar, D. Twells, and S. Wadley. The libraries of the University of Chicago and the India Office, London, are the sources of the items listed in the references.
2. The pathophysiolgy of smallpox is not well known because the disease has been so uncommon in countries where it could most readily be studied. Some nutritional deficiencies are antagonistic to virus infections because of the dependence of the virus on the metabolism of host cells (Scrimshaw, Taylor, and Gordon 1968: 72–73, 81–83, 135, 41). However, any advantage to the host from malnutrition in resistance to smallpox is far outweighed by the disadvantage in reversing the destruction of skin tissue (Dixon 1962: 20).
3. There is a great deal of recent research on variolation motivated by concern with a variety of questions, such as demographic history, the history of immunology, and public health in colonial societies. Razzell (1977: 140 ff.) presents very extensive evidence from the British Isles to show that, before the introduction of the Jenner vaccine, smallpox had largely

been transformed into a nonfatal childhood disease through the widespread practice of variolation. The operation is known to have been introduced into Britain from Turkey early in the eighteenth century, although rural people may well have had versions of their own before that time. Where variolation was invented, and—more interesting—what kind of premodern biological theory made such an invention possible and intelligible, is not settled. Joseph Needham (1980; Needham and Lu 1962: 465–66) presents evidence that it was a Chinese invention, passed to the rest of the world. However, the Chinese usually introduced the virus by blowing powdered pox scabs into the nostril, whereas cutaneous scarification was the method recorded in India and the near East in the eighteenth century. More than one invention of variolation—and, perhaps, different theories of how immunity was engendered—seem quite probable. Wherever the procedure originated, Greenough (1980: 347) has found evidence that it was practiced widely enough in Bengal, even after the introduction of vaccination, to have a significant effect in reducing the smallpox mortality rate.

4. Holwell's transcription, *Gootee ka Tagooran*, leaves some doubt about the language spoken by the inoculators. Since the deity designated is female, *Tagooran* may safely be read as *ṭhākurāṇ*, from *ṭhākurāṇī*, a feminine form of *ṭhākur*, 'lord.' In Hindi, one would then expect *guṭī kī ṭhākurāṇī*, 'Goddess of Smallpox,' but this is awkward and improbable. A preferable reading is *guṭikā ṭhākurāṇī*, 'Smallpox Goddess,' a form that can be produced in several languages. This might all be sterile philology were it not that, nowadays at least, it is only in Orissa that the Smallpox Goddess is known as Ṭhākurāṇī (Roy 1927: 217–23).
5. I am indebted to Dr Jyotindra Jain of the L.D. Institute of Indology, Ahmedabad, who kindly supplied this information as well as an excellent photograph that he made of this image in 1978.
6. There are archaeological suggestions of the goddess's early appearance in the intervening region, such as a Śītalā temple in Gaya containing a late eleventh century inscription of King Yakṣapāla (Kielhorn 1887; Banerji 1915: 95–97; Patil 1963: 40; Sircar 1965–66). But the temple itself is undated, there is no description of the goddess, and the inscription, which makes no mention of Śītalā, may have been originally in another temple.
7. Havell (1905) includes a photograph made within the temple looking outward over a large Śiva *liṅga* through an unadorned rectangular doorway (p. 114). Greaves (1909) has a photograph of the temple seen from the north, probably from the celebrated Daśāśvamedha Ghāṭ (p. 43). Greaves (1909: 55) and later writers on the city (e.g., 'Old Resident' 1918: 85) mention a second Śītalā Ghāṭ south of the Pañca Gaṅgā Ghāṭ.
8. The *Skanda Purāṇa* is one of the longest of the Sanskrit *purāṇas* and was

assembled over a long period of time, beginning as early as the eighth century and extending into the twelfth or thirteenth century AD (Hazra 1975: 165). The *Kāśī-khaṇḍa* includes material from the later part of the period, although Wilson (1864: lxxii) thought most of it to be earlier than AD 1194. The *Śītalāṣṭaka* (Purāṇas n.d. and 1947) is not found in the published versions of the *Kāśī-khaṇḍa* (Purāṇas 1908–09 and 1960–62). The editor of the Bengal edition of the *Skanda Purāṇa* (1911) used the Bombay edition (1908–09) as the basis for his text, but included additional sections found in manuscripts of the work from Bengal (Hazra 1975: 157); apparently, a *Śītalāṣṭaka* was not among them. Thus, the questions of when Śītalā appeared in Banaras and how her verses came to be included in or omitted from the *Kāśī-khaṇḍa* cannot be settled on this evidence. However, the *Āvantya-khaṇḍa* (Pt. 1, *Avantīkṣetra-māhātmya*), the section dealing with Avantī or Ujjayinī in central India, in all three printed *Skanda Purāṇas* includes the following *adhyāya*: 'Sanatkumāra said: To the north of the Vidyādhara *tīrtha* [a place of pilgrimage for bathing] there is a *tīrtha* known as Markaṭeśvara [Lord of Apes]; that *tīrtha* is famous and is a fulfiller of all desires. The person who bathes at that *tīrtha* receives the benefit of donating a hundred cows, and the pustules (*visphoṭa*) of children disappear. If one measures out and grinds *masūra* pulses there, then, by the power of Śītalā, children recover unblemished. The troubled person who views Śītalā with devotion is never again afflicted by evil actions or any kind of poverty; and likewise has no fear of disease or planetary afflictions' (5.1.12).

Markaṭeśvara is not located by the modern authorities on pilgrimage places, but if it belongs to the territory of Avantī (modern Malwa), as the text says then it is likely to have been in communication with the neighboring countries of Gujarat and Rajasthan, and there is no reason to suppose that the text predates the twelfth century images of Śītalā in those locations.

9. The Dutch traveler Baldaeus (1917: 28–33) in 1670 witnessed the worship of the goddess Bhadrakālī as part of the treatment of smallpox in Malabar. By then the disease was evidently well known in that locality, and he relates an elaborate myth concerning its origin.
10. Two other lunar days are mentioned quite often as appropriate for the worship of this goddess, Śītalā *saptamī* (*sīlī sātama* in Gujarati), the seventh day of the bright lunar fortnight in Srāvaṇa (July–Aug.), and Śītalā *ṣaṣṭhī*, the bright sixth of Māgha (Jan.–Feb.). (See Underhill 1921: 105; Stevenson 1920: 306–307; and Wadley 1980, especially the last, for a discussion of textual authorities and full translations of stories appropriate to these occasions.) Both of these dates are, in different regions, considered appropriate for the observance of 'cold-hearth' rites, that is, days on which

no cooking is to be done. The Goddess Śītalā worshiped on these occasions is not treated as mistress of smallpox but as 'The Cool One' who is offended if the hearth is heated. There is a Sanskrit *vrata-kathā* for Śītalā *saptamī* in the *Bhaviṣya Purāṇa*; it is repeated in modern manuals for Bengali priests (Bhaṭṭācārya 1973–1974: 267–69) but the *vrata* is not, to my knowledge, observed in Bengal. It is observed in Gujarat, and a Gujarati version of this story is related by Wadley (1980).

11. Chickenpox is called *pāni-basanta* (waterpox), and measles is called *hām-basanta*, from an Arabic term for the disease.
12. In the Salkia section of Howrah city, the principal worship of Śītalā is done on the fullmoon day of Māgha (Jan.–Feb.). Aditi Nath Sarkar has made a film of the splendid *snāna-yātrā* given to the twenty-two Śītalās of this locality.

Chapter 8
Śītalā and the Art of Printing: The Transmission and Propagation of the Myth of the Goddess of Smallpox in Rural West Bengal

1. The field research on which this paper is based was conducted under the support of a Fulbright-Hays Center Faculty Fellowship awarded through the South Asia Language and Area Center at Michigan State University. I am grateful for this support and to the Asian Studies Center and the Department of Anthropology for facilitating this work in many ways. I would also like to record my debt to my co-worker, Mr Tarasish Mukhopadhyay, and to may wife Marta who collaborated in the fieldwork. Mr Mukhopadhyay was able to check some of the statements made in a draft of this paper against his own extensive knowledge and to interview again some of the performers of the *Śītalā-maṅgal* whom we know. He has corrected a number of errors of fact and interpretation that I made earlier and I am grateful to him. Professor A.K. Ramanujan kindly read and commented on the draft, making helpful suggestions and supplying me with a copy of his still unpublished paper on a topic closely related to this one. The approach that I have taken here is strongly influenced by the ideas laid out by Milton Singer (1958) in his introduction to the volume on *Traditional India: Structure and Change*, as well as by the contributions of Hein, McCormack, Raghavan, and Singer to that volume. Marriott's (1959) analysis of 'Changing channels of cultural transmission in Indian civilization' has been similarly influential.
2. The term 'myth' in this paper follows the customary Western conception rather than the Bengali, which draws finer distinctions among narratives

of this general class than we are accustomed to make. Percy Cohen (1960: 337) characterizes myth in a practically useful way when he says:

> A myth is a narrative of events; the narrative has a sacred quality: the sacred communication is made in symbolic form; at least some of the events and objects which occur in the myth neither occur nor exist in the world other than that of the myth itself: and the narrative refers in dramatic form to origins or transformations. The narrative quality distinguishes a myth from a general idea or set of ideas, such as a cosmology. The sacred quality and the reference to origins or transformations distinguish myth from legend and other types of folk-tale. The narration of events and reference to objects unknown outside the world of myth differentiates myth from history or pseudo-history.

3. Goody and Watt (1965: 326) make a distinction similar to the one that I propose between 'transmission' and 'propagation'; they contrast the 'processes of collective development and transmission' to the 'process of transmission from one individual to another.'
4. Whitehead (1921: 30–31) says that while Mariamma, the Tamil smallpox goddess and village mother, has won her 'way to general respect or fear among the Tamil people,' in the Telugu country, 'as a rule the infliction and removal of epidemics and disasters is a general function of all goddesses alike.'
5. Āśutoṣ Bhaṭṭācārya (1970: 789) says that the *stava of* Śītalā is also found in the second section, fourth part, of the *Bhāvaprakāśa*, an Ayurvedic medical text, as a part of the cure for smallpox. This work appears to be, at the earliest, sixteenth century (Chakraberty 1923: 419), since it describes syphilis as *phiraṅga roga*, the 'Portugese disease.' Bhanj Deo (1954: 1) cites a reference to Śītalā in the *Bṛhadyoginī Tantra*, where she appears as the benign form of the Yoginī Piśitāsanā. The skull-cap (or severed head) and knife carried by the *Yoginī* are exchanged for the pot of nectar and the broom of Śītalā. Both forms have the ass as a vehicle.
6. Crooke's (1968: 125–136) discussion of Śītalā in north India does not suggest that there is any literary authority for the worship and indicates that there is a great deal of diversity in beliefs concerning her.
7. Tārāpada Bhaṭṭācārya (1962: 172) mentions the existence of four other manuscript versions of the *Śītalā-maṅgal*, composed by 'Dayāl,' Akiñcan Cakrabartī, 'Dvijagopāla,' and 'Śaṅkara.' Tamonāś Candra Dās Gupta (1951: 200) mentions versions by 'Rāmprasād' (Sen?), 'Kṛṣṇanāth' (= Kṛṣṇarām Dās?), 'Śaṅkarācāryya' (= Śaṅkara?), and 'Raghunāth Datta.' This last is the name of one of the *pālās* of the Kavivallabh version, according to Āśutoṣ Bhaṭṭācārya (1952: 62).
8. This version consists of three *pālās: Madan Dās Jagātir Pālā, Kājir Pālā,*

and *Hṛṣīkés Sādhur Upākhyāna* (Satyanārāyaṇa Bhaṭṭācārya 1958: lxxvii, 251–285).

9. Later, quoting an article by Byamokesh Mustaphi, Āśutoṣ Bhaṭṭācārya (1964: 734) suggests that Rājnārāyaṇa may have been a 'powerful' but 'book-loving' zamindār dated about 1777 or 1783 AD.
10. Binay Ghoṣ (1957: 405) writes: 'Śītalā Devī's outstanding popularity is visible in the Contai, Tamluk, and Ghatal areas [of Midnapur District]. The Śītalā pūjās of almost all parts of Bengal were introduced [from there]. At the time of smallpox and cholera epidemics, the grand celebration of her special *pūjā* is to be seen. I think that Śītalā is said to be the foremost among village deities in the areas of Contai, Tamluk, and Ghatal. The public worship of Śītalā is the foremost festival of the village and it is celebrated [there] with the greatest pomp of all.'
11. These pustules are called, in euphemistic reversal, *ṭikli*, 'cosmetic ornaments.' *Ṭikli* is derived from *Ṭikā*, 'religious' or 'sectarian mark,' such as are often placed on the foreheads of Hindu worshippers; *Ṭika* also means 'vaccination mark.' Innoculation with live smallpox virus was practiced indigenously in rural Bengal, primarily upon young children, prior to the introduction of the Jennerian vaccine; Śītalā was invoked in connection with the innoculation (Buchanan-Hamilton 1807–08, Book II, 'The People').
12. Gopendrakṛṣṇa Basu (1969: 72–75) reports that Jvarāsur is 'not only Śītalā's; he appears in some villages as the chief minister of Pañcānanda [a terrible, disease-related form of Śiva] and as the companion of Dharmaṭhākur.' He is also sometimes worshiped independently. Occasionally, he is represented as having 'three heads, nine eyes, six hands, and three legs.'
13. Gopendrakṛṣṇa Basu (1969: 25–28), in his chapter on Olāicaṇḍī, asserts that Olāicaṇḍī is generally the name of the goddess of cholera in the Hindu-majority areas. This generalization obviously does not apply to the eastern part of Midnapur District, in which the Hindu Māhiṣya caste constitutes a majority of the population and where even before 1947, Muslims were a relatively small minority. I have heard some Hindus refer to the goddess as Olādevī; I attribute this to a heightened consciousness of religious differences, which is also manifested in the critical attitude that some Muslims take toward the worship of Olābibi by their coreligionists. In his chapter on Olābibi (pp. 185–190), Basu notes that this goddess is found in virtually all of the villages in the southern part of 24 Parganas District. Basu says that there is a middle Bengali text called *Sātbibir Gān* (Song of the Seven Bibis) and that Olābibi often appears as one of seven sisters, similar to the popular Hindu Saptamātṛka (Seven Mother Goddess). However, where a shrine is hers

alone, he says, 'priesthood is most commonly done by Muslim fakirs,' as is the case in eastern Midnapur. See also Hora (1933).

14. I have used the word 'shrine' to translate the rustic Bengali word *thān*. Basu (1969: 193) rightly, I think, says that it is misleading to connect this word with *sthān*, which simply means 'place', since *thān* means the 'temple of a popular deity' although 'no villager calls it a temple (*mandir*).' He describes the ordinary *thān* as being simply an earthen platform at the base of a tree, which is accurate for the Kelomal area except in respect of Olābibir *thāns*, which I describe.
15. The Birāṭ Rājā of the *Śītalā-maṅgal* seems to be the same character as the Virāṭ Rājā of the *Mahabhārāta*; the principal queen and the chief minister both have identical names in the two narratives. Many events and names in Nityānanda's version of the myth are evidently borrowed from the *Mahabhārata*. The effect of such borrowing is probably to lend additional authority to the Śītalā myth, but I cannot take up this problem here.
16. The origin attributed to Śītalā's name in the myth should not, of course, be allowed to obscure its euphemistic reversal: She, whose affliction causes raging fever, is addressed as 'The Cool One.'
17. *Śiraṇi* (alternatively, *śiraṇī*, or more commonly *śirnī* or *śinnī*) is an uncooked mixture of bananas, unboiled milk, wheat flour, molasses or sugar, and spices. It is thought to be an appropriate offering to Muslim saints.
18. A.K. Ramanujan (ms.) relates the story of the 'most influential and probably the most thoroughgoing of the 19th and early 20th century Tamil scholars,' Swaminatha Aiyar, who discovered in 1880 that for years he had been studying relatively late 'second rate religious and grammatical texts' because sectarian strictures prevented his even coming to know of 'the greatest of Tamil literary texts,' the Sangam poetry. He was given, fortuitously, manuscripts of some of these to read. Thereafter, he devoted his life to findings, editing, and publishing Sangam poetry.
19. See note 7 above.

References

Agrawala, Vasudeva S., trans. (1963), *Devī-Māhātmyam: The Glorification of the Great Goddess*. Varanasi: All-India Kashiraj Trust.

Babb, Lawrence A. (1975), *The Divine Hierarchy: Popular Hinduism in Central India*. New York: Columbia University Press.

Baldaeus, Phillipus (1917), *Afgoderye der Oost-Indische Heydenen*. Edited by A.J. DeJong. The Hague: Martinus Nijhoff. (Orig. pub. 1672.)

Banerjea, Jitendra Nath (1956), *Development of Hindu Iconography*. Calcutta: The University of Calcutta.

Banerji, R.D. (1915), 'The Pālas of Bengal.' *Memoirs of the Asiatic Society of Bengal* 5, 3: 43–113.

Bang, B.G. (1973), 'Current Concepts of the Smallpox Goddess Sitala in Parts of West Bengal.' *Man in India* 53: 79–104.

Basu, Gopendrakṛṣṇa (1969), *Bāṃlār Laukik Debatā*. Second printing (First printing 1966). Calcutta: Ānanda Publishers Private Limited.

Basu, Yogeścandra (1940), *Medinipurer Itihās*. 2nd ed. Calcutta: Sen Brothers and Co.

Bengal. Department of Agriculture (1912–1931), *Annual Season and Crop Reports*. Calcutta: Bengal Secretariat Book Depot.

____. Sanitary Commissioner (1912–1931), *Annual Reports of the Sanitary Commissioner*. Calcutta: Bengal Secretariat Book Depot.

Bhanj Deo, Prafulla Chandra (1954), '*Piśitāsana*.' *Journal of the Asiatic Society*, 3rd series 20: 1–5.

Bhaṭṭācārya, Āśutoṣ (1952), 'The Cult of the Goddess of Smallpox in West Bengal.' *The Quarterly Journal of the Mythic Society* 43: 55–69.

____ (1970), *Bāṃlā Maṅgala-kāvyer Itihāsa*. 5th ed. Calcutta: Mukherjee and Co.

Bhaṭṭācārya, Satyanārāyaṇa, ed. (1958), *Kavi Kṛṣṇarāma Dāser Granthavāli*, Calcutta: Calcutta University.

Bhaṭṭācārya, Surendra-Mohana, ed. (1973–1974), *Purohita-darpaṇa*. 37th ed. Revised by Yogendra-candra Vyākaraṇatīrtha Vidyāratna. Calcutta: Satyanārāyaṇa Library.

Bhaṭṭācārya, Tārāpada (1962), *Baṅgasāhityer Itihāsa (Prācīn Parba)*. Calcutta: S. Gupta Brothers (Private) Ltd.

Bhattacaryya, Benoytosh (1958), *The Indian Buddhist Iconography*, 2nd ed. Calcutta: Firma K.L. Mukhopadhyay.

Bhāva Miśra (1958), *Bhāva-prakāśa, with the Hindi Commentary of Pandit Lālacandrajī Vaidya*, 2 vols. Delhi: Motilal Banarsidas.

Bhishagratna, Kunja Lal, ed. and trans. (1911), *An English Translation of the Sushruta Samhita*. 3 vols. Calcutta: Published by the author.

Boyd, Mark F., ed. (1949), *Malariology*. Philadelphia: W.B. Saunders and Co.

Buchanan, Francis (1808), 'An Account of the District or Zila of Dinajpur.' Book II: 'People.' London: India Office Library, MSS Eur. D 71, 'Buchanan Hamilton Collection.'

Cakravartī, Nityānanda (1968), *Bṛhat Śītalā Maṅgal bā Śītalār Jāgaraṇ Pālā* [The great narrative of Shitala or Shitala's Vigil Drama]. Calcutta: Tārācā̃d Dās and Sons.

Carstairs, G.M. (1961), 'Patterns of Religious Observance in Three Villages of Rajasthan.' In *Aspects of Religion in Indian Society*, L.P. Vidyarthi (ed.). Meerut: Kedar Nath Ram Nath. pp. 59–113.

Chakraberty, Chandra (1923), *An Interpretation of Ancient Hindu Medicine*. Calcutta: Published by Ramchandra Chakraberty.

Chatterjee, S.P. (1948), *Bengal in Maps*. Calcutta: Orient Longman.

Clark, T.W. (1967), 'Encounter and Growth in Bengali Literature.' In *Bengal: Literature and History*, E.C. Dimock, Jr. (ed.). East Lansing: Michigan State University Asian Studies Center Occasional Papers, pp. 9–17.

Cohen, Percy S. (1969), 'Theories of Myth.' *Man* n.s. 4:337–353.

Cossigny, Charpentier (1798–1799), *Voyage au Bengale*. 2 vols. Paris: Émery Imprimeur.

Crooke, W. (1968), *The Popular Religion and Folk-Lore of Northern India*. Third reprint ed. from the second ed. of 1806. Delhi. Munshiram Manoharlal.

Das, Veena (1977), *Structure and Cognition: Aspects of Hindu Caste and Ritual*. Delhi: Oxford University Press.

Dās Gupta, Tamonāś Candra (1951), *Prācīn Bāṅgālā Sāhityer Itihāsa*. Calcutta: Calcutta University.

De, Sushil Kumar (1961), *Early History of the Vaiṣṇava Faith and Movement in Bengal*, 2nd ed. Calcutta: Firma K.L. Mukhopadhyaya.

Deutschmann, Z. (1961), 'The Ecology of Smallpox.' In *Studies in Disease Ecology*. J.M. May (ed.). New York: Hafner Publishing.

Dharampal (1971), *Indian Science and Technology in the Eighteenth Century: Some Contemporary European Accounts*. Delhi: Impex India.

Dimmitt, Cornelia, and J.A.B. van Buitenen, ed. and trans. (1978), *Classical Hindu Mythology: A Reader in the Sanskrit Purāṇas*. Philadelphia: Temple University Press.

Dimock, Edward C., Jr. (1963), *The Thief of Love: Bengali Tales from Court and Village*. Chicago: The University of Chicago Press.

____, and A.K. Ramanujan (1964), 'The Goddess of Snakes in Medieval Bengali Literature.' Part II. *History of Religions* 3: 300–332.

____, and Ronald B. Inden (1969), 'The City in Pre-British Bengal, According to the *Maṅgala-kāvyas*.' In *Urban Bengal*, Richard L. Park (ed.). East Lansing: Michigan State University Asian Studies Center Occasional Papers.

____, and P.C. Gupta, eds. and trans. (1965), *The Mahārāshṭa Purāṇa: An Eighteenth-Century Bengali Historical Text*. Honolulu: East-West Center Press.

____ (1969), 'Muslim Vaiṣṇava Poets of Bengal.' In *Bengal: Regional Identity*, David Kopf (ed.). East Lansing: Michigan State University Asian Studies Center Occasional Papers. pp. 23–32.

Dixon, C.W. (1962), *Smallpox*. London: J. and A. Churchill.

Eck, Diana L. (1978), 'Kāśī, City and Symbol.' *Purāṇa* 20: 169–92.

Filliozat, Jean (1964), *The Classical Doctrine of Indian Medicine*. Dev Raj Chanana (trans.). Delhi: Munshiram Manoharlal.

Freed, Ruth S., and Freed, Stanley A. (1962), 'Two Mother Goddess Ceremonies of Delhi State in the Great and Little Traditions.' *Southwestern Journal of Anthropology* 18. 246–77.

Fürer-Haimendorf, Christoph von (1967), *Morals and Merit*. London: Weidenfeld and Nicolson.

Geertz, Clifford (1965), 'Religion as a Cultural System'. In *Anthropological Approaches to the Study of Religion*. Association of Social Anthropologists Monograph No. 3. London: Tavistock. New York: Praeger.

Ghoṣ, Binay (1957), *Paścimbaṅger Saṃskṛti*. Calcutta: Pustak Prakāśak.

Glasse, Robert (1966), 'La Société Musulmane dans le Pakistan Rural de l'Est: Étude Préliminaire.' *Études Rurales*. Nos. 22–23–24: 188–205.

Goody, Jack and Ian Watt (1963), 'The Consequences of Literacy.' *Comparative Studies in Society and History* 5: 304–345.

Greaves, Edwin (1909), *Kashi, The City Illustrious, or Benares*. Allahabad: The Indian Press.

Greenhill, William Alexander, trans. (1847), *A Treatise on the Small-pox and Measles by Abū Bakr Muhammad ibn Zakarīyā al-Rāzī (Rhazes)*. London: The Sydenham Society.

Greenough, Paul (1977), *Prosperity and Misery in Modern Bengal: The Bengal*

Famine of 1943–44. Ph.D. Dissertation, Department of History, University of Chicago.

____ (1980), 'Variolation and Vaccination in South Asia, c. 1700–1865: A Preliminary Note.' *Social Science and Medicine* 14: 345–47.

Hahon, Nicholas (1961), 'Smallpox and Related Poxvirus Infections in the Simian Host.' *Bacteriological Reviews* 25: 459–76.

Hare, Ronald (1967), 'The Antiquity of Diseases Caused by Bacteria and Viruses.' In *Diseases in Antiquity*, D. Brothwell and A.T. Sandison (eds.). Springfield, Illinois: Charles C. Thomas.

Havell, E.B. (1905), *Benares: The Sacred City*. London: Blackie & Son.

Hazra, Rajendra Chandra (1958), *Studies in the Upapurāṇas*, Vol. 1: *Saura and Vaiṣṇava Upapurāṇas*. Calcutta: Sanskrit College.

____ (1975), *Studies in the Purāṇic Records on Hindu Rites and Customs*. 2nd ed. Delhi: Motilal Banarsidas.

Hein, Norvin (1958), 'The *Rām Līlā*.' In Singer 1958: 279–304.

Henderson, Donald A. (1976), 'The Eradication of Smallpox.' *Scientific American* 245, 4 (Oct.): 25–33.

Hilgenberg, Luise, and Willibald Kirfel, eds. and trans. (1941), *Vāgbhaṭas Aṣṭāṅgahṛdayasaṃhitā*, *Ein altindisches Lehrbuch der Heilkunde*. Leiden: E.J. Brill.

Hippocrates (1939), with an English translation by W.H.S. Jones. The Loeb Classical Library. Cambridge: Harvard University Press.

Hirsch, August (1883), *Handbook of Geographical and Historical Pathology*. 2 vols. Trans. from 2nd German ed. by Charles Creighton. London: The New Sydenham Society.

Holwell, J.Z. (1767), *An Account of the Manner of Inoculating for the Small Pox in the East Indies*. London: College of Physicians. (Reprinted in Dharampal 1971: 143–63).

Hora, Sunder Lal (1933), 'Worship of the Deities Ola, Jhola, and Bon Bibi in Lower Bengal.' *Journal of the Asiatic Society of Bengal*, n.s. 29: 1–4.

Hunter, W.W. (1897), *Annals of Rural Bengal*. 7th ed. London: Smith, Elder, and Co.

Inden, Ronald (1967), 'The Hindu Chiefdom in Middle Bengali Literature.' In *Bengal: Literature and History*, Edward C. Dimock, Jr. (ed.). East Lansing: Michigan State University Asian Studies Center Occasional Papers.

____, and Nicholas, Ralph W. (1977), *Kinship in Bengali Culture*. Chicago: Chicago University Press.

India, Archaeological Survey of India (1908–1909), *Annual Report*. Calcutta: Superintendent of Government Printing.

India, Sanitary Commissioner (1918), *Annual Report of the Sanitary Commissioner*. Calcutta: Superintendent of Government Printing.

Ives, Edward (1773), *A Voyage from England to India in the Year 1754*. London: Edward and Charles Dilley.

Jagadīśvarānanda, Svāmī (1955), *The Devī-māhātmyam or Śrī Durgā-saptaśati.* Madras: Sri Ramakrishna Math.

Jolly, Julius (1901), *Medicin. Grundriss der Indo-Arischen Philologie und Altertumskunde.* Vol. 3, part 10. Strassburg: Karl J. Trübner.

Jones, W.H.S. (1909), *Malaria and Greek History.* Manchester: At the University Press.

Junghare, Indira Y. (1975), 'Songs of the Goddess Shitala: Religio-Cultural and Linguistic Features.' *Man in India* 55. 298–316.

Kane, P.V. (1930–1962), *History of Dharmaśāstra.* 5 vols. Poona: Bhandarkar Oriental Research Institute.

Kangle, R.P., ed. and trans. (1969), *The Kauṭilīya Arthaśāstra.* Part I: *A Critical Edition with a Glossary,* 2nd ed. Bombay: University of Bombay.

____ (1972), Part II: *An English Translation with Critical and Explanatory Notes.* 2nd ed. Bombay: University of Bombay.

Karim, Abdul (1959), *Social History of the Muslims in Bengal (Down to AD 1538).* Dacca: The Asiatic Society of Pakistan.

Kaushik, Meena (1979), *Religion and Social Structure: A Case Study of the Doms of Banaras.* Ph.D. dissertation, Department of Sociology, University of Delhi.

Kennedy, Melville T. (1925), *The Chaitanya Movement: A Study of the Vaishnavism of Bengal.* Calcutta: The Association Press.

Kielhorn, F. (1887), 'A Gaya Inscription of Yakshapala.' *Indian Antiquary* 16: 63–66.

Klein, Ira (1972), 'Malaria and Mortality in Bengal 1840–1921.' *Indian Economic and Social History Review* 9: 132–160.

Langer, William L. (1976), 'Immunization for Smallpox before Jenner.' *Scientific American* 234, 1 (Jan.): 111–16.

Leach, E.R. (1960), 'The Frontiers of Burma.' *Comparative Studies in Society and History* 3: 49–68.

Mādhava-kara (1920), *Mādhava-nidānam, with the Commentary Madhu-koṣa of Vijaya-rakṣita and Śrīkaṇṭha-datta, and the Commentary Ātaṅka-darpaṇa of Vācaspati Vaidya.* Edited by Yādava-śarmaṇa. Bombay: Nirnaya-sagara Press.

Majumdar, M.R. (1965), *Cultural History of Gujarat.* Bombay: Popular Prakashan.

Maṇḍal Pañcānan, ed. (1952). *Pūthi Paricay,* Vol. 1. Calcutta: Viśvabhāratī Granthālay.

____ (1958), *Pūthi Paricay,* Vol. 2. Calcutta: Viśvabhāratī Granthālay.

____ (1960), *Haridever Racanāvali.* (*Sahityaprāklaśika,* Vol. 4). Sāntiniketan: Viśvabhāratī.

____ (1963), *Pūthi Paricay,* Vol. 3. Calcutta: Viśvabhāratī Granthālay.

____ (1966), *Dvādas Maṅgal,* (*Sahityaprākaśika,* Vol. 5). Sāntiniketan: Viśvabhāratī.

Marriott, McKim (1959), 'Changing Channels of Cultural Transmission in Indian Civilization.' In *Intermediate Societies, Social Mobility, and Communication*. Proceedings of the 1959 Annual Spring Meeting of the American Ethnological Society. Seattle: University of Washington.

Marshman, John Clark (1850), *A Guide to Bengal*. Calcutta: Government of Bengal.

Mathur, K.S. (1961), 'The Meaning of Hinduism in a Malwa Village.' In *Aspects of Religion in Indian Society*, L.P. Vidyarthi (ed.). Meerut: Kedar Nath Ram Nath. pp. 114–28.

McCormack, William (1958), 'The Forms of Communication in Vīraśaiva Religion.' In Singer 1958: 325–335.

McNeill, William (1976), *Plagues and Peoples*. Garden City, N.Y.: Anchor Press/Doubleday.

McVail, John C. (1893), 'Small-pox and Vaccination.' In *A Treatise on Hygiene and Public Health*, Thomas Stevenson and Shirley F. Murphy (eds.). 3 vols. London: J. & A. Churchill. Vol. 2: 383–463.

Meulenbeld, G.J., ed. and trans. (1974), *The Mādhavanidāna and Its Chief Commentary*. Chaps. 1–10. Leiden: E.J. Brill.

Moore, James (1815), *The History of the Small Pox*. London: Printed for Longman, Hurst, Rees, Orme, and Brown.

Mukherjee, Radhakamal (1938), *The Changing Face of Bengal, A Study in Riverine Economy*. Calcutta: University of Calcutta.

Mukhopādhyāya Bhaktibhūṣaṇa, Gopāladāsa, ed. (1375) [1968] *Śrī-Śrī-Caṇḍī*. Calcutta: Vijanavāsinī Devī.

____, compiler (1965), *Stavakavacamālā*. Revised by Kumāranātha Sudhākara. Third ed. Calcutta: Published by Vijanavāsinī Devī.

Naik, T.B. (1958), 'Religion of the Anavils of Surat.' In Singer 1958: 183–90.

Needham, Joseph (1980), *China and the Origins of Immunology*. Hong Kong: Center of Asian Studies, University of Hong Kong. (First S.T. Huang-Chan Memorial Lecture, Nov. 9, 1979. Department of Anatomy, University of Hong Kong.)

____, and Lu Gwei-djen (1962), 'Hygiene and Preventive Medicine in Ancient China.' *Journal of the History of Medicine* 17: 429–78.

Nepali, G.S. (1965), *The Newars*. Bombay: United Asia Publications.

Nicholas, Ralph W. (1962), *Villages of the Bengal Delta: A Study of Ecology and Peasant Society*. Unpublished Ph.D. Dissertation, University of Chicago.

____ (1967), 'Ritual Hierarchy and Social Relations in Rural Bengal.' *Contributions to Indian Sociology*. n.s. 1: 56–83.

____ (1968), 'Structures of Politics in the Villages of Southern Asia.' In *Structure and Change in Indian Society*, Milton Singer and Bernard S. Cohn, (eds.). Chicago: Aldine Publishing Company.

____ (1973), 'Social and Political Movements.' *Annual Review of Anthropology*, no. 2. Palo Alto: Annual Reviews, Inc. pp. 63–84.

Nirmalānanda (Svāmi) (1967), *Deva-devī o Tā̃der Vāhana*. Calcutta: Bhārata Sevāśrama Saṅgha.

Nityānanda [Cakravartī] ('Dvija Nityānanda') (1878–1879), *Śītalar Jāgaraṇa Pālā*. Calcutta: Trailokyanāth Datta.

____ (1931), *Bṛhat Śītalā Maṅgal bā Śītalār Jāgaraṇa Pālā*. Calcutta: Tarachā̃d Das and Sons.

O'Flaherty, Wendy Doniger (1975), *Hindu Myths*. Harmondsworth: Penguin Books.

____ (1976), *The Origins of Evil in Hindu Mythology*. Berkeley: University of California Press.

'Old Resident' (1918), *All About Benares*. Benares: K.S. Muthiah & Co., Silk House.

O'Malley, L.S.S. (1911), *Bengal District Gazetteers: Midnapore*. Calcutta: The Bengal Secretariat Book Depot.

Orenstein, Henry (1965), *Gaon: Conflict and Cohesion in an Indian Village*. Princeton, N.J: Princeton University Press.

Orth, Johannes (1900), 'Bemerkungen ueber das Alter der Pockenkenntniss in Indien und China.' *Janus*, no. 5: 391–96, 452–58.

Pargiter, F. Eden, trans. and annotator (1904), *The Mārkaṇḍeya Purāṇa*. Calcutta: The Asiatic Society (Bibliotheca Indica).

Patil, D.R. (1963), *The Antiquarian Remains in Bihar*. Patna: Kashi Prasad Jayaswal Research Institute.

Purāṇas. (n.d.) *Śrī Śītalāṣṭakam*. Varanasi: Ṭhākurprasād & Sons, Bookseller.

____ (1908–09), *Skanda Mahāpurāṇa*. Bombay: Veṅkateśvara Steam Press.

____ (1911), *Skanda Purāṇa* [in Bengali characters]. With a Bengali translation by Pañcānana Tarkaratna. Calcutta: Baṅgabāsī Office.

____ (1947), *Śrī Skanda-purāṇokta Śītalāṣṭakam*. Banaras City: Caukhamba Sanskrit Pustakālaya.

____ (1960–1962), *Skanda-mahāpurāṇa*. Calcutta: Manasukha-rāya Mora (Guru-maṇḍala Granthamālā, no. 20).

Raghavan, V. (1958), 'Methods of Popular Religious Instruction in South India.' In Singer 1958: 336–344.

Ramanujan, A.K. (ms.), 'Language and "modernization": the Tamil Example.'

Razzell, Peter (1977), *The Conquest of Smallpox: The Impact of Inoculation on Smallpox Mortality in Eighteenth Century Britain*. Firle, Sussex: Caliban Books.

Rhodes, Andrew J., and C.E. van Rooyen (1958), *A Textbook of Virology*, 3rd ed. Baltimore: Williams & Wilkins.

Risley, H.H. (1891), *The Tribes and Castes of Bengal. Ethnographic Glossary*. 2 vols. Calcutta: Bengal Secretariat Press.

Rogers, Leonard (1926), *Small-pox and Climate in India: Forecasting of Epidemics*. London: Medical Research Council of Great Britain, Special Report Series, no. 106.

Rolleston, J.D. (1937), *The History of the Acute Exanthemata.* London: William Heinemann.

Roy, Satindra Narayan (1927), 'Popular Superstitions in Orissa about Smallpox and Cholera.' *Man in India* 7: 217–26.

Russell, A.J., and E.R. Sundararajan (1929), 'Epidemiology of Smallpox.' *Indian Journal of Medical Research* 16: 559–638.

Śabdakalpadrumaḥ [Sanskrit Encyclopedia in Bengali Characters]. 1931–1934. 7 vols. Compiled by Rādhākānta Deva. Calcutta: New Bengal Press.

Sahai, Bhagwant. 1975. *Iconography of Minor Hindu and Buddhist Deities*. New Delhi: Abhinav Publications.

Sapir, Edward (1949), *Selected Writings of Edward Sapir in Language, Culture, and Personality*. D.G. Mandelbaum, ed. Berkeley: University of California Press.

Scrimshaw, N., C. Taylor, and J. Gordon (1968), *Interaction of Nutrition and Infection*. Geneva: World Health Organization Monograph Series, No. 57.

Sen, Dinesh Chandra (1954), *History of Bengali Language and Literature*. 2nd ed. Calcutta: University of Calcutta.

Sen, Rajendra Nath, trans. (1919), *Brahmavaivartta Purāṇa, Sacred Books of the Hindus*, Vol. 24. Allahabad: The Panini Office.

Sen, Sukumar (1960), *History of Bengali Literature*. New Delhi: Sahitya Akademi.

____, ed. (1975), *Kavikaṅkaṇa Mukunda-viracita Caṇḍī-maṅgala.* New Delhi: Sahitya Academy.

Sengupta, J.C., and Sanat Kumar Bose, eds. (1962), *West Bengal District Records. New Series. Midnapore. Letters Received, 1777–1800.* Calcutta: Government of West Bengal.

Sherring, M.A. (1968), *The Sacred City of the Hindus: An Account of Benares in Ancient and Modern Times.* London: Trübner & Co.

Singer, Milton, ed. (1958), *Traditional India: Structure and Change.* [A special issue of the] *Journal of American Foklore* 71 (no. 281).

____ (1958), 'The Great Tradition in a Metropolitan Center: Madras.' In Singer 1958: 347–388.

Singh, Indera Pal (1961), 'Religion in Daleke: A Sikh Village.' In *Aspects of Religion in Indian Society*, L.P. Vidyarthi (ed.). Meerut: Kedar Nath Ram Nath. pp. 191–219.

Sinha, N.K., ed. (1967), *The History of Bengal (1757–1905)*. Calcutta: The University of Calcutta.

Sircar, D.C. (1965–1966), 'Inscriptions of Two Brahmana Rulers of Gaya.' *Epigraphia Indica* 36: 81–94.

Spate, O.H.K., and A.T.A. Learmonth (1967), *India and Pakistan: A General and Regional Geography*. 3rd ed. London: Methuen & Co., Ltd.

Stavorinus, J.S. (1798), *Voyage par le Cap de Bonne-Espérance à Batavia, à Bantam et au Bengale, en 1768, '69, '70 et '71*. Translated from Dutch by H.J. Jansen. Paris: H.J. Jansen, Imprimeur Libraire.

Stevenson, [Mrs.] Sinclair (1920), *The Rites of the Twice-Born*. London: Oxford University Press.

Sukul, Kubera Nath (1970), 'Original Sites of Some Important Temples in Varanasi.' *Journal of the Ganganath Jha Research Institute* 26: 717–24.

Suśruta (1915), *The Suśruta Saṃhitā, with the Nibanda Saṃgraha Commentary of Śrī Ḍalhaṇācārya*. Edited by Jādavjī Trikuñjī Ācārya. Bombay: Nirnayasagara Press.

Tattwananda, Swami, trans. (1962), *Sri Sri Chandi*. Calcutta: Nirmalendu Bikash Sen Gupta.

Underhill, M.M. (1921), *The Hindu Religious Year*. Calcutta: Association Press.

Varenne, Jean, trans. and comm. (1975), *Célébration de la Grande Déesse* (Devī-māhātmya). Paris: Société d'Édition 'Les Belles Lettres.'

Wadley, Susan S. (1980), 'Śītalā: The Cool One.' *Asian Folklore Studies* 39, 1: 33–62.

Ward, William (1970), *A View of the History, Literature, and Mythology of the Hindoos*. New ed. 3 vols. Port Washington, N.Y.: Kennikat Press. (Reprint of 1822 ed.)

Weber, Max (1968), *Economy and Society*, 3 vols. New York: Bedminster Press.

Whitehead, Henry (1921), *The Village Gods of South India*. 2nd ed. Calcutta: Association Press.

Wilson, Charles R., ed. (1895), *The Early Annals of the English in Bengal*. 2 vols. London: W. Thacker and Co.

Wilson, H.H., ed. and trans. (1864), *The Vishṇu Purāṇa*. 7 vols. London: Trübner & Co.

Wise, Thomas Alexander (1867), *Review of the History of Medicine*. 2 vols. London: J. Churchill.

Index